Prescription Drug Abuse: What Is Being Done To Address This New Drug Epidemic?

United States Congress House of Representatives Committee on Government Reform, Subcommittee on Criminal Justice, Drug Policy, and Human Resources

PRESCRIPTION DRUG ABUSE: WHAT IS BEING DONE TO ADDRESS THIS NEW DRUG EPIDEMIC?

HEARING

BEFORE THE

SUBCOMMITTEE ON CRIMINAL JUSTICE, DRUG POLICY, AND HUMAN RESOURCES

OF THE

COMMITTEE ON GOVERNMENT REFORM

HOUSE OF REPRESENTATIVES

ONE HUNDRED NINTH CONGRESS

SECOND SESSION

JULY 26, 2006

Serial No. 109–237

Printed for the use of the Committee on Government Reform

Available via the World Wide Web: http://www.gpoaccess.gov/congress/index.html
http://www.house.gov/reform

U.S. GOVERNMENT PRINTING OFFICE

35–338 PDF   WASHINGTON : 2007

For sale by the Superintendent of Documents, U.S. Government Printing Office
Internet: bookstore.gpo.gov   Phone: toll free (866) 512–1800; DC area (202) 512–1800
Fax: (202) 512–2250   Mail: Stop SSOP, Washington, DC 20402–0001

COMMITTEE ON GOVERNMENT REFORM

TOM DAVIS, Virginia, *Chairman*

CHRISTOPHER SHAYS, Connecticut
DAN BURTON, Indiana
ILEANA ROS-LEHTINEN, Florida
JOHN M. McHUGH, New York
JOHN L. MICA, Florida
GIL GUTKNECHT, Minnesota
MARK E. SOUDER, Indiana
STEVEN C. LaTOURETTE, Ohio
TODD RUSSELL PLATTS, Pennsylvania
CHRIS CANNON, Utah
JOHN J. DUNCAN, JR., Tennessee
CANDICE S. MILLER, Michigan
MICHAEL R. TURNER, Ohio
DARRELL E. ISSA, California
JON C. PORTER, Nevada
KENNY MARCHANT, Texas
LYNN A. WESTMORELAND, Georgia
PATRICK T. McHENRY, North Carolina
CHARLES W. DENT, Pennsylvania
VIRGINIA FOXX, North Carolina
JEAN SCHMIDT, Ohio
BRAIN P. BILBRAY, California

HENRY A. WAXMAN, California
TOM LANTOS, California
MAJOR R. OWENS, New York
EDOLPHUS TOWNS, New York
PAUL E. KANJORSKI, Pennsylvania
CAROLYN B. MALONEY, New York
ELIJAH E. CUMMINGS, Maryland
DENNIS J. KUCINICH, Ohio
DANNY K. DAVIS, Illinois
WM. LACY CLAY, Missouri
DIANE E. WATSON, California
STEPHEN F. LYNCH, Massachusetts
CHRIS VAN HOLLEN, Maryland
LINDA T. SANCHEZ, California
C.A. DUTCH RUPPERSBERGER, Maryland
BRIAN HIGGINS, New York
ELEANOR HOLMES NORTON, District of
   Columbia
   ———
BERNARD SANDERS, Vermont
   (Independent)

DAVID MARIN, *Staff Director*
LAWRENCE HALLORAN, *Deputy Staff Director*
TERESA AUSTIN, *Chief Clerk*
PHIL BARNETT, *Minority Chief of Staff/Chief Counsel*

SUBCOMMITTEE ON CRIMINAL JUSTICE, DRUG POLICY, AND HUMAN RESOURCES

MARK E. SOUDER, Indiana, *Chairman*

PATRICK T. McHENRY, North Carolina
DAN BURTON, Indiana
JOHN L. MICA, Florida
GIL GUTKNECHT, Minnesota
STEVEN C. LaTOURETTE, Ohio
CHRIS CANNON, Utah
CANDICE S. MILLER, Michigan
VIRGINIA FOXX, North Carolina
JEAN SCHMIDT, Ohio

ELIJAH E. CUMMINGS, Maryland
BERNARD SANDERS, Vermont
DANNY K. DAVIS, Illinois
DIANE E. WATSON, California
LINDA T. SANCHEZ, California
C.A. DUTCH RUPPERSBERGER, Maryland
MAJOR R. OWENS, New York
ELEANOR HOLMES NORTON, District of
   Columbia

EX OFFICIO

TOM DAVIS, Virginia

HENRY A. WAXMAN, California

MARC WHEAT, *Staff Director*
MICHELL GRESS, *Counsel*
WILLIAM COLLUM, *Acting Clerk*
TONY HAYWOOD, *Minority Counsel*

CONTENTS

PRESCRIPTION DRUG ABUSE: WHAT IS BEING DONE TO ADDRESS THIS NEW DRUG EPIDEMIC?

WEDNESDAY, JULY 26, 2006

HOUSE OF REPRESENTATIVES,
SUBCOMMITTEE ON CRIMINAL JUSTICE, DRUG POLICY,
AND HUMAN RESOURCES,
COMMITTEE ON GOVERNMENT REFORM,
Washington, DC.

The subcommittee met, pursuant to notice, at 9:30 a.m., in room 2154, Rayburn House Office Building, Hon. Mark E. Souder (chairman of the subcommittee) presiding.

Present: Representatives Souder, McHenry, Foxx, Cummings, Watson, and Norton.

Staff present: Marc Wheat, staff director and chief counsel; Michelle Gress, Dennis Kilcoyne, and Jim Kaiser, counsels; Scott Springer and Mark Fedor, congressional fellows; William Collum, acting clerk; Tony Haywood, minority counsel; and Cecelia Morton, minority office manager.

Mr. SOUDER. The subcommittee will come to order. Good morning and thank you for being here today.

This hearing addresses a very important aspect of drug abuse in our country and one that I do not believe is getting enough attention, and that is a nonmedical use of prescription drugs, a form of drug abuse. This somewhat quiet form of drug abuse today is so common it is exceeded in prevalence only by marijuana use. Moreover, nonmedical use of prescription drugs now supercedes marijuana as a pathway for initiates into this underworld of drug abuse. It is a problem facilitated by ease of access to the drugs and a perception that prescription drugs are safe because these are FDA approved.

Nonetheless, the statistics about prescription drug abuse are incredibly alarming. To start with, according to the most recent household survey approximately 6 million people were currently users of prescription drugs for nonmedical purposes.

Of the 6 millon people abusing prescription drugs, most of them were abusing pain relievers such as OxyContin, 4.4 million.

The Drug Abuse Warning Network reported that 495,000 emergency room visits in 2004 related to the nonmedical use of prescription drugs.

The most recent Monitoring the Future Survey, measuring drug use amongst our Nation's adolescents, found high rates of nonmedical use of prescription pain relievers in each of the 8th, 10th and

(1)

12-grade groups surveyed. The prevalence of OxyContin use in particular has increased 40 percent since 2002.

The National Center on Addiction and Substance Abuse at Columbia University, CASA, found that between 1992 and 2003 the number of people abusing controlled prescription drugs increased 94 percent, twice the percentage increase of people using marijuana, five times the number of people abusing cocaine, and 60 times the number of people abusing heroin.

CASA also found that teens who abuse controlled prescription drugs are twice as likely to use alcohol, five times more likely to use marijuana, 12 times more likely to use heroin, 15 times more likely to use Ecstasy, and 21 times more likely to use cocaine than teens who do not abuse prescription drugs.

The most recent Attitude Tracking Study by the Partnership for a Drug Fee America found that teen abuse of prescription drugs stems from the ease of availability, the lack of stigma associated with street drugs and the false belief that they are safe to use.

I don't believe anyone can consider these very sobering statistics and survey results without concluding that the abuse of prescription drugs is a problem of epidemic proportions that demand focused attention and aggressive action by both the government and the private sectors.

One of the congressional initiatives for addressing the problem targets the issue of obtaining controlled drugs over the Internet without a prescription. H.R. 840, introduced by Chairman Davis and Ranking Member Waxman, amends the Food, Drug and Cosmetic Act to establish disclosure standards for Internet pharmacies, prohibits Internet sites from selling or dispensing prescription drugs solely on the basis of online questionnaires, and provides additional authority for States to take action against illegal Internet pharmacies.

I am interested in hearing from our administration officials here today about the administration's work on the prescription drug abuse problem, and I am interested in concrete actions, not more general statements about, "working closely with other agencies encouraging solutions to the problem or," "developing action plans," to address this issue. I am tired of the empty rhetoric and long delays on important matters like this and let me give you an example.

As part of a hearing on November 18, 2004, I asked the DEA a number of questions regarding methamphetamine abuse. I just received the responses to these questions last month on June 27, 2006. It took DEA 20 months to respond. That is an unreasonable delay in providing crucial information to Congress about methamphetamine abuse.

Moreover, it took the administration almost 2 years after releasing its synthetic drug action plan in October 2004 to come up with what it calls a synthetic drug strategy despite repeated calls from Congress and only after Congress had passed a bill on the subject, the Combat Meth Act.

Despite being 20 months in the making, this strategy is full of platitudes that don't seem to be truly backed up with any assigned responsibility or interim goals prior to the end of this administration.

I don't want to hear platitudes today. I hope the administration witnesses are listening closely to me right now. I want the ONDCP to tell us what it means in terms of concrete steps when it says it is going to call together representatives from the medical and pharmaceutical communities to, "discuss the problem and to encourage them to educate patients." What does ONDCP mean in terms of concrete steps with its recommendations to "continue to support the efforts of firms that manufacture frequently diverted pharmaceutical products to reformulate their products so as to reduce diversion and abuse."

I want to know if the FDA has responded to Congress' year old request for a report on how the agency might handle priority review of abuse resistant formulations of prescription controlled drugs. This report was requested with the FDA appropriations bill last year. Where is it? Why hasn't the FDA provided guidance on this important matter? I am asking FDA to provide this report to Congress and to provide specific legislative recommendations for the reauthorization of this Prescription Drug User Fee Act that will provide incentives for developing and allow for accelerated approval of abuse resistant forms of highly abused drugs. Since the Prescription Drug User Fee Act is important to the FDA's bottom line, I will expect the FDA to provide this information promptly.

I want to know what the DEA really means when it says it is, "working closely with the FDA to urge the rapid reformulation of OxyContin." My staff has asked DEA officials about this on at least two occasions over the last 12 months and DEA could not provide the staff with anything concrete about its statement. I want to know the bar. I want to know what bar the DEA would set for categorizing controlled drug reformulation as abuse resistant.

I know the National Institute on Drug Abuse has devoted significant resources to studying this problem. I want to know what the institute's research is showing about prescription drug abuse and treatment and how we can apply this research to overcoming this tremendous problem.

Despite what has become a standard practice here, I challenge the administration witnesses today to stay for the second panel and listen to the testimony that will be presented. I know that means you have to stay for the entire hearing so you can hear the testimony of witnesses other than the government officials, but I think it would be helpful. I think it would do some good for you to hear from the people who have experienced the devastation of losing someone to prescription drug abuse, to hear from one of the companies actually working to develop drug abuse resistant forms of pharmaceuticals, to hear from the organizations that are on the front lines working to educate doctors, patients and kids or partnering with the private industry to reduce prescription drug abuse. The second panel gives a face to the problem and presents solutions.

Our first panel today consists of Dr. Bertha Madras, Deputy Director for Demand Reduction at the White House Office of National Drug Control Policy; Dr. Sandra Kweder, Deputy Director of the Office of New Drugs, Center for Drug Evaluation and Review at the Food and Drug Administration; Mr. Joe Rannazzisi, Deputy Assistant Administrator for the Office of Diversion Control in the

Drug Enforcement Administration; and Dr. Nora Volkow, Director of the National Institute on Drug Abuse.

Our second panel consists of Ms. Misty Fetko, a registered nurse who lost her 18-year-old son Carl to Robitussin and Fentanyl abuse; Ms. Linda Surks, who lost her 19-year-old son to a prescription drug overdose related death; Ms. Barbara van Rooyan, who lost her 24-year old son Patrick to OxyContin use; Ms. Mathea Falco, president of Drug Strategies; Mr. Stephen Johnson, executive director of Commercial Planning with Pain Therapeutics, Inc.; Dr. Laxmaiah Manchikanti, chief executive officer of the American Society of Interventional Pain Physicians; and Mr. Steve Pasierb, president and CEO of the Partnership for a Drug Free America.

I welcome each of you, and I look forward to your testimony. I yield to the ranking member, Mr. Cummings.

[The prepared statement of Hon. Mark E. Souder follows:]

Subcommittee on Criminal Justice, Drug Policy and Human Resources

Opening Statement of Chairman Mark Souder

"PRESCRIPTION DRUG ABUSE: What is Being Done to Address This New Drug Epidemic?"

July 26, 2006

Good morning, and thank you for being here today. This hearing addresses a very important aspect of drug abuse in our country and one that I do not believe is getting enough attention: that is the non-medical use of prescription drugs as a form of drug abuse.

This somewhat quiet form of drug abuse today is so common, it is exceeded in prevalence only by marijuana use. Moreover, non-medical use of prescription drugs now supersedes marijuana as the pathway for initiates into the underworld of drug abuse. It is a problem facilitated by ease of access to the drugs, and a perception that prescription drugs are "safe," because they are FDA approved.

Nonetheless, the statistics about prescription drug abuse are incredibly alarming:

- To start with, according to the most recent Household Survey, approximately six million people were current users of prescription drugs for non-medical purposes;[1]
- Of the six million people abusing prescription drugs, most of them were abusing pain relievers such as OxyContin (4.4 million);
- The Drug Abuse Warning Network reported 495,000 emergency department visits in 2004 related to the non-medical use of prescription drugs;
- The most recent Monitoring the Future Survey - measuring drug use among our nation's adolescents - found high rates of non-medical use of prescription pain relievers in each of the 8th, 10th, and 12th grade groups surveyed. The prevalence of OxyContin use, in particular, has increased 40% since 2002.
- The National Center on Addiction and Substance Abuse at Columbia University (CASA) found that between 1992 and 2003, the number of people abusing controlled prescription drugs increased 94 percent – twice

---

[1] Substance Abuse and Mental Health Services Administration. (2005). *Overview of Findings from the 2004 National Survey on Drug Use and Health* (Office of Applied Studies, NSDUH Series H-27, DHHS Publication No. SMA 05-4061). Rockville, MD. (Hereafter "NSDUH.") Available at http://oas.samhsa.gov/nsduh/2k4nsduh/2k4overview/2k4overview.htm#ch5 (last visited July 21, 2006).

the percentage increase of people abusing marijuana, five times the number of people abusing cocaine and 60 times the number of people abusing heroin;

- CASA also found that teens who abuse controlled prescription drugs are twice as likely to use alcohol, five times more likely to use marijuana, 12 times more likely to use heroin, 15 times more likely to use Ecstasy, and 21 times more likely to use cocaine than teens who do not abuse prescription drugs;
- The most recent Attitude Tracking Study by the Partnership for a Drug-Free America found that teen abuse of prescription drugs stems from the ease of availability, the lack of stigma associated with street drugs, and the false belief they are safe to use.

I don't believe anyone can consider these very sobering statistics and survey results without concluding that the abuse of prescription drugs is a problem of epidemic proportions that demands focused attention and aggressive action by both the government and the private sectors.

One of the Congressional initiatives for addressing this problem targets the issue of obtaining controlled drugs over the internet without a prescription. H.R. 840, introduced by Chairman Davis and Ranking Member Waxman, amends the Food, Drug, and Cosmetic Act to establish disclosure standards for Internet pharmacies, prohibits Internet sites from selling or dispensing prescription drugs solely on the basis of an online questionnaire, and provides additional authority for states to take action against illegal Internet pharmacies.

I am interested in hearing from our Administration officials here today about the Administration's work on the prescription drug abuse problem, and I'm interested in the concrete actions, **NOT** general statements about "working closely" with other agencies, "encouraging" solutions to the problem, or "developing action plans," to address this issue. I am tired of empty rhetoric and long delays on important matters like this – and let me give you an example: As part of a hearing on November 18, 2004, I asked the DEA a number of questions regarding methamphetamine abuse; I just received responses to these questions last month, on June 27, 2006; it took DEA twenty months to respond. That is an unreasonable delay in providing crucial information to Congress about methamphetamine abuse.

Moreover, it took the Administration almost two years after releasing its Synthetic Drug Action Plan in October, 2004, to come up with what it calls a Synthetic Drug "Strategy," despite repeated calls from Congress, and only after Congress had to pass a bill on the subject – the Combat Meth Act. Despite being twenty months in the making, this "strategy" is full of platitudes that don't seem to be truly backed up with any assigned responsibility or interim goals prior to the end of this Administration.

I don't want to hear platitudes today. And I hope the Administration witnesses are listening closely to me right now.

I want the ONDCP to tell us what it means in terms of concrete steps when it says in it is going to "*call together* representatives from the medical and pharmaceutical communities to *discuss* the problem and to *encourage*" them to educate patients.[2] What

---

[2] *Synthetic Drug control Strategy: A Focus on methamphetamine and Prescription Drug Abuse*, June 2006, Office of National Drug Control Policy, U.S. Government Printing Office, Washington, DC. Available at

does ONDCP mean in terms of <u>concrete steps</u> with its recommendation to "continue to support the efforts of firms that manufacture frequently diverted pharmaceutical products to reformulate their products so as to reduce diversion and abuse."[3]

I want to know if the FDA has responded to Congress's year-old request for a report on how the agency might handle priority review of abuse-resistant formulations of prescription controlled drugs.[4] This report was requested with FDA's appropriations bill *last year*. Where is it? Why hasn't FDA provided guidance on this important matter? I am asking FDA to provide this report to Congress, and to provide specific legislative recommendations for the reauthorization of the Prescription Drug User Fee Act that will provide incentives for developing, and allow for the accelerated approval of, abuse-resistant forms of highly-abused drugs. Since the Prescription Drug User Fee Act is important to the FDA's bottom line, I'll expect the FDA to provide this information promptly.

I want to know what the DEA really means when it says it is "working closely" with the FDA to urge the rapid reformulation of OxyContin.[5] My staff has asked DEA officials about this on at least two occasions over the last twelve months, and DEA could not provide staff with anything concrete about its statement. I want to know what bar the DEA would set for categorizing a controlled drug reformulation as "abuse-resistant."

I know that the National Institute on Drug Abuse has devoted significant resources to studying this problem; I want to know what the Institute's research is showing about prescription drug abuse and treatment, and how we can apply this research to overcoming this tremendous problem.

Despite what has become standard practice around here, I challenge the Administration witnesses today to stay for the second panel and listen to the testimony that will be presented. The four Administration witnesses together requested that we reserve fifteen seats in this hearing room. These come at the expense of public attendance, so I hope that means you intend to stay for the entire hearing so you can hear the testimony of witnesses other than government officials. I think it will do some good for you to hear from people who have experienced the devastation of losing someone to prescription drug abuse, to hear from one of the companies actually working to develop abuse-resistant forms of pharmaceuticals, to hear from the organizations that are on the front lines working to educate doctors, parents and kids, or partnering with private industry, to reduce prescription drug abuse. The second panel gives a face to the problem and presents solutions.

Our first panel today consists of Dr. Bertha Madras, Deputy Director for Demand Reduction at the White House Office of National Drug Control Policy; Dr. Sandra Kweder, Deputy Director in the Office of New Drugs, Center for Drug Evaluation and Review, at the Food and Drug Administration; Mr. Joe Rannazzisi, Deputy Assistant Administrator for the Office of Diversion Control in the Drug Enforcement

http://www.whitehousedrugpolicy.gov/publications/synthetic_drg_control_strat/ (last visited July 25, 2006).
[3] *Id.*
[4] H.R. Rep. No. 109-102, at 81 (2005).
[5] U.S. Department of Justice, Drug Enforcement Administration, Office of Diversion Control, Drugs and Chemicals of Concern. Available at
http://www.deadiversion.usdoj.gov/drugs_concern/oxycodone/abuse_oxy.htm (last visited July 21, 2006).

Administration; and Dr. Nora D. Volkow, Director of the National Institute on Drug Abuse.

Our second panel consists of Ms. Misty Fetko, a Registered nurse who lost her 18-year-old son Carl to Robitussin® and Fentanyl abuse; Ms. Linda Surks, who lost her 19-year old son Jason to a prescription drug overdose related death; Ms. Barbara van Rooyan, who lost her 24-year old son Patrick to OxyContin use; Ms. Mathea Falco, President of Drug Strategies; Mr. Stephen Johnson, Executive Director of Commercial Planning with Pain Therapeutics Inc.;
Dr. Laxmaiah Manchikanti, Chief Executive Officer of the American Society of Interventional Pain Physicians; and Mr. Steve Pasierb, President and CEO of the Partnership for a Drug-Free America.

Welcome to each of you and I look forward to your testimony.

Mr. CUMMINGS. Thank you very much, Mr. Chairman, and I do thank you for holding this hearing today. And as you were speaking, I could not help but be reminded of so many years ago when I was a high school student working in a pharmacy in south Baltimore when people would come in to the neighborhood and buy high volumes of Robitussin. And even back then it was a problem and I shall never forget at 17 trying to figure out why would anybody want to come and buy 10 or 15 bottles of Robitussin in the middle of July.

So this problem is not a new one. The abuse and illegal diversion of prescription drugs is not new, but due to a number of factors it has been increasingly prevalent.

A number of factors have been cited by the National Institute on Drug Abuse and others as contributing to the expansion of non-medical use of pharmaceuticals. These factors include the growing number of drugs being marketed to treat a seemingly ever expanding list of treatable illnesses and conditions; increasingly easy access to pharmaceuticals by way of use of the Internet, including from on-line pharmacies that do not require a prescription and do not verify the identity of the buyers; the relatively low stigma associated with nonmedical use of prescription drugs versus the use of elicit substances; and the common misperception that pharmaceutical drugs are not dangerous.

As I have said many times, the person who improperly uses prescription drugs and abuses them is just as bad and puts themselves in just as much danger as a person who was sitting in a corner snorting cocaine.

The fact is that any drug can be dangerous when used in the absence of appropriate medical evaluation, guidance and supervision.

This is why the recent estimate that some 43 million Americans have used prescription drugs for nonmedical purposes is so very, very disturbing.

Moreover, 2004 National Household Survey of Drugs and Alcohol indicated that 6.3 million Americans, 12 years of age or older, reported nonmedical use of prescription drugs in 2003.

Data suggested that the elderly, young adults between the ages of 18 and 25, and young women between the ages of 12 and 17 may be particularly at risk.

Perhaps recent trends of the abuse of DXM, an ingredient found in over-the-counter cough suppressant medicines and Fentanyl, another opiate, have also caused great concern. Reports indicate that the latter drug is used sometimes unknowingly in conjunction with heroin and it has been linked to numerous overdose death in cities across the country.

Sadly, we will hear testimony from three mothers of sons whose lives were lost as a result of prescription drug abuse.

They represent a tiny fraction of the universe of people who have lost loved ones to prescription drugs, and their compelling testimony will help us understand how this problem plays out in individual cases.

Hopefully, it will also serve as a stark warning to the public that abuse of prescription drugs is, in fact, dangerous.

I think it is clear, Mr. Chairman, the problem warrants a multi-faceted response, and I would like to see Congress and the administration pursue the following actions. And before I go into that list, I agree with you, Chairman Souder, so often we have a motion come and no results.

And then we come later on, 10 years from now, we are dealing with the same problems. More people have suffered, more have died and more have abused these prescription drugs.

So in the light of trying to get something done and push this ball down the field, I would suggest that we enact legislation to require that every on-line purchase of a prescription drug involves a valid prescription and verification of the purchaser's identity, that we provide Federal funding to support prescription monitoring programs in the States, that we support and promote efforts to educate the public, the medical community and pharmacists about the risk of prescription drug abuse and diversion, we encourage efforts to develop drug invasions that are non-resistant and addictive to abuse, and we encourage all parties involved in the drug supply chain and the consumer purchase transactions to take steps to prevent illegal diversion of pharmaceutical products.

Granted, some of these measures may be more complex than they may sound at first blush. The devil always lies in the details. But I am confident that we can summon the will to overcome whatever obstacles there may be to moving forward on all these fronts.

Certainly today's hearing offers a valuable opportunity to hear recommendations from a variety of different viewpoints concerning how the Federal Government should approach these tasks.

As I close, Mr. Chairman, I cannot help but think about the many people that came into that south Baltimore drugstore. Many of them a little older than I was back then but many of them are dead. With that said, Mr. Chairman, I want to close by extending my deepest sympathies to our witnesses who have lost a child to prescription drug abuse and by applauding all of our witnesses for their work. They are going to address this issue. I think we can all agree that more must be done. The question is whether we will have the will and whether we will do it.

With that, Mr. Chairman, I yield back and thank you.

Mr. SOUDER. Thank you. I ask unanimous consent that all Members have 5 legislative days to submit questions and answers for the hearing record. Any answers to written questions provided by the witnesses also will be included in the record. Without objection, so ordered.

I also ask consent that all exhibits, documents and other materials referred to by witnesses may be included in the hearing record, that all Members be admitted to revise their statements. Without objection, so ordered.

Under the House rules, we will have to adjourn for Iraq's Prime Minister. Our intention is to get through the first panel and then we may have to suspend if we do not get into the second panel before we need to suspend. I intend to reconvene the hearing at 12 promptly, which should give us time to have completed the Prime Minister's address.

With that, I thank each of the witnesses for coming and first I need to swear everybody in. If you would just raise your right hands. We will do it sitting. It is our standard practice to swear in our witnesses.

Let the record show that each of the witnesses responded in the affirmative, and we will start with Dr. Madras. Thank you for coming here.

[Witnesses sworn.]

STATEMENTS OF DR. BERTHA K. MADRAS, DEPUTY DIRECTOR FOR DEMAND REDUCTION AT THE WHITE HOUSE OFFICE OF NATIONAL DRUG CONTROL POLICY; DR. SANDRA KWEDER, DEPUTY DIRECTOR IN THE OFFICE OF NEW DRUGS, CENTER FOR DRUG EVALUATION AND REVIEW AT THE FOOD AND DRUG ADMINISTRATION; JOE RANNAZZISI, DEPUTY ASSISTANT ADMINISTRATOR FOR THE OFFICE OF DIVERSION CONTROL IN THE DRUG ENFORCEMENT ADMINISTRATION; AND DR. NORA D. VOLKOW, DIRECTOR OF THE NATIONAL INSTITUTE ON DRUG ABUSE

STATEMENT OF BERTHA K. MADRAS

Ms. MADRAS. Chairman Souder, Ranking Member Cummings, and members of the subcommittee. Thank you for the invitation to testify before you today regarding the abuse of prescription drugs. The abuse, sometimes called nonmedical use of prescription drugs, is a significant national problem. In sheer number of users it is now America's No. 2 drug problem, second only to marijuana.

Last year the National Survey on Drug Use and Health indicated more new initiates of nonmedical prescription drug use than of marijuana.

Opiates, pain killers like OxyContin, stimulants like Ritalin, and sedative sleeping aids such as Ambien are examples of prescription drugs which are legal and beneficial when lawfully used as indicated. They nevertheless have potential for abuse and for addiction.

The administration's response to this problem strives to balance two important policy concerns: First, that prescription drugs have strong medical benefits when used lawfully and in accordance with medical direction; second, these same drugs can be harmful, even deadly, when abused. And the rate of abuse is growing rapidly.

The administration has set an objective of reducing prescription drug abuse by 15 percent over the next 3 years. The Synthetic Drug Control Strategy released last month describes the administration's plan to accomplish this ambitious goal. To reduce those illicit supply of prescription drugs, traditional law enforcement and interdiction activities, including at our border, are important and an additional element for this class of drugs is regulatory. For example, the administration strongly supports State run prescription drug monitoring programs which seek to reduce doctor shopping, prescription fraud, and ultimately diversion opportunities through State level regulation designed to improve the sharing of prescription information between prescribers and dispenser.

At the beginning of the President's term, there were approximately 15 of these programs. Now there are 33 States where programs exist or have been authorized and the administration hopes to see a prescription drug monitoring program in every State by the end of the President's second term.

The administration is also focused on reducing other avenues for diversion. Federal law enforcement targets both rogue Internet pharmacies and the very small percentage of physicians who circumvent law and sound medical practice to violate certain medical provisions for nonmedical reasons. Preventions for treatment are strong for our strategy. Public health messages, the identification of prescription drug abusers and treatment capacity are major components of the synthetic strategy.

The administration is concerned about the sharing of prescription drugs among family and friends. Our strategy involves a partnership with the pharmaceutical and medical communities to educate Americans as to the importance of monitoring, disposing of unneeded, unused medications.

We are holding a medical education conference in December in which we are inviting the deans of major medical schools as well as State medical boards in order to educate them on this issue. The theme of this medical conference is in fact prescription drugs.

We are also holding a conference this Friday on physician control in which we bring together a multidisciplinary task force of researchers, policemen, medical examiners and treatment providers to educate them in the problem of potential associated death. In Philadelphia, which is a State that has had a very high rate of often continual associated deaths, the National Youth Anti-Drug Media Campaign launched an open letter in People Magazine last Friday encouraging parents to be aware of the number of people abusing prescriptions and other drugs. This letter to parents will run in numerous other publications in the near future and a copy of it is on exhibit to the right in this room.

Drug Free Communities is working on prescription drugs and other educational and teaching materials in over 365 of these communities.

Programs and initiatives which are not drug specific are also important tools in reducing this public health problem. Random student drug testing can help screen young people for prescription drug abuse and offer positive appropriate counseling. The screening brief intervention referral to treatment programs is a key component of expanding our capacity to identify, counsel and refer to treatment persons with substance abuse disorders. It identifies a cohort of prescription drug abusers who enter hospitals or clinical environments seeking treatment for reasons other than prescription drugs. federally supported treatment programs such as the Access to Recovery and Drug Courts can help heal those addicted to prescription drugs.

To achieve a 15 percent reduction in prescription drug abuse we need to increase public awareness and collaboration with the medical community, the pharmaceutical community, all of the risks associated with nonmedical use of prescription drugs. And we have concrete plans to further this goal.

Toward this end, I thank Congress for its support of both the President's National Drug Control Strategy and Synthetic Drug Control Strategy.

[The prepared statement of Ms. Madras follows:]

WRITTEN TESTIMONY

Dr. Bertha K. Madras
Deputy Director, Demand Reduction
Office of National Drug Control Policy

Before the House Committee on Government Reform
Subcommittee on Criminal Justice, Drug Policy, and Human Resources
July 26ᵗʰ 2006 9:30 am
Rayburn House Office Building

"Prescription Drug Abuse: What is Being Done to Address this New Drug Epidemic?"

I.   INTRODUCTION

Chairman Souder, Ranking Member Cummings, and distinguished members of the Subcommittee. I appreciate the opportunity to appear before you today to discuss the Federal response to Prescription Drug Abuse.

Several classes of controlled prescription drugs, prescribed by physicians for legitimate medical purposes, have abuse and addiction potential: narcotic opioid analgesics (for management of pain, cough and other indications), stimulant drugs (to treat attentional disorders, narcolepsy and, less frequently, depression), tranquilizing drugs (to treat anxiety) and sedative drugs (to promote sleep). These drugs are safe, effective and necessary when used according to doctors' prescriptions and advice. Abuse or non-medical use of prescription drugs can be defined as use of drugs not prescribed for an individual, use of drugs solely for the experience or feelings they cause, or use of drugs by a person who has made false or inaccurate claims to obtain the drugs.

Last year, the National Survey on Drug Use and Health (NSDUH) uncovered a higher number of new initiates into non-medical prescription drug use than initiates into marijuana use. Statistics described below (Section II. MAGNITUDE OF THE PROBLEM), indicate that misuse and abuse of controlled and certain over-the counter prescription drugs is a significant national problem. Notwithstanding the abuse of a range of controlled and over-the-counter prescription drugs, opioid analgesic drugs are drawing a higher level of national attention and concern, because of the higher absolute population numbers, escalating rate of abuse, high addictive potential, and potential to induce overdose crises or death due to respiratory failure.

Potential causes. Among the factors postulated to fuel increased diversion of legitimate prescription drugs are: 1. public perception that prescription drugs are safer than illicit street drugs, 2. easier availability via web-based sources or theft of legitimate prescriptions, 3. increased direct-to-consumer advertising, which fosters the view that prescription drugs are integral to our lives; 4. increased prescriptions for chronic pain, sleeping and attentional problems, with increased potential for diversion. 5. inadequate public perception on guarding prescription medications. 5. increased web-based sources on how to tamper with medications. 6.

aging of the US population, which requires an increased level of medications to sustain good health.

Potential profiles of abusers and sources of drugs. Different cohorts of users require different strategies to prevent non-medical use of prescription drugs: unintended populations include children, teens, adults and high risk populations, who can become abusers by acquiring prescription medications by forgery, internet purchases, robberies, buying from patients, stealing from home medical sources, and drug rings. Intended populations include patients who suffer pain, but misuse drugs, or are co-morbid for opioid abuse, or opioid abusers who acquire prescription drugs by doctor shopping, pill mills, or by other means.

Response of various sectors: ONDCP, FDA, DEA, DOJ, SAMHSA, NIDA, pharmaceutical companies, medical associations, pain management specialists, medical schools and communities, are developing strategies in response to this mounting problem, with the ultimate goal of attenuating diversion of effective medications with abuse potential, while not compromising the health, comfort and well-being of intended patient populations. The core problem, misuse and abuse of legitimate medications by unintended populations, is complex. This emerging challenge requires surveillance, distribution chain integrity, interventions, and more research by private and public sectors. Coordinated responses that include federal, medical partners, public health administrators, state legislators (e.g. Alliance of States with Prescription Monitoring), and international organizations are needed to implement educational outreach and other strategies targeted to a wide swath of distinct populations, including physicians, pharmacists, intended patient populations, educators, unintended populations, parents, high school and college students, high risk adults, the elderly, among others. Effective risk management plans developed by pharmaceutical companies in collaboration with the FDA, as well as outreach to physicians and their patients and pharmacists, need to be complemented by education, screening, intervention and treatment for those misusing or abusing prescription drugs, the unintended populations. ONDCP is a key contributor to devising policies and funding demonstration programs that can survey, detect, intervene and treat unintended populations that use prescription drugs.

II. MAGNITUDE OF THE PROBLEM

Sources of data. Several Federal agencies generated the data cited below, including the National Survey on Drug Use and Health (NSDUH) which monitored 67,760 persons aged 12 or older, treatment episode data sets (TEDS), Monitoring the Future (MTF) and Drug Abuse Warning Network (DAWN).

Non-medical prescription drug use: general. In 2004, an estimated 2.8 million persons used psychotherapeutics non-medically for the first time within the past year. The numbers of new users of psychotherapeutics in 2004 were 2.4 million for pain relievers, 1.2 million for tranquilizers, and 793,000 for stimulants. An estimated 19.4 percent of past year users of prescription drugs were new users—a statistically significant increase of 13 percent over 2003's 17.2 percent.

The 2004 NSDUH data estimated that 48 million people ages 12 and older had used prescription drugs for non-medical purposes in their lifetimes. Of these, 2.5% (6 million people) were current users. These estimates are unchanged from 2002 and 2003. Among young adults (aged 18 to 25), non-medical use of prescription drugs was significantly higher in 2004 compared with 2002 for lifetime use (an increase from 27.7% to 29.2%) and for past month use (from 5.4% to 6.1%).

The mean age of first use of the various types of prescription drugs is among the highest for any class of drug, equaled only by heroin at 24.4 years: 23.3 years for pain relievers; 24.5 years for Oxycontin®; 25.2 years for tranquilizers; 24.1 years for stimulants; and 29.3 years for sedatives. Only the mean age of first use for tranquilizers showed any change from 2003, increasing from 22.9 years.

Non-medical prescription drug use: opioids. Narcotic analgesic drugs are a type of pain reliever derived from natural or synthetic opioids. Examples of these in common brand names include Vicodin®, Percocet®, OxyContin®, and Darvon®. Pain relievers are the most commonly abused prescription drugs, representing 75% of non-medical use for the past month and past year (2004 data). While the numbers of current (4.4 million) and past year (11.3 million) users of pain relievers in 2004 are unchanged from 2002 and 2003, the estimates for lifetime users increased 7 percent between 2002 and 2004 (from 29.6 million to 31.8 million). Specifically, lifetime use of pain relievers increased (22.1% to 24.3%), as did past month use of pain relievers (4.1% to 4.7%).

The type of drug for new initiates is an important parameter of current and possibly future trends. Of the 2.8 million past year initiates into non-medical use of prescription drugs, 2.4 million (85%) were pain reliever initiates. Equally concerning is that new users represented 21.5% of past year pain reliever users. Focusing on specific opioids, 1.2 million Americans used Oxycontin® non-medically in the past year, and of these, 50.7% were new users.

Monitoring the Future (MTF) data also may portend future drug trends. MTF reports that past year use of Oxycontin® among 12th graders increased 39.2 percent over three years - from 4.0% in 2002 (the first year for which data on Oxycontin® were collected) to 5.5% in 2005. Past year use of Vicodin remained stable, averaging 10% among 12th graders.

Non-medical prescription drug use: other drug classes. Of the other classes of prescription drugs, only sedatives showed any change in 2004 – a 39 percent decrease in the number of current users compared with 2002 (from 436,000 to 265,000 people) was observed in the general household population. However, among high school seniors, lifetime and past year use of sedatives increased 21.5 percent and 25.2 percent, respectively, since 2001 (from 8.7% to 10.5% and from 5.7% to 7.2%, respectively).

Use of tranquilizers decreased among 8th and 10th graders. Lifetime use of tranquilizers among 8th graders decreased 18.8% (from 5.0% to 4.1%), and 22.9% among 10th graders (from 9.2% to 7.1%). Past year use decreased 34.8% among 10th graders (from 7.3% to 4.8%).

Non-medical prescription drug use: treatment consequences. The Treatment Episode Data Set (TEDS) compiles admission to facilities that are licensed by State substance abuse agencies to provide substance abuse treatment and are collected by SAMHSA. Although most admissions for opioid addiction in 2004 were for heroin, TEDS admissions for primary abuse of opioids other than heroin increased from **2.8 percent** of all admissions in 2003 to 3.4 percent in 2004, and increased from 53,730 to 63,853 individuals.

Non-medical prescription drug use: emergency room consequences. Emergency department reports of opioid pain relievers and other prescription drug abuse are increasing. According to SAMHSA's Drug Abuse Warning Network (DAWN) data system, drug abuse related emergency department visits involving narcotic analgesics/combinations increased 163 percent in the nation (from 45,254 visits to 119,185 emergency department visits) between 1995 to 2002. The greatest increases during this period occurred for oxycodone/combinations (512%), methadone (176%), hydrocodone/combinations (159%), and morphine/combinations (116%).

Dependence was the most frequently mentioned motive underlying drug abuse related emergency department visits involving narcotic analgesics (47%), followed by suicide (22%), and psychic effects (15%). The drug abuse motive was unknown for 14% of the analgesic related emergency department visits. Disposition of emergency department patients involving narcotic analgesics was as follows: 53% were admitted for treatment, 44% were treated and released from the hospital, and 3% that either left against medical advice, died, or had an unknown outcome.

Other potential secondary consequences to intended patients include reduced confidence in essential medications, increased physician reluctance to prescribe pain medications and reduced patient access to needed analgesic medications.

III. POSITIVE PROGRESS

These data emerge simultaneously with very encouraging reductions in use of other drugs. Cooperative efforts of the Administration and Congress have led to a historic 19% reduction in teenage illicit drug use over the last 4 years. This reduction means that there are approximately 691,000 fewer 8th, 10th, and 12th graders using illicit drugs than in 2001.

- This includes a 30% reduction in the number of methamphetamine lab incidents, in methamphetamine-positive workplace tests, in lifetime methamphetamine use among youths over the past two years. Furthermore, there is a significant increase in 12th graders who disapprove of using amphetamines (MTF). Details for each drug are presented below:

- Marijuana is the most commonly used illicit drug among this population. Lifetime, past year, and past 30 day marijuana use decreased 12.9 percent, 15.0 percent, and 19.4 percent.

- Reductions in use of the hallucinogens LSD and MDMA (ecstasy) since 2001 have been dramatic, declining as much as a half to nearly two-thirds. Declines in LSD use in all three prevalence categories are nearly two-thirds and declines in the use of ecstasy among these categories range from almost half to nearly two-thirds.

- There were also decreases in some categories of other club drugs, including rohypnol, GHB, and ketamine.

- Use of amphetamines in all three prevalence categories dropped by more than one-quarter: 25.7 percent (from 13.9% to 10.3%), 27.2 percent (from 9.6% to 7.0%), and 30.7 percent (from 4.7% to 3.3%).

- The use of steroids was down 38.2 percent, 36.7 percent, and 29.8 percent for lifetime, past year, and past month use, respectively.

- Lifetime use of heroin and inhalants for all three grades combined declined 13 percent.

IV. SYNTHETIC DRUG CONTROL STRATEGY: INTRODUCTION

The Administration is concerned about the increase in the abuse of controlled substance prescription drugs. In response to the data described above, the Administration released its first-ever *Synthetic Drug Control Strategy* in June 2006, which focuses on methamphetamine and prescription drug abuse. With respect to prescription drug abuse, the *Synthetics Strategy* calls for a 15% reduction in the illicit use of prescription drugs over three years.

The unique nature of this problem, non-medical use of medically approved prescription drugs, requires a creative balance between aggressively reducing abuse of controlled prescription drugs while simultaneously permitting lawful acquisition of controlled prescription drugs in the practice of medicine. To develop an effective equilibrium between the two general policy concerns, the Administration is committed to prevention, education, and enforcement of non-medical, unlawful use of controlled substances while recognizing the need for legitimate access to controlled substance prescription drugs.

V. OVERVIEW OF SUPPLY REDUCTION

A significant challenge in developing a strategy to reduce the non-medical use of controlled substance prescription drugs involves understanding how the prescription drugs are diverted for illicit use, and which of those methods are most commonly used. Unlike drugs such as heroin or marijuana which are presumptively illegal and often obtained through clandestine, secretive transactions, controlled substance prescription drugs are available for legitimate purposes through one's physician and pharmacy. For this reason, mechanisms that are otherwise legal are often manipulated to acquire controlled substance prescription drugs for illegal purposes.

The Administration's strategy to reduce opportunities for the diversion of controlled substance prescription drugs seeks to address each method of diversion. Because reliable data ranking each of these methods of diversion by prevalence does not exist, for the first time in 2005, the NSDUH incorporated questions into the *Survey* to identify sources of diverted prescription drugs. These data are expected to be released in September 2006. The 2006 *Survey* will seek even more detailed data from respondents as to methods of diversion.

Although there are no firm data that rank methods of acquisition of prescription drugs for non-medical purposes by frequency, specific methods of diversion have been identified. The

Administration's *Synthetics Strategy* seeks to address each specific method: doctor shopping or other prescription fraud, shipping illegal prescriptions from online pharmacies, over-prescribing, theft and burglary (from residences, pharmacies, etc.), selling pills to others, receiving at little or no cost, from friends or family.

Strategy to Reduce Doctor Shopping or Other Prescription Fraud: Prescription Drug Monitoring Programs. The *2004, 2005, and 2006 National Strategies* recognized the problem of prescription drug diversion via "doctor shopping." Generally, this term refers to the visit by an individual—who may or may not have legitimate medical needs—to several doctors, each of whom writes a prescription for a controlled substance. The abuser or addict will visit several pharmacies, receiving more of the drug than intended by any single physician, typically for the purpose of using the drug for psychoactive effects. Associated illegal activities may include the forgery of prescriptions, further multiplying the extent of diversion, or the sale or transfer of the drug to others. In many states, physicians and pharmacists have not been able to automatically cross-check other prescriptions given to the same patient.

In 2004, the Administration announced its intent to respond to this problem by supporting Prescription Drug Monitoring Programs (PDMPs). These programs are designed to reduce prescription fraud and doctor shopping by giving physicians and pharmacists more complete information about a patient's controlled substance prescriptions. These programs vary by State, but generally share the characteristic of allowing prescribers (e.g., a physician) and dispensers (e.g., a pharmacist) to input and receive accurate and timely controlled substance prescription history information, while ensuring patient access to needed treatment. Most States also have some mechanism for law enforcement to receive this information in cases where criminal activity is suspected. Health care providers can use this information as a tool for early identification of patients at risk for addiction and initiate appropriate medical interventions. The justice system can use this information to assist in the enforcement of laws controlling the sale and use of controlled substance prescription medication.

At the beginning of this Administration, approximately 15 PDMPs were in existence in the Nation. The program has expanded to 33 States with active or planned PDMPs—more than double the number in existence in 2001.

A critical avenue of Federal support for States is through the Harold Rogers Prescription Drug Monitoring Grants Program at the Department of Justice. These grants can be used to implement or enhance PDMPs at the State level. The 2007 Budget continues funding for the Rogers Program at the Justice Department, following the funding stream approved by the Congress since 2003. The President has requested that Congress provide $9.9 million for the program in fiscal year 2007 in order to expand the program to new States and enhance the program where it already exists. Officials at ONDCP, the Department of Health and Human Services, and the Department of Justice work with state policymakers to better understand best practices where the programs already exist.

Strategy to Reduce Illegal Access to Controlled Prescription Medications: Internet pharmacies. As the number of Americans with Internet access has increased, so too have opportunities for individuals to acquire controlled substance prescription drugs over the Internet.

The benefits of allowing individuals with a valid prescription to get their prescriptions over the Internet, from a legitimate pharmacy are acknowledged, particularly for people living in rural areas or individuals who are homebound due to illness, disability or other factors. There are legitimate pharmacies that provide services over the Internet and that operate well within the bounds of both the law and sound medical practice. The National Association of Boards of Pharmacy has established a registry of pharmacies that operate online and meet certain criteria, including compliance with licensing and inspection requirements of their State and each State to which they dispense pharmaceuticals.

However, the anonymity of the Internet has enabled proliferation of Web sites that facilitate illicit transactions for controlled substance prescription drugs. These rogue online pharmacy Web sites and links to those sites enable controlled substances to be ordered without a valid prescription. The sites have given drug abusers/ drug addicts and illegal providers a venue to circumvent the law and medically approved prescribing practices by physicians.

Also in existence are Web sites that advertise themselves as pharmacies, but do not operate in the same manner as legitimate pharmacies. Many of these Web sites advertise the sale of controlled substances without a prescription. Such online Web sites usually act as a facilitator, or link, between an individual seeking controlled substance prescription drugs and a doctor and a pharmacy willing to provide these drugs without determining whether the individual has a legitimate medical need. Of particular concern is the "pseudoexam", a cursory, abbreviated medical interaction provided by the Internet site to facilitate a cursory consultation by a doctor via computer or telephone for customers. This consultation is unable to elicit meaningful health information, because the doctor writing the prescription does not see the patient to verify the information provided by the individual. For example, Web sites have no independent means to verify the age of the recipient, enabling a minor to log onto a Web site and claim an inaccurate age. Doctors, frequently paid by the number of prescriptions they sign in this system, have no incentive to spend time seeking additional patient information. Law enforcement has discovered Web site-affiliated doctors who sign hundreds or thousands of prescriptions a day. After receiving the prescription from the doctor, the facilitator will then submit the prescription to a cooperating pharmacy. Because there is no identifying information on the Web site, it is difficult for law enforcement to track the individuals supervising the Web site.

The Administration is using available tools to conduct investigations of rogue Internet-facilitator Web sites, with the purpose of intercepting controlled substance prescriptions illegally sent into the United States through the mail system. For example, the DEA's Internet investigation unit at its Special Operations Division coordinates Internet cases. The DEA has issued immediate suspensions of numerous Internet pharmacies. DOJ has prosecuted doctors and pharmacies who illegally distribute via the Internet. States can also play a significant role in addressing the problem of online facilitators, particularly through PDMPs.

As part of the Administration's work with States regarding PDMPs over the next three years, States will be encouraged to consider addressing, either by statute, regulation, or interstate agreement, situations in which:
• Pharmacies in the State dispense or deliver controlled substance prescription drugs to an address of a patient in another State;

- Pharmacies or other dispensers located in another State dispense or deliver controlled substance prescription drugs to an address of a patient in their own State; and
- Pharmacies or other dispensers in another State that dispense or deliver controlled substance prescription drugs to a patient with an official address in their own State.

The Administration will continue to use the tools at its disposal to target, investigate, prosecute, and dismantle illicit online pharmacies.

Strategy to Reduce Improper Prescribing. The overwhelming majority of prescriptions written in America are responsibly issued on the basis of legitimate medical reasons. A small number of physicians over-prescribe controlled substances, either carelessly, or deliberately. This source of prescriptions drugs facilitates drug addiction. The number of physicians responsible for this problem is a very small fraction of those licensed to dispense controlled substances in the United States. Law enforcement conducts investigations to establish whether the prescribing practice is consistent with sound medical judgment and prevailing medical standards. As part of the Administration's strategy to reduce opportunities to divert controlled substance prescriptions, law enforcement will continue to examine situations where prescriptions for controlled substances are unusually and obviously high, in the absence of legitimate circumstances.

VI. OVERVIEW OF PREVENTION AND TREATMENT

Approximately 35% of the Federal drug budget is targeted to prevention and treatment of drug abuse and addiction. These programs give states and local authorities flexibility in meeting drug-related challenges their communities face, including the mounting problem of prescription drug abuse. Our strategies in prevention and treatment of prescription drugs are both targeted specifically to prescription drugs and to programs that enable prevention, intervention and treatment of addictions, which can have a significant impact on prescription drug abuse.

Preliminary data suggests that the most common way in which controlled substance prescriptions are diverted may be through friends and family.[1] A person with a lawful and medical need for a certain amount of a controlled substance may use only a portion of the prescribed amount and responds to a family member's complaint of pain, by sharing excess medication. Alternatively, for a family member addicted to controlled substance prescription drugs, the mere availability of unused controlled substance prescriptions in the house may prove to be an irresistible temptation. The solution to this problem lies with the medical community and the intended recipient of prescription medications: medical education programs that inform the physician on how to identify the opioid-seeker, counsel patients from losing control of their prescription medications, reducing the number of doses, if feasible, refer pain patients to specialists, and monitor opioid use, by biometric analysis. Patients require information on strategies to retain control of their medications.

Strategies Specific for Physicians Prescribing Controlled Prescription Drugs: Medical Education. The Medical Profession has been alerted through a number of organizations,

[1] Special data run for ONDCP, Preliminary data from the 2005 *National Survey on Drug Use and Health;* data are for the first half of the year and are unweighted.

meetings, medical journals, and medical associations and via pharmaceutical companies of the mounting problem of prescription drug abuse. Notwithstanding the responsible and considered response of the medical community, current statistics indicate that a more concerted effort is required to diminish this escalating public health problem in our society. The administration recognizes the need for a closer partnership between the general medical community, and pain and addiction specialists. To this end, we are organizing several events later this year to facilitate the dissemination of pain and addiction information to the general medical community. Representatives of the medical and pharmaceutical communities will be called together to develop an concerted, effective strategy of change to address this public health problem. It will encourages medical professionals, pharmacists and pharmaceutical companies to take a leading role in educating physicians and patients as to the importance of retaining control of prescriptions medications with abuse liability. ONDCP is also convening a medical conference to assemble leading medical professional associations to focus on medical education on addictions, and specifically on prescription medications.

Multi-Disciplinary Dissemination of Prescription Drug Strategies: Fentanyl. In response to deaths reported in eight states to be associated with fentanyl-laced heroin and cognizant of the view that illegal manufacture and distribution of fentanyl poses unique challenges, ONDCP is convening a Demand Reduction Forum in Philadelphia this Friday, July 28/2006. The forum brings together law enforcement and public health officials, treatment providers, and prevention specialists from Federal, State, and local government to discuss response mechanisms and techniques and the threat to public health arising from abuse of fentanyl. By Friday July 21, 2006, over 100 professionals have registered to attend this important conference.

Other recent outreach efforts include two meetings in Chicago convened by the Chicago Police Department, the Drug Enforcement Agency, and the Chicago High Intensity Drug Trafficking Area, a weekly inter-agency telephone conference initially convened by CDC and SAMHSA to share information on recent developments, and warning alerts sent out by SAMHSA to treatment providers and CDC to public healthcare professionals, including state and local health departments and poison control centers.

Prevention Strategies Specific for People with Access to Controlled Prescription Drugs: Media Campaign. Reductions in prescription drug abuse also require the dissemination of information to various sectors of our society that encounter this class of drugs. Foremost, patients in possession of controlled prescription drugs need to be educated about the legal, social, medical and behavioral consequences of providing a controlled substance to a friend or family member. Patient-parents also need to become aware of the need to restrict access to their drugs. Finally, youth and adults need to become aware of the potentially severe adverse consequences of drugs. ONDCP's National Youth Anti-Drug Media Campaign is addressing the rise in prescription drug abuse by teens. Prescription Drug Use is featured on the Youth and Parents Websites visited by almost two million people a month. The Parent Website has extensive information on the dangers of prescription drugs, ways to prevent this drug use, and resources for parents to help teens who have a problem. All of the parenting resources (handbooks, CD-ROMs, brochures, websites, advertisements, press messages) have solid information on monitoring techniques that are effective against prescription drug use, along with other risky behaviors. The Media

22

Campaign recently added a specific advice page on how to deal with prescription drug use into their interactive parenting guide.

The Media Campaign is also reaching parents with press outreach; for example, on July 18th Director Walters held a press conference that focused on the need for parents to monitor their teens internet usage to avoid the drug threat. Starting last Friday, a new open letter ad from ONDCP's National Youth Anti-Drug Media Campaign will run in *People* magazine, alerting parents to the pro-drug influences to which young people are exposed by technologies like the Internet, text messaging, and social networking sites. The ad specifically addresses the risk of prescription and over-the-counter drug abuse by young people. The E-Monitoring Open Letter to Parents also appeared in Sunday's *New York Times*, as well as top newspapers in 27 media markets across the country and consumer publications like *Newsweek*. Seven health, parenting, and media education organizations signed the E-Monitoring Open Letter to Parents, including the PTA and the American Academy of Pediatrics.

Established Programs: Community Coalitions. Communities across the country have formed local anti-drug community coalitions that coordinate prevention and intervention efforts. These coalitions bring together community leaders and professionals in health care, law enforcement, and education to provide local, grassroots solutions to the challenges drug and alcohol abuse pose to their neighborhoods. Coalitions work to develop a model for all sectors to work together to change community norms and send the same no-use messages to young people. The Administration supports the efforts of many of these coalitions by providing $79.2 million in the President's FY 2007 Budget through the Drug-Free Communities (DFC) Support Program. Through the establishment of community coalitions, the DFC program is designed to complement the development and implementation of the Strategic Prevention Framework in communities across America.

Community Coalitions: Prescription Drug Tracking. Currently, there are over 700 funded DFC coalitions, which exist in every state and form the backbone of the Nation's community prevention system. Under this program, each grantee receives up to $100,000 annually for up to five years to develop a comprehensive community plan to address substance abuse problems. Of the over 700 DCF grantees, 365 work on prescription drug abuse, including education efforts to prevent abuse and the tracking of amphetamines, barbiturates, and oxycodone.

Established Programs: Prevention and Intervention by Biometric Identification: Student Drug Testing. The President stated in his 2004 State of the Union Address that drug testing is an effective part of a community-based strategy to reduce the demand for illicit substances. When implemented in combination with other drug abuse prevention measures, this non-punitive public health tool can reduce the number of youth using drugs illicitly and, by preventing or deterring early-initiation, can also decrease the likelihood of adult drug use. Testing can be used to screen for the abuse of prescription drugs. If a student tests positive, the parents can be notified of the result and can take action if they determine the student should not be taking the drug.

Student drug testing is also an important screening tool that can identify youth who have initiated prescription substance use so that parents and counselors can intervene at an early stage as well as those with a drug dependency so that they can be referred to appropriate treatment. The Office of National Drug Control Policy works closely with the Department of Education to help interested schools and communities learn more about how to develop and implement a comprehensive, considerate, and safe random student drug testing policy. Regional and State summits with experts in the field and other outreach activities help spread model program elements and increase awareness about this prevention program.

Grants from the Department of Education in 2003 and 2004 in the amount of $2 million and in 2005 in the amount of $9.9 million have afforded 373 schools around the nation the opportunity to enhance and implement student drug testing programs. All grantees screen for opioids and amphetamines. Once a screen shows an opioid positive, the screen is broken down to determine which drug is present. If it is determined to be a prescription drug, then the parent is notified to verify that the student has been prescribed that particular drug. Many more schools have added this strategy to their existing drug prevention programs. These schools recognize the benefits of stopping drug use before it starts and in promoting a safe and drug-free community.

Established Programs: Screening, Brief Intervention, Referral and Treatment (SBIRT). A key component of expanding the Nation's treatment capacity lies in early detection and engaging health professionals in the identification, counseling, referral, and ongoing medical management of persons with substance use disorders. The Department of Health and Human Services offers grants through the Screening, Brief Intervention, Referral and Treatment (SBIRT) program to States, territories, and tribal organizations to provide effective early identification and intervention in general medical settings. This program is based on research showing that by simply asking questions regarding unhealthy behaviors and conducting brief interventions, patients are more likely to avoid the behavior in the future and seek help if they believe they have problem. The programs are based in clinical settings, a location that has a high propensity to attract higher-risk populations, who through violence, accidents or health-related problems, are seen by medical professionals.

SBIRT expands the continuum of care available for treatment of substance use disorders by matching an individual's stage of illness to the initial treatment experience and improves linkages among general community-health related services and specialized substance abuse treatment agencies. Universal screening of patients in a general medical setting can significantly reduce drug and alcohol use among non-dependent users, even without accompanying intervention.

SBIRT could help identify a cohort of prescription drug abusers who enter hospital or clinical environments seeking treatment for reasons other than for prescription drug abuse. This cohort would have the opportunity to be shepherded into interventions or treatment programs.

Awards for the program were made in September 2003 to six States and one Tribal Council. In addition to these grants, 12 universities and colleges have received funding to develop a screening and intervention model to be used on campuses. These programs will identify drug problems at an early stage and help reduce drug dependency and addiction in this vulnerable age cohort. The Office of National Drug Control Policy works closely with the Substance Abuse and Mental Health Administration to monitor the success of these programs and to highlight the benefits of early screening and intervention. As part of the FY07 budget, approximately $31.2 million is requested for this initiative.

Established Treatment Programs. Stopping use before it starts is a priority of the Office of National Drug Control Policy, but treating drug users is critical to demand reduction efforts. From extensive work in the field of addiction science, we know that treatment for drug dependency and addiction – including to methamphetamine – can be effective. The programs we support make significant contributions to closing the treatment gap. At present 8.1 million of the 34.8 million past year drug users in the United States meet the clinical definition of abuse or dependency. Of these, 1.4 million received treatment at a specialty treatment facility. Continued success in healing America's drug users is predicated on the availability of treatment for the remaining 6.6 million.

Treatment for prescription drug abuse is available. For example, for those who abuse methamphetamine, the Matrix Model is an evidence-based intensive outpatient treatment program created by The Matrix Institute in Los Angeles. It has been tested through research, showing favorable outcomes. It is a manual-based treatment that uses cognitive behavioral therapy, relapse prevention and skill training, all presented in Motivational Interviewing style. Treatment includes educational sessions for client families and other support people. Skill training groups focus on recovery and relapse prevention. The main objective of the program is to provide clients with a behavioral structure and daily skills enabling the eventual development of a clean and sober lifestyle.

Matrix clients were 38 percent more likely to stay in treatment compared with other treatment modalities and were 27 percent more likely to complete treatment. In some sites of the research clinical trail (total of 8 sites), the Matrix condition was associated with significantly longer periods of abstinence. Treatment completion was about 41 percent.

Specific to opioid addiction, SAMHSA's Center for Substance Abuse and Treatment has Opioid Treatment Program (OT) accreditation grants to: (1) reduce the costs of basic accreditation education and accreditation surveys and ongoing reaccreditation for OTPs; (2) ensure that new OTPs and OTPs that did not become fully accredited before the May 19, 2004, regulatory date become fully accredited under 42 CFR Part 8; and (3) ensure that OTPs maintain their accreditation by undergoing the reaccreditation process every three years.

The President's FY 2007 budget request includes $1.76 billion for the Substance Abuse Prevention and Treatment Block grant, of which 20 percent is set-aside for substance abuse prevention. These funds are directed to specialty treatment providers, many of whom provide treatment for abuse and dependence of prescription drugs. The President's budget also includes nearly $556 million in prevention and treatment discretionary grants (Programs of Regional and National Significance), including *Access to Recovery.*

Administered by SAMHSA, the President's *Access to Recovery* (ATR) program is now in 14 States and one Native American organization. Over the three year grant cycle, ATR will provide services to an estimated 125,000 people who seek treatment, but are not able to obtain it, in part, because they cannot afford it. To close the treatment gap, ATR also funds essential recovery support services not generally provided through conventional Federal treatment resources, such as comprehensive relapse prevention services, transportation, or child-care. Many providers are unable to offer "wrap-around" services, even though they are less costly than services required in the initial stages of recovery, and are of paramount significance to those in recovery

The President's FY07 request for ATR is $98.2 million, which includes $24.8 million for an ATR-Methamphetamine initiative. Both the House and Senate appropriations bills eliminated funding for ATR I'd like to take this opportunity to encourage the Committee to look more closely at ATR, and data on outcome measures.

Established Treatment Program: Drug Courts. There are currently in excess of 1,750 drug courts in operation and another 400 in development. Using the coercive power of the courts to alter behavior through a combination of escalating sanctions, mandatory drug sentencing, and rigorous case management to address the individual's overall needs, drug courts divert non-violent, low-level offenders whose underlying problem is drug use away from prison and into supervised treatment The National Center on Addiction and Substance Abuse (CASA) at Columbia University reviewed and synthesized over 120 evaluations and determined that drug courts provide the most comprehensive and effective control of drug-using offenders criminality and drug usage while under the courts supervision. A National Institute of Justice report demonstrated that, within the first year of release, 43.5 percent of drug offenders are rearrested, whereas only 16.4 percent of drug court graduates are re-arrested. This ratio of re-arrest rates persists in year two following graduation from drug court. Drug courts have not traditionally focused on prescription drug abusers. ONDCP will be working with HHS and DOJ to assess the current status of prescription drug abuse in drug courts and will make recommendations based on our findings. There is strong administration support for drug courts. The President's FY 2007 budget requests a funding level of $69.2 million for drug courts programs – an increase of $59.3 million over the 2006 enacted level. This increase reflects a commitment to this program.

VII. CONCLUSION

Scheduled prescription drugs are safe, effective, and necessary for intended patients, when prescribed for legitimate medical purposes. The diversion of prescription drugs for unintended, non-medical purposes is a national public health challenge. We are encouraged by increasing collaboration and cooperation between pharmaceutical companies and federal agencies, the medical community, and state regulators, which have instituted surveillance, pharmaceutical tracking, legal strategies, educational programs, risk management plans, tamper-free formulations and other procedures and polices to attenuate this escalating problem.

ONDCP is committed to eliminate diversion and abuse of potentially addictive prescription medications, by engaging Federal, private, legal and medical sectors in the creation of effective strategies and policies. The Synthetic Strategy focuses on methamphetamine with relevant programs applicable to prescription drug abuse. Screening, brief intervention and referral to treatment (SBIRT), Student Drug Testing and Drug Courts identify and steer methamphetamine or prescription drug abusers/addicts into intervention and treatment programs. Access to recovery (ATR) and State Block grants provide the necessary treatment.

The President's Drug Control Policy is characterized by vigilance, flexibility, adaptability and innovative strategies to address emerging drug threats. The Administration is committed to developing an effective public health strategy that balances the legitimate medical use of prescription drugs by intended populations, while eliminating diversion and abuse of these medications by unintended populations. Multidisciplinary programs that provide surveillance, legal strategies, identification of prescription drug abusers and treatment capacity are major components of the Synthetic Strategy.

Thank you. I welcome questions from the Subcommittee.

Mr. SOUDER. Thank you.
Dr. Volkow.

STATEMENT OF NORA D. VOLKOW, M.D.

Dr. VOLKOW. Good morning, Mr. Chairman, Mr. Souder and Mr. Cummings and other members of the committee. It is a privilege for me to be here to discuss the science behind the abuse of prescription medication.

We heard the problem is quite large; 6.3 million Americans have used prescription medication. We have also heard that it has surpassed prescription medication, surpassed in terms of 2004 the number of new initiates over that. This is the first time this has happened. If you look at Monitor the Future, which surveys 8th, 10th, 12th graders, prescription medication is No. 2 just preceded by marijuana, but No, 3, No. 4, No. 6 in terms of prevalent are also prescription drug medications. So prescription medication abuse is widespread.

What are the prescription drugs that are abused? They are three classes: Pain medications, that's opiates or OxyContin and Vicodin, which are typically used to treat severe or moderate pain; stimulant medication such as amphetamine and Ritalin, which are typically used to treat attention deficit disorders; and sedative hypnotics, such as benzodiazepines and barbituates like Lithium and Valium which are typically used to treat sleeping disorders, anxiety, and muscle spasms.

Why are they abused? They are abused because like illicit drugs, like meth or cocaine, they increase the concentration of the chemical dopamine in required areas of the brain. And they use the same targets that some of these drugs use. For example, Ritalin and amphetamine stimulant use the same targets as cocaine and meth respectively. For the opiates, OxyContin, Vicodin, Hydrocodone use the same targets as morphine, and benzodiazepines use similar targets as alcohol.

So the question is what is the difference between these drugs being therapeutically effective and the potential of abuse? And what we have learned is that there are several factors, but there are two key factors. One of them is dose. When these drugs are abused, they are used at much larger doses and the doses are taken much more frequently than when prescribed therapeutically.

Another important factor is the route of administration. When you take drugs that are for their therapeutic reasons, they are given orally. When they are abused, they are snorted or injected. And why is that so? Because what we have learned is for this type of drug to be rewarded, they have to get into the brain very rapidly and the route of administration affects the rate at which these drugs enter. When they are injected or snorted, they go into the brain much more rapidly than they when they are taken orally.

Who is at risk? Well, this is nondiscriminatory. It affects all ages or genders or socioeconomic classes. It has phases, for example, for the first time with the abuse of opiate individuals. Now lessons which—usually in terms of opiates abuse, heroin abusers are in their 20's or 30's or 40's. This is particularly problematic because the brain is still maturing. So at this stage the abuse of these medications can affect the proper development of the brain making these individuals more vulnerable to the addictive effects of other drugs into the future.

What do we know about why is this happening now? Some of these factors have been mentioned. There has been a dramatic increase in the number of prescriptions for these medications.

Stimulant, the rate of prescriptions have basically doubled every 5 years over the past 15 years. The rate of production has escalated. There has been increased advertisement of these drugs in the media. We have easy access to the Internet. We have generated a culture that not only gives medications for the treatment of disease, but has started to give medications to improve performance. And those that believe that it may be safe to take this prescription drug because, as was mentioned before, they are approved by the FDA; unfortunately, the recent reminder of the deaths from the use of the Fentanyl is a reminder that these drugs are very dangerous.

So what is NIDA doing? NIDA has taken a multi-pronged approach to invest research into the basic neuroscience of what are these drugs doing to the brain. What are the genes that make a person more vulnerable? What is the etiology? Environmental? We are also developing medications that are potent analgesics without having the resultant properties. We are delivering new ways so they can minimize the abuse. At the same time, we are developing treatments to actually deal with a problem of the person that is addicted to prescription medication and to target those individuals that need the medication but become addicted.

Finally, we realize the importance of education and with partners with SAMSHA and with all medical professional communities to educate both the clinicians as well as the public about, yes, the therapeutic volume of the medication but also the importance of proper surveillance.

I thank the committee. This is a problem that has not been given the attention that it deserves. It is urgent. And it is a privilege for me to be able to share with you how science can help with it.

[The prepared statement of Dr. Volkow follows:]

Testimony
Before the Subcommittee on Criminal Justice, Drug Policy,
and Human Resources
Committee on Government Reform
United States House of Representatives

Efforts of the National Institute on Drug Abuse to
Prevent and Treat Prescription Drug Abuse

Statement of
Nora D. Volkow, M.D.
Director
National Institute on Drug Abuse
National Institutes of Health
U.S. Department of Health and Human Services

For Release on Delivery

Expected at 10:00 a.m.
Wednesday, July 26, 2006

Mr. Chairman and Members of the Subcommittee:

Thank you for inviting the National Institute on Drug Abuse (NIDA), a component of the National Institutes of Health (NIH), an agency of the U.S. Department of Health and Human Services, to participate in this important hearing. Prescription drugs are powerful allies in our quest to alleviate human suffering. And psychotherapeutics—those drugs that target the central nervous system (CNS)—are responsible for remarkable advances in our ability to understand and reduce the burden of mental illness and physical pain. However, as is often the case with beneficial technologies, there is a negative side, too. Because some of the psychotherapeutic drugs act, either directly or indirectly, upon the same brain systems affected by addictive drugs, their non-medical use carries a substantial abuse liability that NIDA's efforts are designed to assess, reduce, and make publicly known. I am pleased to have the opportunity today to share with you what we know and where we are relative to the issue of prescription drug abuse in this country.

What is the Scope of Prescription Drug Abuse in this Country?

Several indicators show that prescription drug abuse is a significant problem in the United States and one that has been increasing recently.

- Approximately 6 million persons 12 and older used psychotherapeutic drugs for non-medical purposes in 2004, which represents 2.5 percent of the U.S. population. Most of them reported abusing opiate pain relievers in particular, with young adults (18-25) showing the greatest increases in lifetime use between 2002 and 2004 (National Survey on Drug Use and Health (NSDUH),

conducted by HHS's Substance Abuse and Mental Health Services
Administration).

- In 2004, 2.4 million persons ages 12 or older *initiated* non-medical use of
prescription pain relievers during the past year, surpassing for the first time in
the life of the survey, those who initiated abuse of marijuana (2.1 million)
(National Survey on Drug Use and Health).

- Among 12th graders, in 2005, 9.5% reported past-year non-medical use of
Vicodin, and 5.5% reported past-year non-medical use of OxyContin. Data
show an increase in the abuse of OxyContin between 2002 and 2005 among
12th graders (NIDA's 2005 Monitoring the Future survey [MTF]).

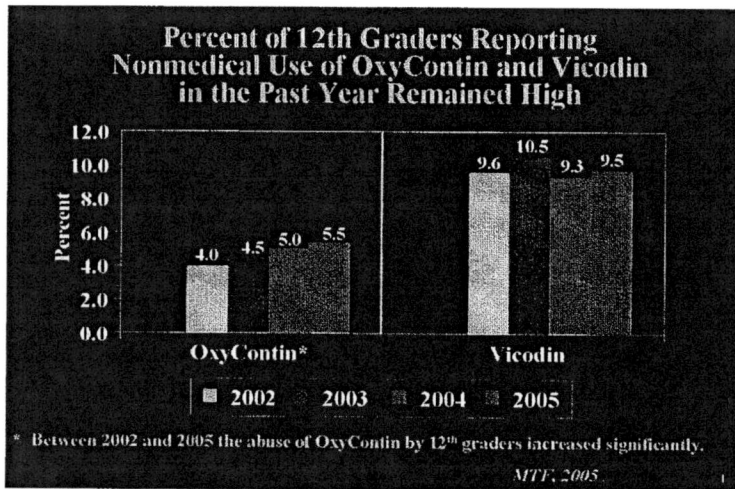

Percent of 12th Graders Reporting Nonmedical Use of OxyContin and Vicodin in the Past Year Remained High

2

- Past-year non-medical use of stimulant medications is also high, with 8.6% of 12th graders reporting abuse of amphetamine (a parent class of drugs that includes methamphetamine), and 4.4% reporting abuse of methylphenidate (Ritalin) (2005 MTF).

Prescription Drugs with Abuse Liability

The psychotropic prescription drugs that present abuse liability fall into three broad categories:

(1) stimulants, which are prescribed to treat attention-deficit hyperactivity disorder (ADHD) and narcolepsy and include drugs such as Ritalin and Adderall; (2) opioids, which are mostly prescribed to treat moderate to severe pain and include drugs such as OxyContin and Vicodin; and (3) CNS depressants, typically prescribed for the treatment of anxiety, panic, sleep disorders, acute stress reactions, and muscle spasms and include drugs such as Valium, Librium, and Xanax.

To understand how these drugs can have both beneficial effects in patients and serious abuse and health liabilities in people taking them for non-medical reasons requires knowledge of how drugs exert their effects in the brain. As noted above, there can be substantial overlap between the brain systems that mediate the therapeutic effects of psychotropic medications and those responsible for the reinforcing effects of drugs of abuse. However, while the molecular targets in the brain for some medications may be the same ones as those for some of the drugs of abuse, differences in how much of the drug gets into the brain and how fast it gets there determine whether desirable (therapeutic) or undesirable (abuse and addiction) effects will follow. Factors such as drug dosage, route of administration (which regulates the speed of drug delivery to the brain), and user expectations are crucial. For example, the stimulant

3

methylphenidate (Ritalin) has much in common with cocaine—they bind to similar sites in the brain and they both increase the brain chemical dopamine through the same molecular targets. And when both drugs are administered intravenously, they cause a rapid and large increase in dopamine, which a person experiences as a rush or high. However, when methylphenidate is taken orally, as prescribed, it elicits a gradual and sustained increase in dopamine, which is not perceived as euphoria and instead produces the expected therapeutic effects seen in many patients.

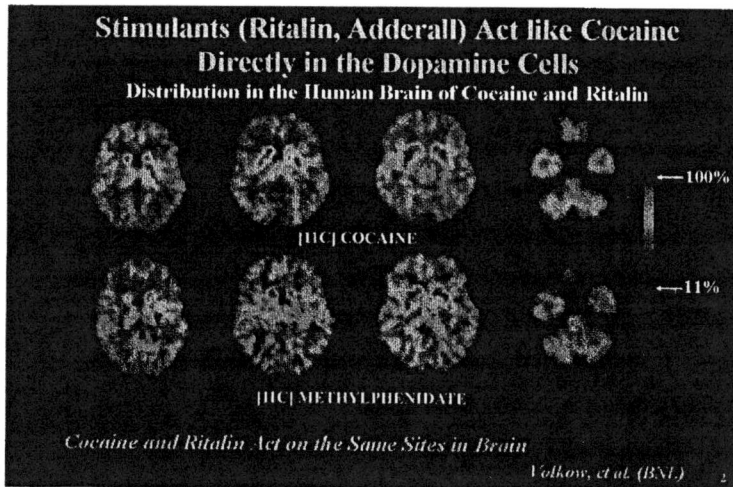

Scientists and physicians are learning how to exploit such differences to develop formulations and dosage regimens for optimal therapeutic value and minimal abuse and addiction potential. Unfortunately, these strategies can sometimes be undermined by sophisticated abusers. Consider OxyContin, a pain medication originally marketed as having a low potential for abuse because it was formulated to ensure a slow and gradual release of the drug. Abusers quickly learned that the pills could be crushed and their contents injected or snorted, releasing the entire dosage at once. What abusers do not realize is the great risk of overdose and other devastating consequences that may result from this practice. Now widespread in its abuse, OxyContin is the only commonly prescribed opioid analgesic that comes with a "black box" warning.

Why is this happening now?

The recent increase in the extent of prescription drug abuse in this country is likely the result of a confluence of factors, such as: significant increases in the number of prescriptions;[1] significant increases in drug availability;[2] aggressive marketing by the pharmaceutical industry;[3] the proliferation of illegal Internet pharmacies that dispense these medications without proper prescriptions and surveillance;[4] and a greater social acceptability for medicating a growing number of conditions. The fact that doctors are prescribing these drugs legitimately and with increasing frequency to treat a variety of ailments leads to the misguided and dangerous conclusion that their non-medical use should be equally safe. This misperception of safety may contribute, for example, to the casual attitude of many college students towards abusing stimulants to improve cognitive function and academic performance.

Notably, between 1987 and 1996, a nearly four-fold increase occurred in the prevalence of stimulant prescriptions among youth; this increase has persisted, but has

---

[1] See, e.g., Zacny et. al., *College on Problems of Drug Dependence taskforce on Prescription Opioid Non-Medical Use and Abuse: Position Statements*, Drug and Alcohol Dependence 69 (2003) 25-232; and Compton and Volkow, *Major Increases in Opioid Analgesic Abuse in the U.S.: Concerns and Strategies*, Drug and Alcohol Dependence 81 (2006) 103-107. These citations include information from IMS Health's National Prescription Audit.
[2] See, e.g., McCabe et al, *Medical Use, Illicit Use, and Diversion of Abusable Prescription Drugs*, Journal of American College Health 54 (2006) 269-278.
[3] See, e.g., United States General Accounting Office, *Prescription Drugs – Oxycontin Abuse and Diversion and Efforts to Address the Problem*, GAO-04-110, 12/2003
[4] See, e.g., Forman et al, *The Availability of Web Sites Offering to Sell Opioid Medications Without Prescriptions*, American Journal of Psychiatry 163 (2006) 1233-1238.

since remained near the 1996 levels. Similarly, the number of oxycodone and hydrocodone prescriptions has more than doubled between 1994 and 2001. While such increases in psychoactive drug prescriptions reflect improved diagnostic practices and treatment options, it would be naive not to also consider the contribution of market forces in the emergence of these trends. For example, sales of ADHD medications in the United States reached $3.1 billion in 2004. But even at this robust level of sales, the number of prescriptions for ADHD medications is less than 20 percent when compared to the 120 million prescriptions written in 2005 for pain medications containing hydrocodone or oxycodone. Such high exposure rates suggest that we need to discover the potential abuse consequences for youth and other populations at risk for addiction.

Special populations, specific risks and consequences

Indeed, the growing problem of prescription drug abuse in this country, which affects individuals at all stages in life, is alarming. In adolescents, the increase in prescription drug abuse reported over the past 5 years contrasts with the steady declines in overall illicit drug abuse that has been reported in this group over this same time period. These trends in adolescent are particularly problematic because adolescence is the period of greatest risk not only for drug experimentation but also for developing addiction. Also at this stage the brain is still developing and exposure to drugs could interfere with these developmental changes.

Today we know that the last part of the brain to fully mature is the prefrontal cortex, a region that governs judgment and decision-making functions. This may help explain why teens are prone to risk-taking and why high rates of risky behaviors,

6

including abuse of alcohol and other drugs, have been reported among those who abuse prescription drugs. The 2001 NSDUH survey reveals that youth who had used prescription drugs non-medically in the past year were almost four times more likely to have also used other illicit drugs.

We are also particularly concerned about older Americans, who currently make up only 13 percent of the population but who receive approximately one-third of all medications prescribed in the Nation. For practical reasons, older patients are sometimes prescribed long-term and multiple prescriptions, which could lead to abuse or unintentional misuse. These medications can interact with over-the-counter medicines and dietary supplements, which older adults tend to consume in significant quantities. Older adults also experience higher rates of other illnesses, normal changes in drug metabolism, and increased susceptibility to toxic effects. It is hardly surprising then that abuse or unintentional misuse of prescription drugs by elderly persons could lead to more severe health consequences. For example, elderly persons who take benzodiazepines such as Valium, Librium, and Xanax are at increased risk for cognitive impairment, leading to possible falls as well as vehicular accidents. Moreover, not all physicians know that prescribing benzodiazepines to elderly people is contraindicated for these reasons. Therefore, physician education is a necessary part of any effort to curb the abuse of prescription medications.

Prescription drug abuse must also be carefully tracked among women because of their combined vulnerabilities. First, women are more likely than men to suffer from depression, anxiety, trauma, and victimization, all of which frequently appear with substance abuse in the form of comorbidities. Second, girls and women report using drugs to cope with stressful situations in their lives. Third, studies suggest that women

7

are significantly more likely than men to be prescribed an abusable drug, particularly in the form of narcotics and anti-anxiety medications. These cumulative risks notwithstanding, adult men and women have roughly similar rates of non-medical use of prescription drugs; 12–17-year-old girls, however, are more likely than boys to abuse psychotherapeutic drugs, including stimulants.

In addition to the risk to women is the potential for harm to the developing fetus. Therefore, more research is needed on the extent and patterns of prescription drug abuse during pregnancy. National projections from survey data collected between 2002 and 2004 suggest that 109,000 pregnant women abused pain relievers in the past year. And past-year abuse of any stimulants (including methamphetamine) or sedatives/tranquilizers was reported by 32,000 and 56,000 pregnant women, respectively. However, there is overall less non-medical abuse of prescription psychotherapeutics among pregnant than among non-pregnant women (6% and 9.3%, respectively), although this is not the case in pregnant adolescent girls (15-17 years), in whom the rate of prescription drug abuse is higher than in those who are not pregnant.

What Abuse of Prescription Drugs Does to the Brain and Body

When taken under the supervision of a physician, prescription drugs can be lifesaving, but when abused, they can be as life-threatening as illicit drugs. Stimulants can elevate blood pressure, increase heart rate and respiration, cause sleep deprivation, and elicit paranoia. Their continued abuse, or even one high dose, can cause irregular heartbeat, heart failure, and seizures. Painkillers and anti-anxiety medications can cause depressed respiration and even death, and CNS depressants can also induce seizures when a reduction in their chronic use triggers a sudden rebound in brain activity.

8

Particularly dangerous is when young people indiscriminately mix and share

prescription drugs, also combining them with alcohol or other drugs. In an environment

where opiate analgesics are the most frequently prescribed medication, with over 100

million prescriptions written every year, this risky practice is likely to contribute to the

growing trend of drug abuse-related emergency room visits involving prescribed

narcotics. And again, these classes of psychotherapeutic drugs have a real potential for

leading to addiction, especially if abused repeatedly, at high doses, and/or by

susceptible individuals.

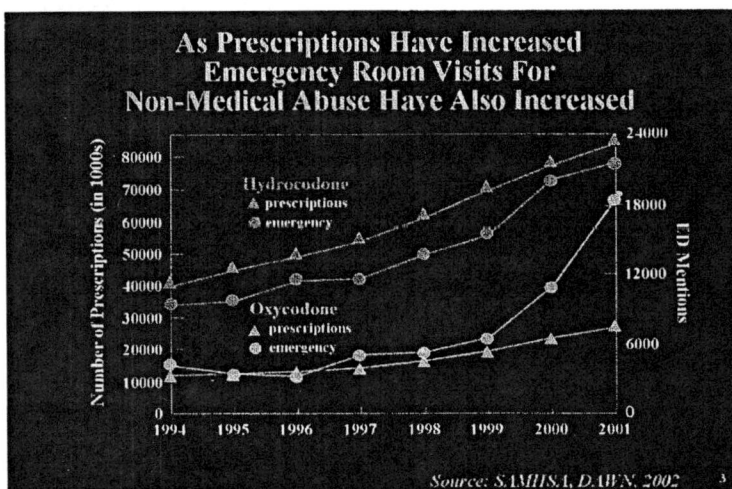

What is NIDA doing about it?

Recent research has revealed an increasing problem with prescription drug abuse, yet

we still must get a better picture of the broader epidemiologic patterns of abuse. We need to learn more about how specific drugs are abused and in what quantities and combinations, why they are abused and how often, as well as other associated medical and health consequences. We also need a better understanding of the regional and local variations in patterns of abuse, and the influence of age, gender, and race/ethnicity—all of which can provide an essential foundation for developing effective and targeted interventions and services.

Epidemiology and surveillance

We have at our disposal a series of surveillance instruments, which we use to continuously monitor trends in all forms of drug abuse, including the abuse of prescribed medications. For example, 21 Community Epidemiology Work Group (CEWG) sentinel sites across the Nation provide ongoing community-level surveillance of drug abuse profiles through analysis of quantitative and qualitative research data. At its 56th semiannual meeting, CEWG representatives held a special conference on patterns and trends in the abuse of prescription drugs, information later disseminated to drug abuse prevention and treatment agencies, public health officials, researchers, and policymakers. The application of this and other tools have allowed NIDA to stay ahead of the curve and to identify potentially troublesome trends as soon as they begin to surface in the population, such as those that have prompted NIDA-supported researchers to investigate the patterns and sources of illicit use of prescription medications in high school and college students.

Research initiatives

In response to the mounting evidence of increased abuse of prescribed medications, NIDA has orchestrated a multi-pronged strategy intended to complement

10

and expand our already robust portfolio of basic, preclinical, and clinical research aimed at better understanding the prescription drug phenomenon. An important item on this agenda is our latest initiative on "Prescription Opioid Use and Abuse in the Treatment of Pain," which encourages a multidisciplinary approach using both human and animal studies from across the sciences to examine factors (including pain itself) that predispose or protect against opioid abuse and addiction. Particularly important is to assess how genetic influences affect the vulnerability of an individual exposed to pain medication to become addicted. This type of information will help develop screening and diagnostic tools that primary care physicians can use to assess the potential for prescription drug abuse in their patients. Because opioid medications are prescribed for all age groups, NIDA is also encouraging research that assesses the effects of their chronic use over the entire lifespan.

Another important initiative pertains to the development of new pain medications or formulations with minimum abuse potential. We have witnessed some remarkable advances in this area of research recently with the introduction of buprenorphine/naloxone, a combined formulation for the treatment of opiate addiction with dramatically reduced abuse liability. Compounds that act on a combination of two distinct opioid receptors (mu and delta), have been shown in preclinical studies to induced strong analgesia without producing tolerance or dependence. Researchers are also getting closer to developing a new generation of non–opioid-based medications for severe pain that would circumvent the brain reward pathways, greatly reducing abuse potential. Included are compounds that work through a cannabinoid receptor subtype located primarily in the peripheral nervous system.

41

Treatment and Prevention

Treatment and prevention of drug abuse and addiction are key NIDA goals. Our efforts to identify effective treatments for prescription opioid abuse and addiction include conducting a multi-center study of more than 600 participants, employing our Clinical Trials Network (CTN) to evaluate treatment regimens using oral buprenorphine/naloxone. In addition, behavioral therapies, an integral part of all treatment strategies, continue to be a mainstay for treating stimulant addiction.

Although scientifically validated prevention programs have been shown to be effective in curbing the prevalence of substance abuse and addiction in general, non-medical use of prescription drugs in some ways presents a more difficult scenario than illicit drugs. Because prescription drugs are safe and effective when used properly and are broadly marketed to the public, the notion that they are also harmful and addictive when abused can be a difficult one to convey. Thus, we need focused research to discover targeted communication strategies that effectively address this problem. Reaching this goal may be significantly more complex and nuanced than developing and deploying effective programs for the prevention of abuse of illicit drugs, but good prevention messages based on scientific evidence will be hard to ignore and will make their mark in time.

In the meantime, the centerpiece of our strategy to curtail the prevalence of prescription drug abuse must center around our efforts to disseminate accurate information about the serious health consequences involved, with particular focus on addiction potential. Our messages aim to reach not only the general public and populations at heightened risk, such as adolescents, but also physicians and other health care providers, whose training on proper diagnostic and monitoring practices is

12

vitally important. We will continue our close collaborations with physicians'
organizations, the Office of National Drug Control Policy (ONDCP), SAMHSA and other
Federal agencies, as well as professional associations with a strong interest in
preserving public health. We regard these preventive efforts an integral part of NIDA's
mission.

Conclusion

In conclusion, we should not be surprised that the availability of more, new, and better
psychotherapeutics has been followed more recently by an upswing in the prevalence of
their non-medical use by varied populations. However, we should be seriously
concerned: prescription drugs can be powerfully addictive and their abuse
accompanied by toxic and sometimes fatal consequences.

Perhaps one of the most challenging aspects of this trend is that prescription
drug abuse affects individuals of all ages. On the other hand, we are fortunate to have
in place an efficient warning system that has helped us to spot this problem at a
relatively early stage and to quickly implement activities designed to keep it in check.
Consistent with one of NIDA's most important goals, our response has been framed by
our commitment to translate what we know from research to help the public better
understand drug abuse and addiction, and to develop more effective strategies for their
prevention and treatment.

The emerging nature of the prescription drug abuse problem, combined with our
substantial but still growing knowledge of its underlying causes and resulting
consequences, make us optimistic about our chances to rationally and successfully
address this challenge.

Thank you for allowing me to share this information with you. I will be happy to answer any questions you may have.

Mr. SOUDER. Thank you.

Dr. Kweder.

STATEMENT OF SANDRA L. KWEDER, M.D.

Dr. KWEDER. Good morning, Mr. Chairman. My name is Sandra Kweder. I am the Deputy Director of the Office of New Drugs and the Center for Drug Evaluation and Research. I appreciate the opportunity to talk about our drug approval process and it's interface with our role in preventing prescription drug abuse.

FDA is a public health agency that is strongly committed to promoting and protecting the public health by assuring that safe and effective products reach the market in a timely way and that the products are marketed for continued safety once out there.

The FDA is aware of and is concerned about reports of and the reality of prescription drug abuse, misuse and diversion. We are aware of data showing that abuse of prescription drugs, including narcotics, is growing.

This is a serious issue and we sympathize with the families and friends of individuals who have lost their lives or otherwise have been harmed as a result of prescription drug abuse and misuse. We have them, too.

While addressing the important issues of drug abuse and misuse, FDA must assure that patients who require these medicines maintain appropriate access to them through informed providers and safeguards.

Under the Food, Drug and Cosmetic Act, FDA is responsible for ensuring that new drugs are safe and effective. Before any drug is approved for marketing in the United States, FDA must decide whether the studies and information submitted by the drug sponsor have demonstrated that the drug is safe and effective when used according to the drug's labeling.

When the drug's benefits outweigh the risks and the labeling instructions and some certain other measures allow for safe and effective use by patients, FDA approves the drugs for marketing. Let me say a little bit more about what I mean by other measures.

At the time of approval and sometimes after approval, FDA may develop in cooperation with the drug sponsor a plan of interventions beyond labeling to help assure the safe and effective use of the drug. This has been referred to as risk management plans or risk maps, but the practice dates back many years.

Interventions that might make up a risk management plan vary, but all are aimed at assuring that known or potential issues regarding proper use of the drug are addressed by prescribers and patients. The agencies' expectation for developing risk maps, including aspects that might include post-marketing surveillance and other strategies, are detailed in a set of guidances that we published in March 2005 as a response to reauthorization of the Prescription Drug User Fee Act.

The provisions of the Controlled Substances Act are a means of actually managing risk of drugs, although they predate this term of risk management plan or risk map. Under the CSA, we at FDA notify the DEA if a new drug application is submitted for any drug having a stimulant, depressant or hallucinogenic effect on the central nervous system. That would include opiates because it is assumed that the drug may have abuse potential. For such drugs, the products' developer or sponsor must provide FDA with all data pertinent to abuse of the drug, a proposal for scheduling under the CSA, and data on overdoses. We then represent a scheduling category, but DEA makes the final scheduling category decision.

In addition to scheduling, it is common though for products with abuse potential to have risk maps that establish interventions to actually prevent misuse, abuse and overdose. Specifically, FDA expects sponsors of applications for any new drug with abuse potential to submit a risk map to address three important areas: Preventing accidental overdose, ensuring proper patient selection for prescription, and preventing misuse and abuse. And we review those proposals very carefully.

While individual programs will vary based on product specific considerations, every risk map for drugs with abuse potential should address those three elements and contain monitoring plans above and beyond the usual for side effects. Specifically to identify misuse, overdose, abuse or potential for diversion. Examples might include specialized training for providers, call centers, or Web sites for reporting problems or obtaining advice, single source distribution, kits for patients to ensure safe storage and disposal, limited marketing roll out plans, targeted surveillance activities to detect excessive prescribing or prescription diversion and additional studies to address development of novel formulations.

Our job is not over after approval. We work diligently to assure that these programs are adhered to and changed if necessary. We monitor our own adverse reactions reporting system for signals of side effects that might suggest abuse or misuse, and we also utilize the DAWN system that SAMSHA operates to continually reasses drug use in the area of abuse.

We work deliberately with the DEA and other agencies. We meet regularly to work on projects to prevent diversion, develop programs for physician education, collaborate with State prescription drug monitoring programs and other task forces. We recognize the serious problem of prescription drug abuse and we are taking steps to address this serious problem.

In conclusion, we share the subcommittee's interest and concerns regarding prescription drug abuse, and I'll be happy to answer further questions.

[The prepared statement of Dr. Kweder follows:]

DEPARTMENT OF HEALTH & HUMAN SERVICES   Public Health Service

Food and Drug Administration
Rockville MD 2085

STATEMENT OF

SANDRA L. KWEDER M.D.
DEPUTY DIRECTOR,
OFFICE OF NEW DRUGS
CENTER FOR DRUG EVALUATION AND RESEARCH
FOOD AND DRUG ADMINISTRATION
U.S. DEPARTMENT OF HEALTH AND HUMAN SERVICES

CONCERNING FDA ACTIVITIES TO CURB PRESCRIPTION DRUG ABUSE

BEFORE THE

SUBCOMMITTEE ON CRIMINAL JUSTI CE, DRUG POLICY AND HUMAN
RESOURCES

COMMITTEE ON GOVERNMENT REFORM

HOUSE OF REPRESENTATIVES

JULY 26, 2006

Release Only Upon Delivery

INTRODUCTION

Mr. Chairman and Members of the Subcommittee, I am Sandra Kweder M.D., Deputy Director of the Office of New Drugs at the Center for Drug Evaluation and Research (CDER), U.S. Food and Drug Administration (FDA or the Agency), an agency of the U.S. Department of Health and Human Services (HHS). My staff works closely with CDER's Controlled Substances Staff, which coordinates CDER's activities related to controlled substances, and the Drug Enforcement Administration (DEA). I appreciate the opportunity to talk to you today about FDA's role in preventing prescription drug abuse.

The Agency is actively involved in the Administration's efforts to prevent abuse and misuse of prescription drugs, while making sure that needed drugs are available for patients who need them. FDA is strongly committed to promoting and protecting the public health by assuring that safe and effective products reach the market in a timely manner and monitoring marketed products for continued safety.

FDA DRUG APPROVAL PROCESS

The Federal Food, Drug, and Cosmetic (FD&C) Act, requires FDA to ensure that all new drugs are safe and effective. Before any drug is approved for marketing in the U.S., FDA must decide whether the studies submitted by the drug's sponsor (usually the manufacturer) have adequately demonstrated that the drug is safe and effective under the conditions of use proposed in the drug's labeling. It is important to realize, that "safe" does not mean free of risk, and that there always is some risk of potential adverse reactions when using prescription drugs. FDA's approval decisions, therefore, always involve an assessment of the benefits and the risks for a particular product. When the benefits of a drug are determined to outweigh the risks, and the labeling instructions allow for safe and effective use, FDA considers a drug safe for approval and marketing.

During the approval process, FDA assesses a drug product's potential for abuse and misuse. Abuse liability assessments are based on a composite profile of the drug's chemistry, pharmacology, clinical manifestations, similarity to other drugs in a class, and the potential for public health risks following introduction of the drug to the general population. If a potential for abuse exists, the product's sponsor is required to provide FDA with all data pertinent to abuse of the drug, a proposal for scheduling under the Controlled Substances Act (CSA), 21 U.S.C. §801 et seq., and data on overdoses.

Under the FD&C Act, FDA is responsible for the approval and marketing of drugs for medical use and for monitoring products for continued safety after they are in use, including controlled substances. DEA is the lead Federal agency responsible for regulating controlled substances and enforcing the CSA. The CSA separates controlled substances into five schedules, depending upon their abuse potential and medical use. Schedule I controlled substances have the highest potential for abuse and have no medical use while Schedule V substances have the lowest abuse potential. Schedule II substances also have a very high potential for abuse but are approved for medical use. Schedules III, IV, and V substances and drugs have lower abuse potential and fewer controls under the CSA. The U.S. Immigration and Customs Enforcement (ICE) is the lead agency for enforcing transborder smuggling laws. ICE focuses its efforts on individuals and organizations involved in the smuggling of counterfeit pharmaceuticals both controlled and non-controlled, scheduled narcotics, medical devices and medical test kits via the Internet.

The CSA requires the Secretary of Health and Human Services to notify the Attorney General, through DEA, if a "new drug application is submitted for any drug having a stimulant, depressant, or hallucinogenic effect on the central nervous system, ..." because it would then appear that the drug had abuse potential (21 U.S.C. §811(f)). HHS has delegated this function to FDA.

FDA assesses preclinical, clinical, and epidemiological data to determine whether a drug under review requires abuse liability studies, scheduling under the CSA, or a risk minimization action plan (RiskMAP) designed to maximize safe use of a drug in part by reducing abuse, overdose, or misuse. FDA's job is not over after a drug scheduled as a controlled substance is approved. The goal of FDA's post-marketing surveillance is to continue to monitor marketed drugs for safety. This is accomplished by reassessing drug risks based on new data obtained after the drug is marketed and recommending ways of trying to manage that risk most appropriately.

THE IMPORTANCE OF RISK MANAGEMENT

Safety or risk assessment combined with efforts to minimize known risks comprise what FDA calls risk management. Risk management is the overall and ongoing process of assessing a product's benefits and risks, taking action as necessary to decrease known risks, and then tracking safety and making adjustments as necessary to assure that risks are kept in line with benefits.

As part of risk management, FDA may ask companies to collect specific information to improve the speed and sensitivity of detecting suspected safety problems. When this enhanced data collection is requested by FDA, it is called a pharmacovigilance plan. These exist for many long-acting and potent opioid products and contribute to safe use of the product by detecting, as rapidly as possible, adverse outcomes, including misuse, overdose, and abuse. Once problems are detected, there need to be actions to address them.

Actions to minimize risks that go beyond labeling changes are called risk minimization action plans or RiskMAPs. These are strategic safety programs designed to decrease known product risks by using one or more interventions, such as specialized education or restrictions on typical prescribing, dispensing, or use. The small number of RiskMAPs that exist are largely customized programs, although consistent approaches are being sought, for example, in the control of drugs that cause birth defects, such as thalidomide and isotretinoin.

FDA IS CONCERNED ABOUT THE INCREASED ABUSE OF PRESCRIPTION DRUGS

FDA is aware that some consumers are able to obtain controlled substances without a prescription, with many people using the Internet to purchase these drugs. FDA is concerned about the increasing abuse of prescription drugs, including opioid drugs. Abuse of opioid analgesics (controlled drugs that include oxycodone, morphine, fentanyl and hydrocodone), has risen steadily over the past five years. By contrast, overall rates of abuse of illicit drugs have been generally stable over the same time period.

FDA's goal is to assure that patients who require opioids for pain control maintain appropriate access to them through informed providers, while limiting misuse and abuse of these products to the extent possible. FDA takes its responsibility in meeting this goal very seriously. Given the broad scope of factors at issue, to achieve this goal, it is essential that FDA work in concert with other government agencies, professional societies, patient advocacy groups, industry, and others to share information and coordinate activities.

The Substance Abuse and Mental Health Services Administration (SAMHSA), another agency within HHS, annually conducts the National Survey on Drug Use and Health (NSDUH) on a random sample of U.S. households to determine the prevalence of non-medical use of illicit and prescription drugs. The 2004 NSDUH reported that 6.0 million persons, or 2.5 percent of Americans age 12 and older, were current users of psychotherapeutic drugs taken non-medically; 14.6 million persons, or 6.1 percent, had used such drugs nonmedically in the past year; and 48 million persons had used such drugs non-medically at least once in their lifetimes.

Also, according to the 2004 NSDUH, the number of people who had used pain relievers non-medically at least once during their lifetime increased 7 percent from 2002 to 2004, for a total of 31.8 million Americans. The prevalence of lifetime non-medical use of oxycodone-containing analgesics increased from an estimated 11.8 million users in 2002 to 13.7 million users in 2003.

The reported rise of prescription drug abuse is corroborated by data on the consequences of such use. SAMHSA's Drug Abuse Warning Network (DAWN) surveys a national sample of emergency departments (EDs). DAWN captures ED visits associated with substance abuse/misuse, both intentional and accidental, as well as visits related to the use of drugs for legitimate therapeutic purposes.

According to the 2004 DAWN Report, nearly 1.3 million ED visits in 2004 were associated with drug misuse/abuse. Non-medical use of pharmaceuticals was involved in nearly a half million of these ED visits. In addition, opiates/opioid analgesics (pain relievers), such as hydrocodone, oxycodone, and methadone were present in 158,281 ED visits, and benzodiazepines such as alprazolam and clonazepam were present in 144,385 ED visits associated with nonmedical use of pharmaceuticals in 2004. Muscle relaxants, particularly carisoprodol and cyclobenzaprine, were involved in an estimated 28,338 ED visits related to nonmedical use. Finally, over two-thirds of ED visits associated with opiates/opioids, benzodiazepines, and muscle relaxants involved multiple drugs, and alcohol was one of the other drugs in about a quarter of such visits.

The Treatment Episode Data Set (TEDS), also administered by SAMHSA, collects data on admissions to Federally funded drug and alcohol addiction treatment programs. Between 1999 and 2003, treatment admissions for primary abuse of opioids other than heroin increased from 1 percent of all admissions (22,637 admissions) in 1999 to 3 percent in 2004 (63,243 admissions).

FDA ACTIONS TO PREVENT ABUSE AND MISUSE OF PRESCRIPTION DRUGS

Support of National Drug Control Strategy

The President's 2006 National Drug Control Strategy continues to recognize the effectiveness of state prescription drug monitoring programs, and called on the pharmaceutical industry, medical community and state governments to become partners in an effort to prevent the illegal sale, diversion, and use of prescription drugs in a way that does not impede legitimate medical needs.

Collaboration with other Government Agencies

FDA is continuing to meet with DEA, ICE, SAMHSA, the National Institute on Drug Abuse (NIDA) at the National Institutes of Health (NIH), the Office of National Drug Control Policy (ONDCP), the Centers for Disease Control and Prevention, the American Medical Association (AMA), and industry to share information and insights needed to address the problem of prescription drug abuse.

FDA and DEA meet regularly to discuss new ways to prevent prescription drug abuse and misuse. In addition to assisting one another with criminal investigations, as described below, FDA (or other components of HHS) is working on the following initiatives:

Task Force Participation – FDA participates in a number of task forces and other groups. Agents of FDA's Office of Criminal Investigations (OCI) frequently participate in and/or assist many DEA-led Federal-State task forces throughout the country focusing on the illegal sale of controlled prescription drugs.

FDA is a long-time participant of the Interagency Pharmaceutical Task Force (with participants from DEA, Customs and Border Protection (CBP), and ICE that meets frequently to devise and implement mutually agreed-upon policies and enforcement strategies for the interdiction and disposition of unlawful pharmaceuticals entering the United States. FDA also works with DEA to address the diversion of pharmaceuticals. DEA and FDA have established working relationships with eBay and internet service providers (ISPs) to prevent internet auction sites from being used to facilitate illegal controlled substance and other pharmaceutical product distributions. FDA has, often in conjunction with DEA and other agencies, met with ISPs couriers, and credit card companies to explore ideas for combating illegal internet drug sales that include, and may go beyond, traditional law enforcement methods.

FDA and DEA are members of the following working groups: Cross Border Pharmacy Working Group, Interagency Pharmaceutical Task Force, Permanent Forum on International Pharmaceutical Crime, Interagency Committee on Drug Control, Federal Trade Commission/FDA Health Fraud Working Group, and a working group composed of representatives from HHS (including FDA, SAMHSA, and NIH), DEA, ONDCP, and other agencies to address issues of drug abuse and control under the CSA. ICE and CBP participate in many of these working groups in an effort to collaborate with FDA in reducing the quantity of illegal dangerous drugs imported into the U.S. as well as to improve information sharing, increase public awareness and work cooperatively with industry.

In October of 2004, a cooperative effort with ONDCP, HHS (including FDA and the Office of the Surgeon General), and DEA was announced with the release of the first National Synthetic Drugs Action Plan. The cooperative effort included various programs aimed at addressing prescription abuse, including careful consideration by FDA of labeling and commercial promotion of opiate drug products, additional efforts by FDA, DOJ, DEA and others to investigate and prosecute "pill mills" (Internet pharmacies that illegally provide controlled substances), and various educational efforts aimed at providing safety, use, and disposal information on prescription drugs. FDA created a web site at: *http://www.fda.gov/cder/consumerinfo/DPAdefault.htm#Misuse* that continues to include updates and alerts on various medications. Consumers also can sign up for specific e-mail alerts.

An important component of FDA's strategic plan is to enable consumers to make smarter decisions by providing them with better information to weigh the benefits and risks of FDA-regulated products. FDA remains committed to ensuring that information on FDA's website is current, useful, and educational and provides consumers with important and timely drug safety information. On FDA's main website (*www.fda.gov*) there is additional information for patients on drug safety and side effects, public health alerts, and general information about major drugs. These web pages provide important information to patients regarding how to use their drug products safely. For example, in an effort to educate health care providers and consumers about the risks associated with OxyContin, FDA created an OxyContin Drug Information web page (*www.fda.gov/cder/drug/ infopage/oxycontin /default.htm*). This page contains valuable information for consumers including the current approved labeling and approval letter, frequently asked questions, and articles on prescription drug abuse.

FDA worked closely with SAMHSA, NIDA, DOJ, DEA, DHS, ONDCP, and other Federal agencies, as part of the Synthetic Drugs Interagency Working Group (SDIWG), which was established to implement the recommendations of the National Synthetic Drugs Action Plan issued in 2004 and to develop the goals of the Synthetic Drug Control Strategy issued in June 2006. Prescription drug abuse is one of the many topics that both the Plan and the Strategy address.

Assessment of New Products With Abuse Potential – As required by the CSA, FDA, on behalf of HHS, provides DEA with a scientific and medical evaluation of a drug's potential for abuse and misuse, whether a drug should be controlled under the CSA, and a recommendation as to the schedule.

FDA Seeks Expert Advice From Non-Agency Experts On Medical Use of Opioid Analgesics

FDA routinely convenes panels of non-Agency experts to seek outside advice through the use of its many advisory committees. Outside experts add a wide spectrum of judgment, outlook, and state-of-the-art experience to drug issues confronting FDA. These expert advisers add to FDA's understanding, so that final Agency decisions more likely will reflect a balanced evaluation. Advisory committee recommendations are not binding on FDA, but the Agency considers them carefully when deciding drug abuse issues.

FDA's Anesthetic and Life Support Drugs Advisory Committee, a panel of experts, has met twice within recent years to discuss the medical use of opioid analgesics, appropriate drug development plans to support approval of opioid analgesics, and strategies to communicate and manage the risks associated with opioid analgesics, particularly the risks of abuse of these drugs. The most recent meeting included DEA participation, and the Committee included both pain specialists and addiction experts. At this meeting, Committee members again advised FDA that opioid medications are essential for relieving pain. Members emphasized that a balanced approach should be taken to both meet the needs of patients with pain as well as to minimize opiate analgesic misprescribing, abuse, addiction, and diversion. They expressed a range of perspectives on the question of imposing restrictions on the prescribing of potent opioids. The pain specialists were concerned about hurting legitimate patients and reversing the progress in the appropriate treatment of pain as efforts were increased to address abuse and misuse, while the drug addiction experts urged more constraints on use.

FDA Monitors Advertising and Promotion

FDA's Division of Drug Marketing, Advertising, and Communications (DDMAC), in CDER, is responsible for regulating prescription drug advertising and promotion. DDMAC's mission is to protect the public health by ensuring that prescription drug information is truthful, balanced, and communicated accurately. This mission is accomplished through a comprehensive surveillance, enforcement, and education program, and by fostering optimal communication of labeling and promotional information to health care professionals and consumers.

FDA continues to monitor promotional materials for controlled substances, particularly for sustained release products, to ensure that claims are not false or misleading. Also, all product promotional materials must include information from "black box" warnings in the approved labeling. For example, the current approved product labeling for

58

OxyContin contains a "black box" to convey serious risks associated with the use of the product. FDA has taken action against sponsors who violate this requirement or otherwise promote their product in a manner that is false or misleading. We will continue to monitor promotional materials for these products and use our regulatory authority to its fullest extent to ensure that healthcare providers and patients are not subjected to false or misleading claims for these products. As well, FDA's Office of Criminal Investigations remains vigilant to the possibility of criminally fraudulent marketing that may contribute to the problem of dependence.

CONCLUSION

FDA recognizes the serious problem of prescription drug abuse. The Agency will continue to take steps to curb abuse and misuse of prescription drugs. Since this is a problem that is broad in its reach and implications, we are committed to collaborating with our partners – Federal, state and local officials, professional societies, and industry - to prevent abuse and help ensure that these important drugs remain available to appropriate patients.

I would like to thank the Subcommittee again for this opportunity to testify today on this important issue. I would be pleased to respond to any questions.

Mr. SOUDER. Thank you.
Mr. Rannazzisi.

STATEMENT OF JOSEPH T. RANNAZZISI

Mr. RANNAZZISI. Chairman Souder, Ranking Member Cummings. On behalf of Administrator Tandy and the Drug Enforcement Administration, I appreciate your invitation to testify today regarding DEA's effort to address the efforts of prescription drug abuse.

Addressing the growing problem of diversion and abuse of controlled programs continues to be one of the top priorities of the Drug Enforcement Administration. DEA has not remained idle in response to this growing threat. DEA has significantly increased the amount of resources and manpower dedicated to investigating the diversion of controlled substances of particular pharmaceuticals. We continue to focus our drug enforcement efforts on the most significant diverter in the drug supply chain. The illustration of the administration's focus on this problem occurred on June 1, 2006, when the Department of Justice along with DOE, DHS and HHS released the Synthetic Drug Control Strategy, which among other threats specifically targets prescription drug abuse.

The DEA is constantly aware of this problem and, as outlined in that strategy, we have committed an ambitious goal of reducing the abuse of controlled pharmaceuticals by 15 percent over the next 30 years. In developing the strategy to attack this problem, it's important to understand that there are distinct differences between drugs such as heroin, marijuana, and controlled pharmaceuticals.

Typical drug control strategies used to attack organizations that focus on distribution of clandestine drugs do not necessarily lend themselves to attacking those organizations that illegally traffic in illegal pharmaceuticals. Distribution channels that are otherwise legal are often manipulated to acquire controlled substance prescription drugs for illegal purposes. Compounding this matter is the perception, particularly among teenagers and young adults, that controlled pharmaceuticals are safe even when used recreationally.

The most common methods of diversion witnessed are through doctor shopping, prescription fraud, improper prescribing and sharing among family and friends. Perhaps the largest growth method for controlled substances diversion is the Internet.

Looking at perhaps the most potentially dangerous and increasingly used method for controlled substances, the Internet, we have discovered that many of these on-line pharmacies do not operate in the same manner as brick and mortar pharmacies. This includes advertising controlled substances for sale without a prescription and not requiring an in-person medical examination by a licensed physician.

There are strong societal benefits to allow individuals with a valid prescription to get their prescriptions over the Internet as long as the pharmacy that fills the prescription is legitimate and there exists a legitimate doctor-patient relationship. There are legitimate pharmacies that provide services over the Net and that operate well within the bounds on both law and sound medical practice. However, what is particularly troubling is the idea that a minor can easily log on to an illicit Web site, provide an inaccurate age and have a controlled substance delivered directly to their door.

No special DEA registration is currently required to market controlled substances on-line, but the tangible aspects of manufacturing, distributing, prescribing and dispensing pharmaceuticals and controlled substances remain squarely under the jurisdiction of the Controlled Substances Act. Any legitimate transaction over the Internet must comply with these laws.

Additional clarification by roles of responsibilities for professionals seeking to use the Internet to meet the needs of clients would not only allow us to more readily identify legitimate on-line pharmacies and persons using them but would also assist in gathering and pointing to abuse patterns.

In addition, there exists no statutory designation of a doctor-patient relationship.

Finally, the potential of those associated with an illegal sale of Schedule III through V substances, which are those most often sold over the Internet, are not as significant as may be warranted.

Finally, it is important to consider DEA's obligation under the law and to the public, which is to ensure that controlled substances are prescribed and dispensed only for legitimate medical purpose and in accordance with the CSA. Understanding the differences and the similarities between prescription drugs and controlled substances is an important aspect of evaluating the causes and policy solutions regarding the rise in prescription drug abuse.

In conclusion, the diversion program of controlled substance continues to be a significant challenge. Nevertheless the DEA is committed to use the necessary tools at its disposal to fight this problem on all fronts while simultaneously ensuring an uninterrupted supply of pharmaceutical controlled substances for legitimate demands.

Chairman Souder, Ranking Member Cummings, thank you again for the opportunity to testify today. I'll be happy to answer any of your questions. Thank you.

[The prepared statement of Mr. Rannazzisi follows:]

Statement of

Joseph T. Rannazzisi
Deputy Assistant Administrator
Office of Diversion Control
Drug Enforcement Administration
U.S. Department of Justice

Before the

House Government Reform Committee

Subcommittee on Criminal Justice, Drug Policy, and Human Resources

July 26, 2006

"Prescription Drug Abuse: What is Being Done to Address This New Drug Epidemic?"

Chairman Souder, Ranking Member Cummings, and distinguished members of Subcommittee, on behalf of Administrator Tandy and the Drug Enforcement Administration (DEA), I appreciate your invitation to testify today regarding DEA's efforts to address the issue of prescription drug abuse.

Overview

Addressing the growing problem of the diversion and abuse of controlled pharmaceuticals continues to be one of the top priorities of the Drug Enforcement Administration. DEA has made great strides in dealing with this ever-changing, global drug issue. We continue to concentrate on identifying, targeting, and dismantling large-scale organizations that seek to divert and distribute controlled pharmaceuticals in violation of the Controlled Substances Act (CSA). An illustration of the Administration's focus on this problem occurred on June 1, 2006, when the Department of Justice, along with the DEA, the Office of National Drug Control Policy, the Department of Homeland Security, the Department of Health and Human Services, and other agencies announced a comprehensive Synthetic Drug Control Strategy, which among other significant drug threats, specifically targets prescription drug abuse. The DEA is keenly aware of this problem.

An examination of youth drug abuse data reveals that the percentage of young Americans abusing prescription drugs is second only to marijuana and ahead of cocaine, heroin, methamphetamine, and other drugs. DEA, as the nation's primary law enforcement agency dedicated to enforcing the Controlled Substances Act, plays an integral role in achieving the goals of the Administration's Synthetic Drug Control

Strategy. As outlined in that Strategy, we have committed to an ambitious goal of reducing the abuse of controlled pharmaceuticals by 15 percent over the next three years.

DEA's obligation under the law and to the public is to ensure that pharmaceutical controlled substances are prescribed and dispensed only for legitimate medical purposes in accordance with the Controlled Substances Act. By carrying out this obligation, DEA strives to minimize the diversion of pharmaceutical controlled substances for abuse while ensuring that such medications are fully available to patients in accordance with the sound medical judgments of their physicians. In this manner, DEA is committed to balancing the need for prevention, education, and enforcement with the need for legitimate access to these drugs.

In developing a strategy to balance these priorities, the Administration has worked to obtain better data on how people acquire and abuse controlled pharmaceuticals. It is important to understand that there are distinct differences between drugs such as heroin or marijuana and controlled pharmaceuticals. As we know, illegal drugs such as cocaine, heroin, and marijuana often are obtained through secretive and dangerous transactions. Typical drug control strategies used to attack organizations that focus on distribution of clandestine drugs do not necessarily lend themselves to attacking those organizations that illegally traffic in controlled pharmaceuticals.

Controlled pharmaceuticals are readily available for legitimate purposes through one's physician and pharmacy. Distribution channels that are otherwise legal are often manipulated to acquire controlled substance prescription drugs for illegal purposes. Compounding this matter is the perception, particularly among teenagers and young adults that controlled pharmaceuticals are safe even when used "recreationally." Abusers of controlled pharmaceuticals are using these medicines for non-medical purposes in a manner for which they were never intended. This practice, coupled with the erroneous perception of safety, makes these medicines much more dangerous.

DEA Initiatives

DEA has not remained idle in response to this growing threat. DEA has made it a priority to disrupt and dismantle organizations that illegally traffic in controlled pharmaceuticals. This priority is reflected in the fact that diversion control is a strategic goal in the DEA five-year Strategic Plan. Part of this strategy is to attack the economic basis of the drug trade by inflicting upon the illicit drug business what every legal business fears: escalating costs, diminishing profits, and unreliable suppliers. To do so, DEA uses all of the tools at its disposal. We have dismantled major pharmaceutical trafficking and distribution organizations through criminal investigations. We have also used our regulatory authority to take action against DEA registrants found to be in violation of regulatory requirements under the CSA. Through regulatory authority, DEA has subjected registrants to significant civil fines, licensing restrictions, or even suspended registrations. Such civil remedies have proven to be an effective deterrent to potential violators.

As we have observed the pharmaceutical controlled substances abuse problem grow, DEA has significantly increased the amount of resources and manpower dedicated to investigating the diversion of controlled pharmaceuticals. We continue to focus our drug enforcement efforts on the most significant diverters in the drug supply chain. Specifically, DEA has increased the number of Special Agent work-hours on diversion investigations by 114 percent between FY-2003 and FY-2005. DEA has increased the number of Intelligence Analyst work-hours by 234 percent during that same period. Enforcement efforts undertaken by the DEA are also aimed at the economic base of drug traffickers, and strong emphasis is placed on seizures of financial and other assets. In FY-2002 DEA seized approximately $1.8 million in assets related to diversion investigations. In FY-2005 that increased to approximately $32.4 million, an 1,800 percent increase.

In early FY 2005, the DEA began working with its industry partners to develop public service announcements that now appear automatically during Internet prescription drug searches. These announcements are designed to alert consumers of the potential dangers and the illegality of purchasing controlled substances, particularly pharmaceuticals, over the Internet. Both Yahoo and Google have responded by instituting voluntary compliance measures and corporate commitments to taking affirmative steps to curtail the illicit sale of pharmaceuticals on their networks.

In addition, DEA's Demand Reduction office has produced an anti-drug website for teens, www.justthinktwice.com. This site provides young people with straightforward information on the consequences of drug use and trafficking, including health, social, legal consequences. It is continually updated to provide current information to teens and will be expanded and refined to reflect the needs of teens. This site has been a valuable (and popular) resource for teens seeking information on drugs for their own education or for school research projects. The Demand Reduction Program also continues to provide the public and school age children with a variety of demand reduction presentations on a national and local level regarding the abuse of controlled prescriptions.

Finally, the DEA has met with the leading certifying medical boards and encouraged them to develop educational programs concerning the prescribing of controlled substances, especially high-dose opioids.

Sources of Abused Pharmaceuticals

Pharmaceutical investigations and surveys of state and local law enforcement agencies and state medical boards have revealed that the most common methods of controlled substance prescription drug diversion include "doctor shopping" or other prescription fraud, illegal online pharmacies, theft and burglary (from residences, pharmacies, etc.), stereotypical drug dealing (selling pills to others), receiving from friends or family, and negligent or intentional over-prescribing by physicians or other practitioners. What is not yet adequately understood is the relative proportion of these methods.

Doctor Shopping and Prescription Fraud

"Doctor shopping" by drug addicts is one of the most common ways that addicts get illegal controlled substances. Generally, this term refers to the visit by an individual—who may or may not have legitimate medical needs—to several doctors, each of whom writes a prescription for a controlled substance. The individual will visit several pharmacies, receiving more of the drug than intended by any single physician, typically for the purpose of feeding an addiction.

Associated illegal activities may include the forgery of prescriptions, or the sale or transfer of the drug to others. Unfortunately, in many states, physicians and pharmacists have not been able to automatically cross-check multiple prescriptions given to the same patient.

To address this problem, Congress first appropriated funds to the Department of Justice in 2003 to promote the deployment of Prescription Drug Monitoring Programs (PDMPs) by States. That commitment continues as part of the Administration's National Drug Control Strategy for 2006. PDMPs help cut down on prescription fraud and doctor shopping by giving physicians and pharmacists more complete information about a patient's prescriptions for controlled substances.

While the specifics of these programs vary from state to state, they generally share the characteristic of allowing prescribers (for example, a physician) and dispensers (for example, a pharmacist) to input and receive accurate and timely controlled substance prescription history information while ensuring patient access to needed treatment. Most states also have some mechanism for law enforcement to receive this information in cases where criminal activity is suspected. Some states also allow health care providers to use this information as a tool for the early identification of patients at risk for addiction in order to initiate appropriate medical interventions. In other states the justice system can use this information to assist in the enforcement of laws controlling the sale and use of controlled substance prescription medication.

The PDMP program has steadily expanded through the Harold Rogers Prescription Drug Monitoring Program, with a total of 33 states with active or planned PDMPs as of July 1, 2006. These grants can be used to implement or enhance PDMPs at the state level. The Administration plans to continue its work with states that have PDMPs to obtain better data as to the extent and nature of the controlled substance prescription drug abuse threat, to encourage the expansion of the PDMP program nationwide, and to share best practices information with states that already have PDMPs (e.g., on cost effectiveness, the benefits to monitoring all scheduled controlled substances, and measuring performance).

Improper Prescribing

Improper prescribing is another method of controlled substance diversion. Improper prescribing differs from doctor shopping and prescription fraud in that the latter situations, the abusers are attempting to deceive or mislead the medical professionals who are doing their jobs responsibly.

The overwhelming majority of prescribing in America is conducted responsibly. Often these responsible doctors and pharmacists are the first to alert law enforcement to potential prescription problems. However, the small number of physicians who over prescribe controlled substances—carelessly at best, knowingly at worst—help supply America's second most widespread drug addiction problem. Although the problem exists, the number of physicians and pharmacists responsible for this problem is a very small fraction (less than 1 percent) of those licensed to prescribe and dispense controlled substances in the United States.

Sharing Among Family and Friends

As DEA increases its understanding of where abusers acquire prescription drugs, preliminary data suggest that the most common method in which controlled substance prescriptions are diverted may be through friends and family. For example, a person with a lawful and genuine medical need for a controlled substance may use only a portion of the prescribed amount. A family member or friend may complain of similar symptoms, and the former patient shares excess medication. Alternatively, for someone addicted to controlled substance prescription drugs or to an inquisitive youngster, the mere availability of unused controlled substance prescriptions in the house may prove to be an irresistible temptation.

The solution to this aspect of the problem lies both with the medical community and the legitimate patient population. Greater educational efforts are needed regarding quick and safe disposal of unused and unneeded medications. Prescribers need to carefully consider the potential for abuse of controlled substances and prescribe only the amount of a controlled substance required medically. Patients must also be educated about the legal and social ramifications of providing a controlled substance to a friend or family member. It is not merely illegal, but could feed, or lead to, an addiction, and place that loved one in a life threatening situation.

Illegal Online Pharmacies

Perhaps the most potentially dangerous and increasingly used method for the diversion of controlled pharmaceuticals is through the Internet. As the number of Americans with Internet access has increased, so too have opportunities for individuals to acquire controlled substance prescription drugs over the Internet. There are strong societal benefits to allowing individuals with a valid prescription to get their prescriptions over the Internet, as long as the pharmacy that fills these prescriptions is a legitimate one and there is a legitimate doctor-patient relationship. This may be helpful in rural areas or

66

for individuals who are homebound due to illness or other factors. However, the anonymity of the Internet, and the proliferation of websites that facilitate illicit transactions in controlled substance pharmaceutical drugs, have given drug abusers the ability to circumvent both the law and sound medical practice.

There are legitimate pharmacies that provide services over the Internet and that operate well within the bounds of both the law and sound medical practice. The National Association of Boards of Pharmacy has established a registry of pharmacies that operate online and meet certain criteria, including compliance with licensing and inspection requirements of their state and each state to which they dispense pharmaceuticals.

By contrast, other websites used by Internet facilitators will often advertise themselves as pharmacies, but they do not operate in the same manner as brick-and-mortar pharmacies. Many of these websites advertise controlled substances without a prescription, and none include an in-person medical examination from a licensed physician.

Of particular concern is the cursory and abbreviated nature of the medical interaction. Often, if there is any interaction with a medical professional at all, the Internet facilitator will provide only a cursory doctor consultation by computer or telephone for customers. This brief interaction is not meant to elicit meaningful health information, and is generally done by way of a "questionnaire" filled out by the "patient" without any face-to-face meeting between the doctor and the patient. Without this face-to-face interaction, it is not possible for the doctor writing the prescription, who has never met the patient, to verify the information provided by the individual and assess legitimate medical need. This is particularly troubling in the context of youth drug abuse. Unlike when the patient visits the doctor, a minor can easily log onto a website and provide an inaccurate age.

Doctors, who are often paid by the number of prescriptions they sign in these situations, have no incentive to spend time seeking additional patient information. Law enforcement has discovered website-affiliated doctors who sign hundreds or thousands of prescriptions a day. After receiving the prescription from the doctor, the facilitator will then submit the prescription to a cooperating pharmacy. Because there is often no identifying information on these rogue websites, it is very difficult for law enforcement to track any of the individuals behind them.

The Administration is using all available tools to go after the operators of these rogue Internet-facilitator websites. We are conducting investigations and working to intercept controlled substance prescriptions illegally sent into the United States through the mail system. For example, the DEA's Internet investigation unit at its Special Operations Division continues to coordinate Internet cases, and the DEA has issued a number of immediate suspensions of the DEA registrations of doctors and pharmacies operating illegally via the Internet. The Department of Justice has prosecuted doctors and pharmacies who illegally distribute via the Internet.

The tangible aspects of manufacturing, distributing, prescribing, and dispensing pharmaceutical controlled substances remain squarely under the jurisdiction of the CSA. Any legitimate transaction over the Internet must be in compliance with these existing laws.

Additional clarification of the roles and responsibilities for professionals seeking to use the Internet to meet the needs of clients would not only allow us to more readily identify legitimate online pharmacies and persons operating and promoting them, but it would also assist in gathering information pointing to abuse patterns. Such clarification would also help us investigate drug traffickers hiding behind the façade of an otherwise legitimate practice.

Additionally, there exists no statutory definition of a valid "doctor/patient" relationship. Finally, the penalties associated with the illegal sale of Schedule III-V substances, which are those most commonly sold controlled substances over the Internet, are not as significant as may be warranted.

States can play a significant role in addressing the problem of online facilitators, particularly through PDMPs. As part of the Administration's work with states regarding PDMPs over the next several years, states will be encouraged to consider addressing, either by statute, regulation, or interstate agreement, a number of scenarios that primarily involve pharmacies dispensing or delivering controlled substance prescription drugs to patients across state lines. To be effective, laws must be updated to reflect the changing ways people live and in which business is conducted.

Coordinating Regulatory Responsibilities

As the DEA fights against diversion and drug abuse across the nation, the proper regulatory control of new pharmaceuticals is vital. Appropriate control mechanisms are particularly important given the strength and formulations of products as they become available to the consumer. This is important to the DEA as we are seeing an overall increase in the commercial dispersion of pharmaceuticals which results in a significant increase of pharmaceutical doses available for diversion. Understanding the differences– and the similarities–between prescription drugs and controlled substances is an important aspect of evaluating the causes and possible policy solutions regarding the rise in prescription drug abuse.

Congress signaled its full recognition of the abuse potential of certain prescription drugs in 1914, when it passed the Harrison Narcotic Act, regulating the sale of opiates for the first time. With the passage of the Federal Food, Drug and Cosmetic Act (FDCA) in 1938 and in subsequent amendments, the United States Congress recognized the critical importance of indicating the medically proven uses of prescription drugs for legitimate medical needs.

The CSA is the legal foundation for the United States fight against abuse of drugs and other substances. It was passed to minimize the quantity of abuseable substances

7

available to those likely to abuse them, while providing for legitimate medical, scientific and industrial needs for those substances in the United States. Control under the CSA encompasses both licit and illicit substances and regulates chemicals used in the clandestine production of controlled substances. The Department of Justice (DOJ), through the DEA, and the Department of Health and Human Services (HHS), through the FDA, both have a role in implementing the CSA.

The CSA requires that substances be scheduled by a determination made by the Attorney General, after a scientific and medical evaluation and recommendation by the Secretary of HHS (See 21 USC 811(b)). Substances with a substantial potential for abuse are considered for control under Schedules II through V. Schedule II substances have the highest abuse potential and dependence profiles with the most restrictive regulatory requirements, while III through V drugs have progressively less abuse potential and dependence profiles and are subjected to less restrictive regulatory requirements.

The placement of a substance in a given schedule is based on its medical use, safety, potential for abuse, or dependence liability, and consideration of specific factors as listed in the CSA. For drug products containing substances that are not already controlled under the CSA, as in the case of new molecular entities, HHS will forward their scientific and medical evaluation and a scheduling recommendation to the DEA. FDA has the statutory responsibility to determine the safety and effectiveness of new drug products for medical use in the United Sates. As a part of their evaluation, FDA also examines the abuse potential of drug products.

The CSA includes seven major control mechanisms. They are scheduling, registration, quotas, records and reports, import and export authorizations, security and investigational authority. These mechanisms allow DEA to monitor and regulate a controlled substance and its movement: in the case of the most potentially dangerous drugs, in Schedule II, we register all persons who handle them; we inspect the documentation of their distribution; we control their import and export; and we control the amount produced, bought, sold, and otherwise transferred.

These controls have been extremely effective in preventing diversion at the importer, manufacturer, and distributor levels. However, as described earlier, the vast majority of diversion occurs at the retail level, once the product is in the hands of practitioners and patients.

Conclusion

The diversion of pharmaceutical controlled substances continues to be a significant challenge. Nevertheless, the DEA is committed to using the necessary tools at its disposal to fight this growing problem on all fronts, while simultaneously ensuring an uninterrupted supply of pharmaceutical controlled substances for legitimate demands. DEA's core competency, the disruption and dismantlement of drug trafficking organizations impacting the United States, is an integral component to the Synthetic Drug

Control Strategy and we will continue to implement this aspect of the Strategy with our inter-agency partners to combat controlled substance pharmaceutical diversion.

Chairman Souder, Ranking Member Cummings, and distinguished Members of the Subcommittee, thank you again for the opportunity to testify before you today. Prescription drug abuse is an increasing threat that we must face, and DEA looks forward to working with you to address this important issue. I'll be happy to answer any questions you may have.

Mr. SOUDER. Let me ask a basic question first. Maybe if Dr. Volkow and maybe Mr. Rannazzisi will know the answer to this question. In the overdose-misuse categories in particular, do we know how many of these people have a legitimate prescription and then move on to abusing it as opposed to just starting with abuse?

Dr. VOLKOW. No. That information, to my knowledge, is not accessible. One of the problems that happens in emergency rooms where you are recording these numbers is that in general, I mean the individual that comes in with an overdose, may not necessarily state this was for diversion purposes and many times they won't want to admit it. So the physicians don't even have the information about what may be wrong with the particular individual. So the numbers are not clear in terms of what percentage constitutes the diversion versus proper medication. It is likely that in most cases it will come from diversion because if you are properly prescribing the medications they have guidelines about how to instruct the patients to ensure that they will take it safely. However, there is a subgroup where that is a higher risk and that is elderly individuals which may forget that they've taken their medication or, on the other hand, may be taking multiple medications and then combine them in an inappropriate way. So that is the subgroup that is at risk for developing medical complications even when properly prescribed.

But otherwise, I would predict the numbers are not there just on the standard practices of medicine that when used properly, these medications are quite safe.

Mr. SOUDER. Because that defines our problem substantially different when you make certain assumptions. I mean if you have small percentage who might decide to self-medicate, that the treatment wasn't enough. You have seniors that you mentioned, may be that case. But it leads to a whole different type of a strategy depending on that data, and I would think gathering that data becomes fairly critical here, if nothing else kind of doing a post-analysis of people out of the emergency rooms trying to figure out whether they in fact had legal prescriptions and where they got it because that would seem such a basic piece of information. Any background is business, that is how you would approach it. You'd say what is my target group and try to figure out where it came from.

Another related question to that is my understanding the moral conflict. You said was that one of the big reasons people do this is the way they need to inhale it to get it into the brain faster. That suggested to me that if you are doing that, that probably you weren't using it for—you didn't start with that as a legitimate pain medication because that sounded more like a recreational use question or perceived recreational use question, and that means that the market and the strategy, whether it's a treatment question, a prevention question, youth education question, law enforcement question is substantially different because we have people who really don't want to know how to use it.

Therefore, my guess is, for example, ONDCP announcing a conference, they are going to pull all of the manufacturers together, may be in fact irrelevant because they already know the dangers of the problem. The question is how do you in this at risk market reach them? And let me ask a fundamental question of Dr. Kweder.

Dr. VOLKOW. Can I answer you? Just one point. I want you to be aware of this. This is something that struck me when I first heard about it, which is I wanted exactly the same numbers. What are the numbers on the emergency rooms that are accounting for overdoses? I wanted those numbers badly. We couldn't get them. Part of the problem is that many States, most of the States, and in the emergency room, if someone comes in with an illegal substance that they have taken for illegal purposes, the insurance will not reimburse. So in the United States you have a physician that wants to treat that particular individual, you may not necessarily want to ask the question because you are a physician who needs to take care of that individual. So the rules themselves that we currently have in emergency rooms do not necessarily help to be able to get an idea of the problem.

Mr. SOUDER. Dr. Kweder, one of the requirements I mentioned in my opening statement is from the Appropriations Committee is you look at the abuse of recently formulated prescription drugs. Do you believe you have the authority to grant priority review for these products, and has it considered requests to do so and, if so, have you granted priority review for any of the types of products that in fact would make it more abuse resistant?

Dr. KWEDER. Mr. Chairman, the abuse—a product that came in with a formulation that appeared to have any potential to mitigate abuse potential would be something that we would consider appropriate for a priority review. I don't know off the top of my head which products we have granted such review for, but I can provide that information.

Mr. SOUDER. But you believe you have granted some?

Dr. KWEDER. I believe we have.

Mr. SOUDER. We would appreciate that soon for the record.

Mr. Rannazzisi, in this, the DEA has said in your publication that you are working closely with FDA for rapid reformulation of OxyContin. We have asked DEA about the statements in the past and DEA hasn't provided us with any response. I'll ask you again. Specifically, have you worked closely with the FDA to urge this and what do you have to show for your efforts of reformulation of OxyContin?

Mr. RANNAZZISI. I can't specifically comment on OxyContin. I can tell you that we work very closely with FDA on all different issues regarding scheduling and new drugs. Our scientists are continually in contact with them on all different matters concerning the scheduling or new drug approval process. The fact is that we have a special testing lab in Virginia that would be able to take these formulations and look at them and see if we could leach or remove the final product from the tablets and we have offered that to pharmaceutical companies in the past.

You know, abuse resistance, we could make a determination in our labs if the product could be removed easily or with difficulty and that information would be passed on to FDA. And, again, that was offered to the companies. We do work closely with FDA when it comes to that. We have to because that is how we come up with what schedule the drug is going to be put into and how it is going to be scheduled.

Mr. SOUDER. Here's what my frustration is. As mentioned in the opening statement, of the 6 million people abusing prescription drugs, 4.4 million were pain relievers such as OxyContin. OxyContin in particular among youth is showing up 40 percent in the action plan to prevent the diversion and abuse of OxyContin. It says DEA continues to work closely with the Food and Drug Administration in strongly urging rapid reformulation of OxyContin to the extent it is technically possible in order to reduce abuse of this product, particularly by injection. And the question is since this has been testimony under oath and what your action plan is, what are you doing—I mean, OxyContin is the major pressure point. Is anything happening?

Mr. RANNAZZISI. The key statement is to the extent it is technically possible. The Drug Enforcement Administration does not dictate how a company is going to formulate or reformulate.

Mr. SOUDER. I asked a more particular question. It says, you said the agency, DEA, continues to work closely with the FDA in strongly urging the rapid reformulation of OxyContin. What I asked, my original question was what action points have you had with FDA in the context to work with OxyContin? Not did they find it. Did you ask them to find it? Do you have memos you showed to ask them to find it? Has there been a task force working to do it? Have they pulled it in? Have they tried to reformulate two or three times and it didn't work? Is anybody doing anything?

Mr. RANNAZZISI. I'll have to get back to you on that, sir.

Mr. SOUDER. In your testimony you already said you were doing it, in the testimony before. And your action plans. That is—this is the major hearing. It's not like you got 10 hearings on this subject. It's not like this is a huge shock that this question might come up. That is the frustration.

As you know, I've been a major supporter of DEA. I have remained a major supporter of DEA. This type of thing is frustrating. You can't make assertions and action plans that you are doing something, then when you have your big hearing that usually what happens is everybody scrambles after a 2-year request to get it, and when the hearing finally comes we get an answer and usually I am complaining that the answer came 1 hour before the hearing. In this case, it still isn't here, and that is what is frustrating. It's not like OxyContin—Fentanyl is kind of a new one popping up on this, and we are trying to get on Fentanyl, but on OxyContin it's not like we haven't had a warning. Pharmacies are being robbed in my district. They have been for a long time and all over the country, and we're saying well, we will check out and see if we have done anything. That is basically what my question was.

Ms. MADRAS. I wonder if I can march in here for a moment. There is a manuscript that was published just a few weeks ago by a Dr. Cohen on trying to define one of the problems of formulations, and what he quotes is the number of Internet sites that teach, instruct people how to circumvent effective formulations. And for OxyContin, there are two or three mechanisms that the Internet tells potential users how to get around these. I do accept your view that this is a very significant problem, but I think the program companies, which take years and years to develop new formulations, are trying to catch up to some of these strategies, and I think we have to——

Mr. SOUDER. You are telling me that multi-billion dollar program companies, some of which happen to be in my home State, and I am very proud of them with all of their buildings of researchers, that kids and people can come up with multi-reformulations and so they should just kind of say well, tough luck. Kids are dying. That is kind of what you said that they get—that I haven't had, and quite frankly the idea that the Federal Government's big response here is that they read an article about the difficulty of reformulations doesn't explain are they trying. Have you asked them? What have you done? Are you pushing them? Have they tried some reformulations and then showed on the Internet they can get around those reformulations?

That is what my question is. What actions have you done? Not did you read an article, not did you wring your hands. I understand it is difficult. When we try to stop trafficking of the Internet, people are going to come up with a solution. That is the business of crime, is to try to figure out how to get around it. The question is do we say oh, well, I guess they are going to get around anything we do so let's keep doing it the way we are doing?

Ms. MADRAS. That is not.

Mr. SOUDER. So what are we doing?

Ms. MADRAS. Well, our goal is to develop a——

Mr. SOUDER. To have a conference.

Ms. MADRAS. No. A conference from my vantage requires an action plan. And from our vantage what we are going to do is have a consortium of program industries come together. SAMSHA organized this a week ago and ONDCP has an intention to do this as well. But without simply talking and devising strategies in order to circumvent some of these obvious problems——

Mr. SOUDER. Mr. Cummings.

Mr. CUMMINGS. Thank you very much, Mr. Chairman. Dr. Volkow, tell me something. Do you think we have an epidemic here?

Dr. VOLKOW. I think we have an epidemic. I mean people get caught up with the term "epidemic," but I would just determine this one and I think, as you mentioned, it is not a new one. What is new, it was dramatic increases that are seen in the opiate analgesics.

Mr. CUMMINGS. You said something that struck me when you were testifying. You were talking about the parts of the brain that are affected by I guess overdosage of these prescription drugs and, you know, I couldn't help and as I listen to Chairman Souder I could not help but wonder about how powerful these combinations are, this overdosage is. And the reason why that is so significant to me is because thousands, literally thousands upon thousands of inner city folks in my district are sitting in jail for having possession of or distributing things that I guess would be just as powerful as some of these combinations. And it is interesting because you know, Mr. Souder, Chairman Souder, said, I said it, I think all of us said it, there is no stigma attached to this. The housewife picks up the kids after school from the private school, then dashes off to the ball in the evening.

When it's found that she is taking these dosages of OxyContin, for example, there is no real—I mean a stigma. Compared to the person who's shooting up dope in the alley in Baltimore, he goes to jail; people just say "poor little Amy."

And I guess what I'm trying to get to is, is there—the combinations of drugs, the things that we're talking about, are they just as powerful or can they be just as powerful as the drugs like crack cocaine, heroin, methamphetamines, you know, as far as damage to the body and mind?

Dr. VOLKOW. Well, very challenging question. And when used properly, these drugs—with the prescribed doses and for the purpose intended—these drugs are safe and very beneficial. They can save people's lives. When they are abused, however, they are utilized in very different circumstances. Some of these drugs can be as damaging in terms of their addiction potential as legal substances.

We've all heard about OxyContin. We've all heard about fetanyl. Fentanyl is a potent opiate, it can produce addiction. No difference of that in heroin in terms of the consequences of overdose. It is as dangerous because you have a potent drug.

So these drugs, pharmacologically, when they are injected pharmacologically, you cannot say this is worse than the other one. In some instances, yes, there are some drugs that are as potent, but some of these drugs can be as potent as the others, and that is why that question comes around.

One of the important issues, though, which is very challenging, we have people that even when properly prescribed some of these medications for pain—and the numbers exactly we don't know, precisely but it's between 5 and 7 percent of those people with properly prescribed pain medications will become addictive, following their physician. We are trying to understand why. That chronic use of these drugs produces changes in the brain that leads to the process of addiction, I don't know yet.

Mr. CUMMINGS. But you're talking 7 percent; is that what you said?

Dr. VOLKOW. Five to 7 percent. We do not know exactly. I'm very conservative, 5 to 7 percent.

Mr. CUMMINGS. And that's one group, but that leaves 93 percent of others; is that right? If I'm doing my math right.

You said there is a group that may take these drugs properly and may become addicted. There are others who go out and make a choice; they make a choice to use these drugs the way they are not supposed to be used. And I can understand Chairman Souder's frustration, because basically what we have is a group of people who make a choice to do this, and they can, in many instances—just let me finish—skirt the law, while that other person who goes and shoots up crack cocaine or heroin can go to prison, but yet still they're—one is just as dangerous as the other.

Dr. VOLKOW. You are absolutely right. As I said, there is no justification of choosing to take that drug for a diversion in some instances from other drugs. However, I do not believe in stigmatizing the drug, whether it is a heroin addict or whether it is an OxyContin addict. I think that what I believe is important is to recognize this is a disease where that individual, because of the effects of drugs, has lead to changes that affect their behavior. And so I do not see justification for stigmatizing the person that is addicted to heroin as I don't see stigmatizing the person that is addicted to OxyContin.

Mr. CUMMINGS. But the fact is that in this country, if a dope addict came in here right now on heroin, nodding, saliva dripping from his face, as I've seen in my district, that person is stigmatized as a bad person. I'm just telling you, whether we like it or not.

So now the question becomes is, I do believe that education is so significant in this because I think maybe a lot of times people don't even realize what we just talked about, how—I mean, they think I'll do a little here, a little something here, and I'll add it and I'll get this buzz; and a lot of times may not even realize the full impact of what is happening to them. I mean, what do you see as the most practical solutions?

Now, considering what I said in my testimony, that I was dealing—I was looking at this problem as a 17-year-old, I'm 55 now, and being realistic of what this government will or will not do, and we in the Congress, it is our job, as you well know, to try and make policy to help protect the citizens of this country. I mean, what would you have us do that you think is practical and that you know can happen before we go to dance with the angels?

Dr. VOLKOW. Well, to start with, I was delighted that you organized this hearing. It's not that I need more work, but I've been actually very proactive to try to make people aware of the importance of this problem that, in my view, is not recognized to the extent of the impact. So I spoke with the FDA. I personally spoke with a doctor at NIH to alert him about it.

So the notion of educating the different agencies is extraordinarily important, like we're doing by this hearing; it's a very important beginning.

In the process, also being coordinated. This is something that we're not—again, it's not one agency by themselves; it really needs that concerted effort of the multiple agencies. And it does need the concerted effort of partnership with the private industry because it's in their ultimate interest. They don't want their OxyContin labeled as something that is negative; it's bad for the reputation. So, taking advantage of that to bring them into the process.

And it is really going to take, again, a systematic, multiprong approach where, as we develop science, as we develop programs which are in the FDA and for regulating, you have to take that leadership position that bring this to the floor and say we cannot ignore it, we need to address it, and we need do address it and we need achievables, we need certain timeframes.

Mr. CUMMINGS. In light of the time, Mr. Chairman, I yield back.

Mr. SOUDER. Is this—is abuse of prescription drugs disproportionate compared to others like heroin, cocaine?

Dr. VOLKOW. Yes. And I was mentioning that in terms of monitoring the future, because when I saw the numbers, it's very telling. You have, No. 1, 33 percent of kids, marijuana. No. 2, it's Vicodin, 9.5 percent. No. 3 is amphetamine, 8.5 percent. No. 4 is—I think it's another opiate or a benzoate. No. 5 is OxyContin at 4.5 percent. And then you have inhalants and cocaine and prescription medications. So they are overwhelming. And again, the notion of exposure to these drugs which are very potent—and in this case most are taking them not because they medically need it, but because of a diversion situation is particularly vulnerable, because it can interfere with the normal development; and what we know, it does make early exposure to drugs, it makes the risk for addiction much greater. So it's a very venerable period. So yes, those are the numbers.

Mr. SOUDER. Ms. Watson.

Ms. WATSON. I want to thank the chairman for his responsible behavior because I see this as oversight, and we don't do enough of this kind of oversight in Congress. And I want to thank all of the witnesses here.

Dr. Volkow, since you seem to be the person that we're targeting to give us some answers, you know as I've been listening to your testimony, I'm thinking we are always dealing after the fact and I don't hear enough in the front end about prevention.

As I was reading the brochure on Jason Surks, he went on the Internet and he was researching all these different new medications and he thought he could use them without risk. Now there is a memorial search center named after him.

The question is, What can we do to prevent young people from looking outside of themselves to get a buzz on? Should we do it through our schools or should we get our courts—you know, we throw people into jail who we figure they're drug users, drug sellers, and we're not doing a thing to rehabilitate; in fact, lockups don't rehabilitate. But should we, maybe throughout our county and your departments that are represented here, maybe have walk-in drug abuse centers, both prescription drugs and over-the-counter drugs? Should we require across the educational spectrums—which is the only mandatory program in this country—that we do a lot—starting with K and going up the scale—to talk about the effect of using these drugs on body functions and brain development?

And I'm really concerned about—I have a degree in school psychology in my other life, and I saw the effects of drugs on children. I tested them, and the result is poor performance in school and, pretty soon, drop-out. So where do we go from here? And any of you that have information, insight or vision, please respond.

Dr. VOLKOW. Again, I am a strong believer of the importance of prevention to tackle the problem of substance abuse and addiction; in fact, it's our No. 1 priority, and we've been doing research and prevention for many years.

What we've learned is yes, indeed, the educational system is extraordinary to teach children and adolescents at different stages of their life about the knowledge of what drugs can do, but also teach them the skills that will enable them to behaviorally be able to say no when they're in a peer-pressure situation. And these programs have been shown to work.

At the same time, we've come to recognize that the aspect of prevention—again, we need a multiprong approach, and we should not just rely on the educational system, even though it is very effective; we also need to involve the parents, we also need to involve the medical community. As bizarre as it may sound to you—because it sounded very bizarre to me when I first heard about it—pediatricians don't necessarily evaluate kids for abuse of substances. So the medical community, which could play a very important role in the early detection of abuse and substance abuse is not doing it. So this issue of preventing drug abuse is a responsibility at multiple levels.

Now, definitely, we should take advantage of the education system, but we also should alert—should involve the families and the medical community into it.

Ms. MADRAS. I'd like to add to that.

As Dr. Volkow said, there are multiple means in which we can educate young people through schools. Student drug testing is an effective way, and we're been advocating and promoting this program because it can provide children with an excuse for not using drugs. Second, it can identify children who are using drugs and steer them into counseling and into treatment if necessary.

The second issue, as Dr. Volkow said, is parents. And our media campaign is targeting parents, particularly in and specifically with regard to prescription drugs, because we are aware that parents have the No. 1 influence on children's drug behavior.

The third issue which we are dealing with now with regard to our medical conference that I would like to just add some more detail is that we are profoundly concerned that the majority of medical schools in this country, the majority of residency training programs in this country, do not teach physicians how to screen for drugs, how to screen for adolescent drug abuse, and what to do once they screen for it.

So we have a two-pronged approach to trying to solve this very significant void in medical education. No. 1 is to try to enlist medical schools to develop these programs. And one of the ways in which we can enlist medical schools to develop these programs is to work toward reimbursing physicians for the screening.

The second issue is, we are supporting programs throughout the country in 14 States to conduct brief screening and interventions in trauma centers and emergency rooms as well as colleges, and we think that this program is an effective mechanism for catching people who are using drugs and will be identified by the medical community.

What is striking about the data that has emerged from SAMSHA is that the number of people who are addicted, who do not feel they have a problem, is a vast majority. It's estimated between 70 and 90 percent of people addicted do not come forward because they don't feel they have a problem. And by screening people within the medical community—and most Americans, more than 80 percent, see a physician at least once every 2 years. By screening people in the medical community, we will be able to identify and intervene and provide treatment for them. I think this is one of the great voids that we can fill that the administration and my office is working very, very significantly toward.

Ms. WATSON. Thank you.

This question goes to Dr. Kweder; is that the correct pronunciation? You are the Deputy Director of the Office of New Drugs Center for Drug Evaluation and Review at the Food and Drug Administration. How about having an engagement from the pharmaceutical manufacturers that when they put out a new drug that has the potential of becoming an addictive kind or has ingredients that the person using would become addicted to—and there appears to be something in the American psyche that leads them to using drugs; you know, you can't turn on your television or your radio that they're not plugging something: If you want to go to sleep, if you want to wake up, if you want to stay awake, if you want to feel good, take this. So it goes into our psyche. But how about talking to our pharmaceutical companies about having a fund that the more profit they make the more they add to that fund? Because I hear that after 9/11 the profits were astronomical for the pharmaceutical manufacturers.

This fund, then, would support these walk-in counseling centers. It wouldn't cost the consumer anything. But I would think that the courts could direct people to those rather than to lockups. And would you see the pharmaceutical manufacturers engaging in that kind of thing? It's not a tax.

Dr. KWEDER. The kinds of things that—we have not specifically explored that as an option. What we have done is we have looked at—when we evaluate drugs that have the potential for abuse, we look at each one uniquely, to try and ensure that the company is involved in activities that will do everything possible to prevent diversion, to prevent overdose, to prevent abuse. And we might use all kinds of measures. Those might include limited marketing rollouts, for example, to prevent that. They might include specific kinds of safety measures or distribution systems that might prevent diversion.

For example, the only way for a hospital to obtain a prescription drug would be directly from the company, without a middle wholesaler or distributor. We have not specifically explored with them a collaboration across companies to have some sort of a fund.

I think another area that we might explore is how companies can collaborate to look at tamper-resistant formulations. Although we have participated in meetings and conferences sponsored by the industry and by academia to do those things, we have an example of a recent approval that was well out in the press, where several companies got together to be able to produce a formulation that would allow once-a-day administration of three drugs to treat HIV. These are three drugs that have been on the market by different companies for over 10 years. Putting those together in one pill once a day was a monumental effort, and it required all of the resources of three very large pharmaceutical companies. But they did it because they saw that there was an interest, and it's a huge public health benefit. Those are the kinds of things, some of the collaborations that we've been involved in with ONDCP, NIDA and SAMSHA.

Ms. WATSON. And this is my last comment, if I have——

Mr. SOUDER. We have to adjourn in 10 minutes.

Ms. WATSON. Let me close it out.

I just to want say that if you could approach the pharmaceutical manufacturers—and I notice now when they're talking about a particular over-the-counter, a new prescription drug, they do give the side effects, but it's always at the last, at the end, and very quickly and very softly do they tell you the side effects. Maybe if we played out the effect of this medication on one's system, it might really garner that kind of attention.

And thank you for the time, Mr. Chairman, and then I think Dr. Kweder has a response.

Dr. KWEDER. Thank you for saying that. We're actually doing that. We have just implemented a new regulation that completely changes the format of how information is presented both to patients and providers so that the risk information, the key information is right up front.

In recent approvals that we've had of drugs that have the potential for abuse, we have also included in labels the kinds of information about how to screen patients for evidence that the drug may be being abused and how to address that once it is detected, something that is really a departure from tradition and I think is a real step forward.

Mr. SOUDER. Which is all nice, except that our testimony said that the people we're talking about here are mostly abusers of prescriptions, where people are getting the drug illegally. Educating the doctors when they give us a prescription, we have a whole different problem here—I'm not saying it's not nice; this is not the major problem we're addressing.

Ms. Foxx.

Ms. FOXX. Well, thank you, Mr. Chairman. You have led very nicely into the comment that I wanted to make and the question I wanted to ask.

I am very troubled by Dr. Volkow's comments that you do not want to stigmatize anyone who is a drug abuser, and yet you're saying that 70 to 90 percent of the people who are addicted to drugs don't feel like they have a problem, and we want to spend a lot of time educating young people about the problems of drug abuse. It seems to me that you will never, ever get people to believe that there is a drug problem if you don't stigmatize drug abuse. And I cannot understand how you can say that it is wrong to stigmatize people who abuse drugs. What is that saying to the people who are trying to stop people from becoming drug abusers? And I'd like to have a reaction to that.

And then I'd also like to know, do we have some sort of composite study that's been done? I understand that there has been—that compares programs that focus on personal responsibility, such as the AA 12-step process and all these other programs that just say to people, it's OK if you're a drug abuser. So tell me what the results are in terms of getting people off of—stop getting—getting people to stop being drug abusers with those two programs, one that promotes personal responsibility and the other that says it's perfectly all right for you to be a drug abuser.

Dr. VOLKOW. Let me give you an explanation about why I do not believe in stigmatization of the person who is addicted to drugs. For the past 25 years of my life, never have I encountered a drug-addicted person that wanted to be addicted. The consequences of addiction to the person are devastating, including suicide, loss of children, incarceration. I ask why are you taking the drugs, and they say Doc, I don't even know; it's no longer pleasurable, I just cannot control it.

Drug addiction is the result of changes in the brain of the person that erode their ability to exert control. As a result of that, even though they know that they shouldn't take the drug, they don't

want to take it, 24 hours later after being released from prison—
5 years, no drugs—they're taking it. It is no longer a choice the
way that we see it.

What is the problem of stigmatizing? What we're saying is that
it's a disease and it needs to be treated, and you need to take responsibility over this disease. So by labeling it as a medical disorder, we're not saying to the person it's OK, we're not removing
the responsibility; we're changing the framework, we're highlight-
ing the importance of treatment, both that person needs help, and
that the person needs to take responsibility of that treatment.

As for your question, how effective are treatments? Drug addiction can be treated, and some of the problems that you mentioned
that use 12-step bases like the Alcoholics Anonymous are very beneficial for many drug-addicted people. They're not a panacea, not
everybody responds to it.

The other thing about drug addiction is it is a chronic disease,
which means that treatment would need to be continuous, that you
cannot just discontinue and expect a cure.

On the other hand, stigmatizing, what is the problem of stigmatizing? The problem of stigmatizing is that the person who is addicted to drugs is much more likely to recognize and admit and
stand up and say I need help because no one likes to be stigmatized. So we have 85, 90 percent of people that are addicted that
are not seeking treatment. Part of the problem is that the stigmatization can be difficult to overcome if you're an addicted person
that requires treatment. So we are not helping anyone by stigmatizing.

This prevention, what we need is to educate children and adolescents and the general population about the dangers of drugs, the
devastating consequences that drugs can have. That, in my view,
is what will make the change.

We did it with smoking in this country, we brought down smoking by 50 percent. The moment we recognize and we mount a
multiprong approach to say we cannot afford this, this is just too
harmful to the person, too harmful to the society—we have been
successful with nicotine, not completely, we still have significant
numbers, but we have been successful, we need to do the same
thing for other drugs including prescription drug abuse.

Ms. FOXX. Just a followup. You can call it a semantics difference
if you want to, but I think one of the reasons that we brought down
smoking is we've stigmatized smoking. You know, there is just no
other way around it, we have said it is bad for you. If you call drug
addiction a disease and people have no control over it, I think you
have just exactly the opposite problem, and I think the statistics
show that. It just is incomprehensible to me that you cannot see
the connection between those two. And I know the chairman——

Mr. SOUDER. I need to go to Ms. Norton—are you done?

Ms. FOXX. Yes.

Mr. SOUDER. Ms. Norton.

Ms. NORTON. Well, I just to want say that, unfortunately, smoking worked because it shows that you die from cancer from it. You
didn't stigmatize people, you scared them into it, and a new generation stopped smoking.

What you had to say was very instructive and I think very well said about stigma; break through their disease and taking responsibility for it. Your Alcoholics Anonymous is the best example. The first thing you do is to get up and say, I am an alcoholic and take responsibility for it, you admit it, and you have been reached. And the real question is how to reach these many Americans who—some of them are elderly and unintentionally, apparently, becoming addicted—where the addiction isn't even defined as such because they are taking medicine; and thus when they begin to take more and more of it, it may be very difficult to recognize that you have become addicted to something the doctor prescribed. How can I be addicted if the doctor prescribed this?

I'm not sure that the ordinary ways of going at addiction are so very different when we're dealing with drugs and alcohol that would work here. Is there a different way of reaching people who are addicted to medicines that someone has said is good for you and they just keep taking it without recognizing that this has become an addiction? Is there a way to reach them that has anything in common with the way we reach addicts, or is this a different kind of addiction requiring a different approach?

Dr. VOLKOW. Well, it has similarities and differences. And I think you put the finger on one of the most complex issues, how do we—and it is one of the ones that we're talking about clinical trials—how do you treat the person that requires a medication that becomes addicted to it? And more important, how do you even recognize that person is addicted to it? And that's one of the points that Dr. Madras brought out, the importance of educating medical students as well as residents in their specialty in recognizing the problem of substance abuse and addiction, so that when they are prescribing these medications, they can tell their patients there is a risk potential for addiction with them, and these are the symptoms that you need to watch, so that the individual themselves can recognize when this is happening to them and alert the physician.

We don't have a standard yet, nor are we educating, unfortunately, our medical students of the problem of drug addiction, but bringing it to the medical community is of extraordinary importance.

Ms. NORTON. Shouldn't there be something on the label of medicine that warns that addiction could result if this medicine is taken beyond when it is prescribed?

Dr. VOLKOW. You, as a physician, when you're prescribing this medication——

Ms. NORTON. But I'm talking about the physician prescribes it—you're speaking about the physicians who are rushed. If there is something on the label cautioning people about trying to get this prescription beyond when it is prescribed, and saying that it could become addictive—people read those little things that come with our prescriptions these days that are very informative. Why not put that on it rather than trusting some individual physicians—physicians may be very rushed and in the process not always give the warning——

Mr. SOUDER. I'm sorry. The answer is going to be have to be written. We have to suspend. The Prime Minister is in the Chamber.

I think it is important to establish that earlier in the hearing they testified that prescribed drugs going through a doctor are not really a major problem here, it's more an outside. But I don't think anybody disagrees that having some kind of a label would be helpful for those cases, seniors and a few others.

We are adjourned. We will reconvene at 12 o'clock promptly.

[Recess.]

Mr. SOUDER. The subcommittee will come to order. We thank you for your patience.

First, I need to swear in the witnesses first. Our witnesses on this panel are Misty Fetco, who is a registered nurse who lost her 18-year-old son Carl to DXM and fentanyl abuse; Linda Surks, who lost her 19-year-old son Jason to a prescription drug overdose-related death; Barbara van Rooyan, who lost her 24-year-old son Patrick to Oxycontin use; Mathea Falco, who is president of Drug Strategies; Stephen Johnson, executive director of commercial planning for Pain Therapeutics, Inc.; Dr. Manchikanti, who is chief executive officer of the American Society for Interventional Pain Physicians; and Steve Pasierb, the president and CEO for the Partnership for a Drug-Free America.

If you would each raise your right hands.

[Witnesses sworn.]

Mr. SOUDER. Let the record show that the witnesses responded in the affirmative.

As an oversight committee, we always swear in our witnesses. Ms. Fetco, you are sitting where Mark McGuire sat and couldn't remember the past. I am hoping that you can today and are willing to talk about it, because I think it is very important that we learn from those experiences. Thank you for being here today. And our sympathy goes out to all your families. I know this is difficult, but we appreciate your being willing to talk to the American people and to Congress about the challenges you faced.

Ms. Fetko, if you want to go ahead.

STATEMENTS OF MISTY FETCO, REGISTERED NURSE, WHO LOST HER 18-YEAR-OLD SON CARL TO DXM AND FETANYL ABUSE; LINDA SURKS, WHO LOST HER 19-YEAR-OLD SON JASON TO A PRESCRIPTION DRUG OVERDOSE-RELATED DEATH; BARBARA VAN ROOYAN, WHO LOST HER 24-YEAR-OLD SON PATRICK TO OXYCONTIN USE; MATHEA FALCO, J.D., PRESIDENT, DRUG STRATEGIES; STEPHEN E. JOHNSON, EXECUTIVE DIRECTOR, COMMERCIAL PLANNING, PAIN THERAPEUTICS, INC.; LAXMAIAH MANCHIKANTI, M.D., CHIEF EXECUTIVE OFFICER, AMERICAN SOCIETY FOR INTERVENTIONAL PAIN PHYSICIANS; AND STEVE PASIERB, PRESIDENT AND CEO, THE PARTNERSHIP FOR A DRUG-FREE AMERICA

STATEMENT OF MISTY FETCO

Ms. FETKO. Good afternoon, Chairman Souder, Congressman Cummings, and members of the committee. My name is Misty Fetko, and I'm a registered nurse who works in a very busy emergency room in central Ohio. But more importantly, I am a mother of two wonderful boys.

I am here today to tell you the story of my oldest son Carl. Carl was my beautiful boy, eyes like large dark chocolates, an infectious smile and an insatiable curiosity. I spent years protecting him from harm, but 3 years ago harm found a way to sneak in and steal the life of this gifted young man.

It was the morning of July 16, 2003. Carl had just graduated from high school and was getting ready to leave for Memphis College of Art in 2 days. The college had courted him after he won an award for artwork he created in his junior year in high school. The night before, Carl and I had sat in his room and talked with each other about his day at work and the pending trip to Memphis. He smiled and hugged me and said, "Good night, Mom, I love you."

The next morning I decided to walk the dog before waking Carl. While walking next to his car I noticed an empty bottle of Robitussin in Carl's back seat. Instantly I knew something was wrong. I had been vigilant for signs of drug abuse in the past and hadn't seen many. I rushed to his bedroom door, only to find it locked. After finding my way in, I discovered Carl lying peacefully in bed, motionless, with legs crossed, but he wasn't responding to my screams and he wasn't breathing.

I quickly transformed from mother to nurse and began CPR, desperately trying to breathe life back into my son. I could not believe my worst fear was happening, my son was dead, but I still did not know what had caused this nightmare.

We are a very close family and I am a very involved mother. Carl always assured me that he wasn't using alcohol or drugs. And I, the ever-watchful mother, believed him, as there really wasn't any evidence to prove differently.

During Carl's junior year of high school, I found the first evidence of marijuana in his room. After all the talks and reassurances between us, what had changed? I intervened and didn't see anything else suspicious until the summer after his junior year, when I found two empty bottles of Robitussin in our basement after a sleepover with friends. I was determined to keep drugs out of our house; but cough medicine?

I went to search for answers on the Internet but found nothing and confronted my son instead. Carl had explained that he and his friends had experimented, but nothing had happened, and I was reassured once again that he wasn't using hard drugs. Finding no further evidence, I believed him.

During his senior year I knew Carl had developed an interest for marijuana, but thought we had addressed it. So why on that dreadful July morning did I discover that my son had passed away during the night?

The next several months after Carl's death I frantically searched for answers. During my search I found two more empty bottles of cough syrup, but it wasn't until after talking with friends and finding journal entries on his computer did I discover that Carl had been abusing cough medicines intermittently over the past 2½ years.

Through the Internet and his friends, Carl had researched and educated himself on how to use these products to get high. He read about and enjoyed the hallucinations achieved by abusing cough and cold products. But I wouldn't find out until the morning of

Carl's death what he and many others knew about his abuse of cough medicine. The danger that I so desperately tried to keep out of our house had found a way to sneak in secretly, but there were no needles, no powders, no smells, none of the typical signs associated with drug abuse.

Carl's autopsy report revealed that he had died from a lethal mix of drugs. Fentanyl, a strong prescription available in a patch, cannaboids, found in marijuana, and DXM, the active ingredient in cough medicines, were found in his system. To this day, I don't know where Carl obtained the narcotic fentanyl. There are no journal entries that talk about his use of pain killers. Was this his first time? We will never know why he made the choice to abuse prescription and over-the-counter drugs; we only know parts of his story by the words he left behind in his journal. His words are now silent.

I've spent many hours trying to find a reason for this unexplainable tragedy. If loving my son were enough, Carl would have lived forever. But I know now that the abuse of over-the-counter and prescription drugs is rapidly emerging. Access to information about this type of drug abuse is prevalent on the Internet. Availability to obtain these drugs—which can be lethal and abusive—is even more prevalent, but what is even scarier is that these teens have a false sense of security; they have the mindset that these drugs provide a safe high.

We as parents need to be aware of these lurking dangers, and we need to make other parents and teens aware of them, too.

It is with a heavy heart and eternal love for my son that I share his story today to hopefully prevent other families from having to suffer the same heartache.

Thank you for calling this hearing today to examine the problem of prescription drug abuse in our country. I appreciate you listening, and I'll be happy to answer any questions.

Mr. SOUDER. I thank you for your willingness to testify. I can see it's very difficult.

[The prepared statement of Ms. Fetko follows:]

Testimony of Misty Fetko
"Prescription Drug Abuse:
What is Being Done to Address This New Drug Epidemic?"
House Government Reform Subcommittee on
Criminal Justice Drug Policy & Human Resources
July 26, 2006

Good morning Chairman Souder, Congressman Cummings and Members of the Committee. My name is Misty Fetko and I am a registered nurse who works in a very busy Emergency Room in Central Ohio, but, more importantly, I am a mother of two wonderful boys.

I am here today to tell you the story of my oldest son, Carl.

Carl was my beautiful little boy; eyes like large, dark chocolates, an infectious smile, and an insatiable curiosity. I spent years protecting him from harm, but two and a half years ago, harm found a way to sneak in and steal the life of this gifted young man.

It was the morning of July 16, 2003. Carl had just graduated from high school and was getting ready to leave for Memphis College of Art in two days. The college had courted him, after he won an award for artwork he created his junior year of high school.

The night before, Carl and I had sat in his room and talked with each other about his day at work and the pending trip to Memphis. He smiled and hugged me goodnight. He said, "Goodnight Mom. Love you."

The next morning, I decided to walk the dog before waking Carl. While walking next to his car, I noticed an empty bottle of cough medicine in Carl's backseat. Instantly, I knew something was wrong. I had been vigilant for signs of drug abuse in the past and hadn't seen many. I rushed to his bedroom door only to find it locked. After finding my way in, I discovered Carl lying peacefully in bed, motionless with legs crossed. He wasn't responding to my screams, and he wasn't breathing.

I quickly transformed from mother to nurse and I began CPR, desperately trying to breathe life back into my son. I could not believe my worst fear had happened. My son was dead, but I still did not know what had caused this nightmare.

We are a very close family. I was a very involved mother. Carl had always assured me that he wasn't using alcohol or drugs. I, the ever watchful mother, believed him, as there wasn't really any evidence to prove differently.

During Carl's junior year of high school, I found the first evidence of marijuana in his room. After all the talks and all the reassurances between us; what had changed? I intervened, and didn't see anything else suspicious until that summer when I found two empty bottles of cough medicine syrup in our basement after a sleepover with friends. I was determined to keep drugs out of our house, but cough medicine? I went to search for answers on the internet, but found nothing and confronted my son instead. Carl explained that he and his friends had experimented, but that nothing happened. I was reassured, once again, that he wasn't using "hard" drugs and not to worry. Finding no further evidence, I believed him.

During his senior year, I knew Carl had developed an interest for marijuana, but I thought we had addressed it. So why on that dreadful July morning did I discover my son had passed away during the night?

The next several months after Carl's death I frantically searched for answers. What signs did I miss?

During my search, I found two more empty bottles of cough syrup. But it wasn't until after talking with his friends and finding journal entries on his computer, that I discovered that Carl had been abusing cough medicine intermittently over the past 2 ½ years. He documented his abuse in his computer journal. Through the internet and his friends, Carl had researched and educated himself on how to use these products to get high. He wrote about and enjoyed the hallucinations achieved upon intentionally abusing cough and cold products. Carl had described the "pull" that he felt towards the disassociative effects of abusing the cough medicine and seemed to crave the effects.

According to the journal, Carl gradually increased the amount of cough medicine he abused. He wrote that he was increasingly "pulled" to the effects of escape more and more.

As his abuse increased, many things in his life were changing: graduation, college, his parents' divorce, and increasing pressures in his life.

I wouldn't find out until the morning of Carl's death what he and many others knew about his abuse of cough medicine. The danger that I so desperately tried to keep out of our house had found a way to sneak in secretly. But there were no needles, no powders, no smells, no large amounts of money being spent – None of the "typical" signs associated with drug abuse.

Carl's autopsy report revealed that he had died from a lethal mix of drugs: Fentanyl, a strong prescription narcotic available in a patch, that is removed and eaten to achieve an abusive high. Cannaboids found in marijuana, and DXM, the active ingredient in cough medicine were found in his system.

To this day, I still don't know where Carl obtained the narcotic Fentanyl. There are no journal entries that talk about his use of painkillers. Was this his first time? Was he looking for a different high? We will never know why Carl made the wrong choice to abuse prescription and over-the-counter drugs. We only know parts of his story by the words he left behind in his journal; his words are now silent.

I have spent many hours trying to find the reason for this unexplainable tragedy. If loving my son were enough, Carl would have lived forever. But I know now that abuse of over-the-counter and prescription drugs is rapidly emerging. Parents and their children need to be made aware of these lurking dangers. It is with a heavy heart and eternal love for my son that I share his story today to hopefully prevent other families from having to suffer the same heartache.

Thank you for calling this hearing today to examine the problem of prescription drug abuse in our country. I appreciate you listening to my testimony and I am happy to answer any questions.

Mr. SOUDER. Ms. Linda Surks, thank you for coming also.

STATEMENT OF LINDA SURKS

Ms. SURKS. Thank you.

Good afternoon, Chairman Souder, Congressman Cummings, and members of the committee. Thank you for holding this hearing today to examine the problem of prescription drug abuse, a subject which is very close to my heart.

My name is Linda Surks, and I'd like to tell you about my son, Jason.

Jason was the kind of person that people were drawn to. He made friends easily and had a great sense of humor. He was a caring person and a loving son. He was active in his youth group and participated in several community service projects. He even volunteered at NCADD where I work, a community-based organization in Middlesex County, New Jersey, that works to prevent substance abuse.

When Jason was a little boy, he would lie about little things; like the time he was 7 years old and he swore he had taken a shower, even though I showed him that the tub was completely dry. He was caught in lies like that all the time. As he grew into a young man, we talked about it, and he said he realized how silly it was. I was convinced he had outgrown it.

In December 2003 I discovered that he had not. At the time, Jason was halfway through his second year at college as a pre-pharmacy major. Since his dorm was only 45 minutes away, he came home frequently on weekends, to work at the pharmacy where he had a job since high school. On one Sunday night I remember saying goodbye to him at our front door. As I often did, I put my hand on his cheek. I loved the scruffy feel of his stubble, it reminded me that my little boy was growing up. I caressed Jason's cheek that night and told him I love him.

Three days later, on the morning of December 17, 2003, my husband called me at work to tell me that the hospital had called to say Jason was brought to the emergency room and we should come as soon as we can. We met nearby and drove to the hospital together, in silence. We couldn't imagine what had happened. My husband had spoken to Jason the day before and he said he sounded fine.

When we arrived at the hospital, the first thing I remember was being referred to as "the parents" and being ushered into a private office. I used to work in hospital administration, and I knew what that usually meant, but this had to mean something different. We asked to see Jason and were told we had to wait to speak to the doctor; again, a sign I knew but I could not accept.

I have relived that day in my mind so many times, but I really can't tell you exactly what the doctor said. The message was clear: My beautiful son was gone. Apparently Jason had been abusing prescription drugs and had overdosed. He was 19 years old.

This couldn't be possible. I work in prevention. He knew the dangers, we talked about it often. I was so convinced that he was not using drugs, it became a sort of joke between us. As he would leave home at the end of a weekend I would say, Jason, don't do drugs. And he would say, I know, Mom; I won't. But he did.

While speaking with dozens of Jason's friends after his death, we learned that his abuse of prescription drugs may have started after he began college, and apparently started to escalate the summer before he died.

I know he believed he was being safe. He used the Internet to research the safety of certain drugs and how they react to others. As a pre-pharmacy major, he probably thought he knew more about the drugs than he actually did. We also learned that he had visited several on-line pharmacies to order drugs from a Mexican pharmacy on the Internet that automatically renewed his order each month.

I think back to the last several months of my son's life, trying to identify any signs I might have missed. During his first year of college I discovered an unlabeled bottle of pills in Jason's room. After some research, I identified them as a generic form of Ritalin. When I confronted Jason, he told me he had gotten them from a friend who had been prescribed the medication; he wanted to see if they would help him with his problem focusing in school. I took that opportunity to talk to him about the dangers of abusing prescription drugs. I told him that if he really thought he had ADD, we should pursue it with a clinician. He promised he would stop using the drug, and even called the counseling office at school to make an appointment for evaluation.

The only other sign I can remember was that 1 weekend when Jason was home, I passed him in the kitchen and noticed that his eyes looked strange. I confronted him right then and there and asked him if he was on something. He said, No, what's wrong? And he went over to a mirror to look and see what I was talking about. He said he didn't know what was wrong, maybe it was because he was tired. I was suspicious but his behavior was perfectly normal, so I let it go. There were no other signs until we got that horrible call on December 17, 2003 that changed our lives forever.

There are things being done to address this new drug epidemic, but we need to keep moving forward. With the support of my office, we have developed a number of initiatives in our community to raise awareness about the dangers of prescription drug abuse. Something as simple as a mouse pad in a high school has already made a difference in someone's life. Something as profound as supporting the Ryan Haight Internet Pharmacy Consumer Protection Act can save so many lives.

Jason touched so many lives in such a short time. He had many friends who cared deeply for him but just didn't know how to help. I believe education is key to preventing this tragedy from repeating. By sharing Jason's story, I hope we can help other families avoid the kind of heartache that my family his suffered.

Thank you for listening. I'm happy to answer any questions you might have.

Mr. SOUDER. Thank you.

[The prepared statement of Ms. Surks follows:]

Testimony of Linda Surks
"Prescription Drug Abuse:
What is Being Done to Address This New Drug Epidemic?"
House Government Reform Subcommittee on
Criminal Justice, Drug Policy and Human Resources
July 26, 2006

Good morning Chairman Souder, Congressman Cummings, and Members of the Subcommittee. Thank you for holding this hearing today to examine the problem of prescription drug abuse, a subject which is very close to my heart. My name is Linda Surks and I'd like to tell you about my son, Jason.

Jason was the kind of person that people were drawn to. He made friends easily and had a great sense of humor. He was a caring person and a loving son who respected his family. He was helpful around the house and in the winter he always shoveled our neighbor's walk. He was active in his youth group and he often volunteered for various community projects – he even worked for NCADD where I work, a community-based organization in Middlesex County, New Jersey that works to prevent substance abuse.

When Jason was a little boy, he'd lie about little things. Like the time he was seven years old and swore he had taken a shower, even though I showed him that the tub was completely dry. He got caught in little lies like that all the time. As he grew into a young man, we talked about it and he said he realized how silly it all was. I was convinced he had outgrown it. In December of 2003, I realized that he had not.

At the time, Jason was finishing the first semester of his second year as a pre-pharmacy major at college. Since his dorm was only 45 minutes away, he came home frequently on weekends, often to work at the pharmacy where he had a job since high school. On one Sunday night in December, I remember saying goodbye to him at our front door. As I often did, I put my hand on his cheek. I loved that scruffy feel of his stubble – it reminded me that my little boy was growing up. I caressed Jason's cheek and told him I love him.

Three days later, on the morning of December 17, 2003, my husband called me at work to tell me the hospital had called to say Jason was brought to the emergency room and we should come as soon as we can. We met near the turnpike and drove to the hospital together in silence. We couldn't image what had happened – my husband had spoken to Jason the day before and said he sounded fine.

When we arrived at the hospital emergency room, the first thing I remember is being referred to as "the parents," and being ushered into a private office. I used to work in hospital administration and I knew what that usually meant – but this had to mean something different. We asked to see Jason, but were told we had to wait to speak to the doctor. Again, it was a sign I knew, but I could not accept.

I have relived that day in my mind so many times, but I really can't tell you exactly what the doctor said - the message was clear – my beautiful son was gone. Apparently, Jason had been abusing prescription drugs and had overdosed. He was 19 years old.

This couldn't be possible. I work in prevention. He knew the dangers. We talked about it often. We believed that he was not using drugs. I was so convinced that he was not using, it became a sort of joke between us – as he would leave home at the end of a weekend, I would frequently say, "Jason, don't do drugs." Then he would say, "I know, Mom, I won't." But he did.

In speaking with dozens of Jason's friends after his death, we learned that his abuse of prescription drugs may have started after he began college, and apparently started to escalate the summer before he died. I know that he believed he was being safe. He used the internet to research the safety of certain drugs and how they react with others. As a pre-pharmacy major, he probably felt that he knew more about these drugs than he actually did, and perhaps had a "professional curiosity" about them. We also learned that he had visited several online pharmacies and ordered drugs from one Mexican pharmacy online. We found indications that this pharmacy automatically renewed his order each month. It was a simple process of a few clicks and the drugs were delivered right to his door.

I think back to the last several months of my son's life, trying to identify any signs I might have missed. I remember that sometime during his first year in college, I discovered an unlabeled pill bottle in Jason's room. I took the pills to my computer and identified them as a generic form of Ritalin. When I confronted Jason, he told me he got them from a friend who'd been prescribed the medication. He wanted to see if they would help him with his problem focusing in school. I took that opportunity to talk to him about the dangers of abusing prescription drugs. I told him that if he really thought he had A-D-D, we should pursue this with a clinician. He promised he would stop using the drug; and he even called the counseling office at school to make an appointment for an evaluation.

The only other sign I can remember is that one weekend when Jason was home I passed him in the kitchen and noticed that his eyes looked odd – his pupils were as small as pinpoints. I confronted him right there and then, asked him if he was on something. He said, "no, what's wrong?" and went over to a mirror to see what I was talking about. He said that he didn't know what was wrong – maybe it was because he was tired. I was suspicious, but his behavior was perfectly normal, so I let it go.

There were no other signs until we got that horrible call on December 17, 2003 that changed our lives forever.

Jason touched so many lives in such a short time. He had many friends who cared for him deeply but just didn't know how to help. I believe that education is key to preventing this tragedy from continuing. With the support of my office, we have developed a number of initiatives in our community to raise awareness about the dangers of prescription drug abuse. Something as simple as a mouse pad in a high school has already made a difference in someone's life. By sharing Jason's story, I hope we can help other families avoid the kind of heartache that my family has suffered.

Thank you for listening. I am happy to answer any questions that you might have.

Mr. SOUDER. Next is Barbara van Rooyan.

STATEMENT OF BARBARA VAN ROOYAN

Ms. VAN ROOYAN. Chairman Souder and other members of the subcommittee, my name is Barbara van Rooyan. I'm a California college faculty member and a mother of two sons.

My son, Patrick Stuart, died in 2004 after ingesting just one OxyContin. He had no other drugs in his system, and only a small amount of alcohol.

He was a college graduate, a graphic designer, and a certified personal trainer. He made the tragic mistake of believing someone at a Fourth of July celebration when he was told that OxyContin was prescription and FDA approved, and therefore safe. As happens with someone who is intolerant to opioids, he stopped breathing in his sleep. After 5 days in a coma, Patrick was reported to have no brain activity. We arranged for organ donation as we said our last goodbyes. Only his lungs could not be shared; the OxyContin had destroyed them.

In my grief, I learned very quickly about OxyContin and prescription drug abuse. And what I learned I felt compelled to share with others. So during a partial sabbatical leave from the college, focusing on prescription drug education, I told Patrick's story to hundreds of college and high school students, faculty, staff, and administration. I learned from them as they learned from me. I learned that young people believe prescription FDA-approved drugs are safe, and that taking them is not doing drugs.

Contrary to the testimony of the first panel at this subcommittee hearing this morning, young people are getting prescriptions from their doctors and they are getting them from the medicine cabinets of other family members who are getting prescriptions from their doctors. Overprescribing is a huge problem with OxyContin.

I also found that most teachers, counselors, administrators, and parents are in the dark about prescription drug abuse.

Soon after Patrick's death, I requested that the Anesthetic and Life Support Drugs Advisory Committee of the FDA meet to discuss OxyContin, as they had new membership. Repeated contacts with FDA officials, including a letter from Senator Feinstein, yielded no results. So in February 2005, my husband and I submitted a Citizen Petition to the FDA requesting that OxyContin and Palladone be reformulated as "abuse resistant" and be relabeled "for use with severe pain only." The relabeling alone would powerfully reduce the number of deaths and addictions to OxyContin without compromise to terminally ill or dying patients' access to the drug. I received only one communication from the FDA regarding the Citizen Petition. That was a letter stating that they needed more time for review.

Subsequently, Palladone has been targeted for reformulation. However, last month the FDA approved Opana, a sustained-release opioid, without first resolving OxyContin problems.

It has now been over 10 years since OxyContin first came on the market. The deaths and addiction continue, unabated.

The 2005 Castle Report states about half of all doctors do not receive medical school training in prescribing controlled substances, addiction or diversion of drugs. Yet in 2002, OxyContin was one of the most widely prescribed opioid medications, with an increase of 380 percent in a 10-year period. Purdue Pharma's greed and FDA approval of OxyContin for moderate pain are primarily responsible for this increase.

I'd also like to mention that, again, contrary to the testimony of the first panel this morning, the 2005 Waismann Opiate Dependency Survey indicates that 71 percent of their patients who are addicted to opioids were originally prescribed an opioid by their doctor.

In 2001, the Attorney General of Connecticut pleaded with Purdue Pharma and the FDA to take steps to stem the tide of death and addiction to OxyContin. In 2004, Fred Pauzar, another parent who lost a son to OxyContin, came before this very subcommittee and asked the same.

Today, more than a decade after OxyContin was first unleashed, I am asking the same once again. There must be, at the very least, more assertive and comprehensive actions by the FDA to protect citizens, increase mandatory physician education regarding selective opioid prescribing and a balanced approach to pain management, youth and family prescription drug education.

I come before this committee today because my son is dead. I will forever mourn. I also come before this committee today because my son stands at my right shoulder and each day he tells me, "Mother, it is better to light one candle than to curse the darkness." I will light as many candles as necessary, and I hope that you will too.

Mr. SOUDER. Thank you for the testimony. And if you could get us some more information on the survey, we'll make sure we get that in the record.

[The prepared statement of Ms. Rooyan follows:]

95

Testimony of Barbara Van Rooyan
Before the
Subcommittee on Criminal Justice, Drug Policy and Human Resources

July 26, 2006

Introduction

Chairman Souder and other distinguished members of the Criminal Justice, Drug Policy and Human Resources Subcommittee, thank you for the opportunity to testify today regarding the problem of prescription drug abuse.

My name is Barbara Van Rooyan. I am a California Community College faculty member and counselor, the wife and daughter of physicians, the mother of two sons. My first-born son, Patrick Stewart died on July 9, 2004 at 24 years of age after ingesting just one OxyContin. He had no other drugs in his system and only a small amount of alcohol. He was a SDSU graduate, a graphic designer and a certified personal trainer. His friends described Patrick as "the one who puts you back on your bicycle after you fall off". He made the tragic mistake of believing someone at a 4th of July celebration when he was told that OxyContin was "sort of like a muscle relaxant, that it was prescription and FDA approved, so therefore safe". Close friends say that Patrick had never before taken an OxyContin, did not know it was equivalent to "heroin in a pill". As happens with some who are intolerant to opioids he stopped breathing in his sleep. Found by his friends he was rushed to the ER at UC San Diego Medical Center. There he remained in a medically induced coma to control seizures resulting from lack of oxygen to his brain. After five days Patrick was reported to have no brain activity. As I believed would be his wish we arranged for organ donation as we said our last goodbyes. Only his lungs could not be shared; the OxyContin had destroyed them. At the time I knew next to nothing about OxyContin, prescription drug abuse or grief.

But in my grief I learned very quickly.

And what I learned I felt compelled to share with others. Therefore in the two years since Patrick's death I have become involved in youth and family education regarding prescription drug abuse, governmental regulation of controlled substances, and physician education regarding pain management. In addition I gained knowledge of expansion of the California Prescription Monitoring Program facilitated by other parents who lost both a son and daughter.

Youth and Family Education

As a counselor, employed by a college district of 80,000 students, I applied for and was granted a partial sabbatical to concentrate on prescription drug abuse education for students, faculty, staff and administration. This past year I have told Patrick's story hundreds of times and upon hearing his story, people tell me theirs. From them I learned that...

1

- Many young people think taking a prescription drug is not the same as "doing drugs"

- Many teachers, counselors and administrators are not aware of the abuse of prescription drugs, the scope of the problem, nor the signs of misuse (no odor, no paraphernalia = no drugs)

- Many young people have a friend or relative who was prescribed OxyContin for an injury, back pain or arthritis and now is unable to stop taking the drug.

- High school health classes include segments on illicit drugs but in most classes prescription drug abuse is not addressed.

- Some people obtain OxyContin from their own family doctors by "faking pain".

- Most physicians have very little training in opioid prescribing or addiction; as a result many are not selective in prescribing opioids nor do they make adequate use of non-drug interventions.

- Easy availability of prescription drugs from doctors, family medicine cabinets and the Internet, combined with young people's feelings of invincibility has led to more deaths and addictions than I ever imagined.

- Prescription drug abuse education needs to target parents as well as youth.

DrugTalk programs and tools, particularly, "The New Face of Drugs" DVD are valuable educational tools that I discovered during this sabbatical year. They can be used in schools or homes.

Governmental Regulation
In the fall of 2004, just a few short months after Patrick's death I learned that stories of hundreds of OxyContin deaths could be found on the website of Ed Bisch (www.oxyabusckills.com) who lost his son Eddie to OxyContin in 2001. I also learned from the website that the Anesthetic and Life Support Drugs Advisory Committee of the FDA had voted in September 2003 NOT to restrict OxyContin for use with severe pain only. *Such a restriction would powerfully reduce the number of deaths and addictions to OxyContin without compromising terminally ill or dying patients' access to OxyContin.* Yet the FDA has failed to take this step. When I discovered that the membership of the Advisory Committee had changed since the 2003 vote I began to contact FDA members with Patrick's story and a request for the new committee members to meet to discuss OxyContin. Although I was put in touch with an FDA ombudsman and although Senator Feinstein wrote the FDA requesting that the committee meet, our requests went unheeded.

In February 2005 my husband and I submitted Citizen Petition 2005P-0076 to the FDA requesting that OxyContin and Palladone be reformulated as abuse resistant and relabeled for severe pain only. Despite many attempted contacts with the FDA I have received only one communication from the agency- a letter stating that more time was needed to review the petition requests and I would be notified of any decision. Subsequently, Palladone has temporarily been removed from the market for reformulation. However, in June 2006, without first addressing the continuing problems with OxyContin, the FDA approved an additional sustained release opioid, Opana, manufactured by Endo Pharmaceuticals.

In the fall of 2005 a meeting of the Advisory Committee was tentatively scheduled for November 10, 2005. I contacted the executive secretary and was informed that it was to be a closed meeting; therefore the agenda was not available to the public. She indicated that there would be a short public session prior to the closed meeting; I could attend or submit a written statement. I chose the latter, registered for the open session and submitted a written statement and the Citizen Petition for each committee member. Transcripts of the open session contain no mention of my written statement or of OxyContin and of course, there is no public transcript of the closed session. To my knowledge the Anesthetic and Life Support Advisory Committee has not, to date, responded to many requests to address OxyContin or Citizen Petition 2005P-0076.

In May 2005 HR 2195 was introduced in The House of Representatives, asking for a recall of OxyContin. After communications with Congressman Lynch's staff it is my understanding that the recall would be temporary, for the purpose of reformulation such as requested in Citizen Petition 2005P-0076. The bill currently resides with the Health Subcommittee of Energy and Commerce. I have sent letters to Chairman Waxman and all subcommittee members requesting support for HR 2195 and have asked others to do so also.

Just five months before my son Patrick died, Fred Pauzar, another parent who lost his son to OxyContin, also gave testimony before this subcommittee. Mr. Pauzar made an impassioned plea for Congress to be wise and courageous in taking steps to monitor and curb the improper marketing and use of OxyContin. Today, two years later, OxyContin remains on the market for use with moderate pain and new sustained release opioids continue to receive FDA approval.

Physician Education
In California, since October 2001, physicians have had a one time only requirement of 12 hours of continuing education in pain management and treatment of terminally ill and dying patients that must be completed by December 2006. Not all states require even this minimal education.

The July 2005 report from the National Center on Addiction and Substance Abuse at Columbia University states that 4 in 10 doctors surveyed say they received no training in medical school on prescribing controlled substances; more than half received no training on identifying prescription drug abuse or addiction and three fourths said they had no training in medical school identifying diversion of prescription drugs for illicit purposes.

Yet in 2002 OxyContin was, by far, one of the most widely prescribed opioid medications in the U.S. with an increase of 380% between 1992 and 2002. Purdue Pharma's false and aggressive marketing of OxyContin and the FDA's approval of OxyContin for moderate pain are primary reasons for this increase.

In addition, the Waismann 2005 Opiate Dependency Survey indicates that 71% of patients with opiate dependency were originally prescribed opioid medications by their doctors.

The question becomes, "How can so many prescriptions for opioids be written by so many doctors with so little training?

Consider that:

- The majority of physicians do not know that the long term safety and effectiveness of opioids for management of non-malignant pain have NOT been substantiated.

- The majority of physicians do not know that patients seeking pain relief for chronic, non malignant pain often have underlying psycho social problems and need psychological or rehabilitation services or would respond well to other non-drug interventions.

- In busy medical practices, particularly primary care and family practice office settings, a thorough diagnosis of the cause and type of pain and a balanced, multifaceted pain treatment program are often difficult to achieve. The result is that often pain therapy is based not on science but on intuition or hearsay, and ends up aggravating rather than ameliorating prescription pain medication abuse and addiction.

- Many good physicians relied upon false marketing information regarding OxyContin from an aggressive Purdue Pharma sales force that was prompted by greed. The result was an expansion of opioid therapy for patients who might benefit more from non-drug interventions or alternate drugs, without the accompanying risks of opioids.

My husband, a plastic surgeon and consultant for The Medical Board of California, and I have taken some initial steps to help improve and expand California's continuing medical education regarding pain management. Other physicians, such as Dr. Stephen Gelfand, a South Carolina rheumatologist who works with a large population of chronic pain patients, are working to educate general practitioners of the efficacy and safety of non-drug therapies, alternate medications and multidisciplinary care. However, the surface has only been scratched.

Comprehensive pain management education with a balanced, multi-faceted approach is needed for all physicians.

Prescription Drug Monitoring Programs

Prescription drug monitoring programs are also essential to combat the tide of death and addiction from prescription drugs.

In California, Bob and Carmen Pack, with the help of State Senator Torlakson introduced SB 734 which expanded California's Prescription Drug Monitoring Program into the current Controlled Substance Utilization Review and Evaluation System, known as C.U.R.E.S. SB 734 became effective January 2006 but is only the "first leg of the program". The "second leg" of the program is essential and would provide an online narcotic prescription drug-monitoring program. Unfortunately, state funds for this portion of the program are not available. The Packs are looking to the pharmaceutical companies and the federal government for financial assistance. Tragically, the new program comes as a result of the death of the Pack's two children, age 7 and 10. The children were hit and killed by a car driven by a woman addicted to Vicodin and under the influence at the time. Prior to the crash the woman had been given six Vicodin prescriptions from six different doctors at the same HMO; the physicians had corroborated none of the injuries she complained about.

Conclusion

There is no ONE culprit in this epidemic of prescription drug abuse. It would be simple and understandable for a grieving parent to hold only one party responsible and focus efforts on that one party. However, I believe that it will take a concerted effort by many individuals, groups and agencies to stem the tide of deaths and addiction to prescription drugs, most notably OxyContin, that continues to plague our country. Sadly, correspondence from Richard Blumenthal, Connecticut State Attorney General, dated July 31, 2001 to Richard Sackler, President of Purdue Pharma (access at: www.ct.gov/ag/lib/ag/press_releases/2001/health/oxy.pdf) was ignored. Had Mr. Blumenthal's suggestions been heeded my son and many others might be alive today.

Based on my work of the past two years I believe that necessary steps include but are not limited to:

1) Substantial unrestricted grants from pharmaceutical companies and increased federal appropriations for:

- Youth/family prescription drug abuse education

- Increased mandatory physician education regarding selective opioid prescribing and a balanced, multifaceted approach to pain management

- Treatment and Rehabilitation Programs

- Nationwide prescription monitoring programs

2) More assertive and comprehensive implementation by the FDA of its basic responsibility to protect citizens by increasing restrictions such as those requested in Citizen Petition 2005P-0076.

I come before this committee today because my son is dead; I will forever mourn. I also come before this committee today because my son stands at my right shoulder and tells me each day, "Mother, It is better to light one candle than to curse the darkness". I will light as many candles as necessary and hope that you will too.

Thank you.

Mr SOUDER. Next is Ms. Falco.

STATEMENT OF MATHEA FALCO

Ms. FALCO. Thank you, Mr. Chairman, and thank you all for your leadership on this very, very important issue. The testimony that we just heard I think overwhelmingly makes the case that action is needed.

I am the president of Drug Strategies, a nonprofit research institute, and we have put together in the last year and a half a collaboration, including the Weill Medical Center in New York City, the Treatment Research Institute at the University of Pennsylvania, and Harvard Law School to develop a private/public partnership to try to look at ways in which we can curtail the sale over the Internet of these highly addictive, lethal narcotic drugs, without prescription. If you type in the term "OxyContin without prescription" in any search engine, you will immediately get hundred of ads willing to sell you—without even pretending to go through a prescription process—these drugs. So we are very concerned about this. We believe in our collaboration that the government has a vital role to play, the Federal agencies do. But we thought perhaps progress could be made immediately, even in small ways, by engaging the key points along the chain of Internet commerce that basically got the drugs off the Internet, through the Internet into the homes of what are essentially adolescents. Nora Volkow testified this morning that this is an epidemic among teens; that, I think, has been proved beyond question.

Our partnership looked at the key targets, really. How are these drugs purchased over the Internet? Well, with credit cards for the most part. So we've been working with MasterCard, Visa, American Express to look at steps they can take, without any formal governmental action, to try to track down who these illicit sellers really are. The Internet service providers are also very concerned that, in effect, they have become a river which connects this illicit traffic which increasingly, I must point out, comes from Web sites hosted overseas. So this is rapidly becoming an international, not just a domestic problem.

The ISPs have been extremely responsive in trying to think of technological ways in which they can help filter out some of this solicitation. We are also working with, as I said, government agencies; with the State Department. I talked to the Department of Justice about things that might be done, but I think that the profound point here is that this is such a huge problem, we're at the beginning of what everyone agrees is an epidemic, we need to look for as many targets as we can. And I think everyone today has very specific suggestions about what might be done. Clearly education and prevention, the Partnership For a Drug-Free America, all of these things are very important.

We convened a conference 2 weeks ago at Harvard Law School of this collaboration, and very high-level representatives of many of these companies were in the process of refining recommendations. We hope very much at the end of the year to come up with some very specific recommendations which the private companies have already bought into, so to speak, so that we can come forward with a combined voice, because we do believe very much in the business response to these things.

And we would like very much to continue to work closely with your staff. The staff has been extremely helpful along the way. And we think that even down the road we might need to come back and ask for specific legislation; we aren't quite there yet. And we've called our initiative, Keep Internet Neighborhoods Safe. And with the same notion that we try to protect our children from the terrible dangers of society today, even getting run over by cars when they're little children, we need to try to make the Internet safe for our children. And that's essentially what this private/public collaboration is doing.

I thank you very much, and I hope we'll come back to you very soon.

Mr. SOUDER. Thank you very much for your actions and your testimony.

[The prepared statement of Ms. Falco follows:]

⚡ Drug**Strategies**

"Keep Internet Neighborhoods Safe"

Preventing the Illegal Internet Sales of Controlled Substances to Youth

Testimony of Mathea Falco, President, Drug Strategies

House of Representatives Committee on Government Reform

Subcommittee on Criminal Justice, Drug Policy and Human Resources

July 26, 2006

Chairman Souder and members of the Committee, I am pleased to testify before you today about the important initiative we have undertaken to address the growing tragedy of addiction and death from powerful narcotic painkillers bought without prescriptions over the Internet. Drug Strategies, a nonprofit research institute founded in 1993 that promotes more effective approaches to the nation's drug problems, became actively involved a year and a half ago when Dr. Thomas McLellan, President of the Treatment Research Institute (TRI) at the University of Pennsylvania and his colleague Dr. Robert Forman, described to our Board of Directors the extensive research TRI had conducted since 2002 that specifically identified more than 300 unique websites offering to sell prescription narcotics without prescription. TRI verified that these websites actually deliver what they promise and will even replace without cost any shipments that are intercepted. Although key government agencies were aware of this growing problem and have undertaken actions to try to curtail emerging internet drug traffic, the tragic costs in terms of wasted lives and teen deaths continued to mount. Drug Strategies decided that a new, unique collaboration between the private and public sectors could make a critical difference.

Drug Strategies, the Treatment Research Institute at the University of Pennsylvania, the Center for International Criminal Justice at Harvard Law School and the Weill Medical Center at Cornell University formed a core leadership group in January 2005. Since then, we have brought together leaders of companies that play key roles in internet commerce. These include Internet Service Providers (ISPs), such as Verizon Online; AOL; AT&T, Earthlink; Microsoft, and Comcast; search engines, such as Google and Yahoo; banks, such as UBS and JP Morgan Chase; credit card companies, such as Mastercard, Visa and Paypal; and private carriers, such as UPS, DHL and Fed Ex. We have also included officials of key U.S. government agencies, such as the National Institute of Drug Abuse, the Department of Justice, the Drug Enforcement Administration, Customs and Border Protection, the Department of State, and the U.S. member of the United Nations International Narcotics Control Board. Senior staff members from

key Senate and House Committees have also participated. In addition, our collaboration is informed by academic, legal, and technology experts as well as leaders in public education through the media, such as the Partnership for a Drug Free America. The goal of this collective effort is to develop new strategies to curtail Internet drug trafficking to youth, taking into consideration such issues as Internet regulation, online advertising, payment transfers, delivery services, U.S. and international law as well as prevention initiatives.

The "Keep Internet Neighborhoods Safe" collaboration has involved more than fifty participants and has held six plenary meetings at Harvard Law School and several specialized meetings with government officials and private company executives in Washington, D.C. since early 2005. On July 6-7, 2006, we convened a major conference to discuss potential strategies to curtail illegal Internet sales of controlled substances to youth by targeting key points of control. (The list of conference participants is attached.) We are continuing to refine our recommendations, which will be announced before the end of this year.

Why We Are Concerned

1. Sales of <u>Psychoactive Prescription Drugs over the Internet is Becoming a Major Enterprise, Presenting New Challenges to Drug Abuse Prevention and Treatment.</u>

Adolescent use of highly addictive prescription opioid drugs, such as Vicodin and Oxycontin; sedatives, such as Ambien; and tranquilizers, such as Valium and Xanax, without prescription is increasing, according to annual national surveys. Despite the encouraging news that past month illicit drug use overall has declined 19% among youth ages 12 to 17 since 2001, there has been a significant increase in adolescent non-medical use of addictive prescription drugs. These drugs are widely advertised and sold over the Internet without prescription and ready availability through "non-prescription websites (NPWs)" may be one important contributing factor to increasing adolescent use of these drugs.

The global reach of the Internet now makes it as easy for an adolescent to buy drugs as it is to buy a book or CD with a credit card, PayPal, or even cash. Some sites provide drugs initially free without immediate payment. Unlike many scams on the Internet, there is ample evidence that these drugs of abuse are real, potent, and actually delivered to buyers. Of particular concern is the role that NPWs might play in initiating opioid and other non-medical drug use among adolescents, the age group that

- 2 -

most frequently uses the Internet. For example, a sixth grader researching a school paper might enter the term "Vicodin" in a major search engine, like Google or Yahoo, and see a majority of the retrieved websites aggressively advertising to sell these drugs without prescription (Forman 2003, Forman in press).

2. Prevalence of Adolescent Substance Abuse in the United States.

Two major federally funded annual surveys provide information on adolescent drug, alcohol and tobacco use nationwide. *Monitoring the Future* (MTF), begun in 1975, interviews approximately 50,000 8th, 10th, and 12th grade students (Johnston et al 2005). The *National Survey on Drug Use and Health (NSDUH)*, begun in 1971, interviews approximately 70,000 randomly selected individuals aged 12 and older in order to provide national and state-level estimates of past month, past year, and lifetime drug, alcohol and tobacco use (Substance Abuse and Mental Health Services Administration 2005). The *NSDUH* collects data by age group (12-17; 18-25; 26 and older) rather than by grade level.

Both national surveys confirm that non-medical drug use is pervasive among American adolescents. According to MTF, 50 percent of 12th graders, 38 percent of 10th graders and 21 percent of 8th graders reported in 2005 that they had used an illicit drug at least once in their lifetime (Johnston et al 2005). The *NSDUH* reported that 11 percent of youths ages 12-17 (over 2.6 million adolescents) said they had used an illicit drug in the month prior to the survey, and 1.3 million youth ages 12-17 said they had abused or were dependent on an illicit drug at some point during the previous year (SAMHSA 2005). In 2004, a majority (58 percent) of the approximately 2.8 million persons who reported using an illicit drug for the first time within the year prior to the survey were younger than age 18 when they first used (SAMHSA 2005).

The *MTF* survey reported that there was almost a 19 percent decline in past month use of any illicit drug by 8th, 10th, and 12th graders between 2001 and 2005. This trend is driven largely by decreasing rates of marijuana use among these students: since 2001, past month marijuana use has fallen by 28 percent among 8th graders and by 23 percent among 10th graders (Johnston et al 2005). The *NSDUH* reported that between 2002 and 2004, past month marijuana use by males ages 12 to 17 declined (9.1 percent in 2002, 8.6 percent in 2003, and 8.1 percent in 2004), but remained level for female youths (7.2, 7.2, and 7.1 percent, respectively) during the same time period. The *NSDUH* survey also found that current rates of illicit drug use among teens in 2004 varied significantly by major racial/ethnic groups. Native American or Alaska Native youths reported the highest rates (26 percent), compared to 12 percent for youths identified with two or more races. White youths reported 11 percent; Hispanic youths, 10 percent; African-American youths, 9 percent, and Asian youths, 6 percent.

In 2004, approximately 2 million people reported using marijuana for the first time within the past year (SAMHSA 2005). The *NSDUH* also found a significant decline in the number of recent marijuana initiates between 2002 and 2003 (about ten percent). Of the 2 million recent marijuana initiates, almost two-thirds (64 percent) were younger than age 18 when they first used.

The *NSDUH* reported that about one million people used cocaine for the first time within the past 12 months. About one-third of these recent cocaine initiates were under 18 when they first used. The survey shows growing use of psychoactive drugs: an estimated 2.8 million people reported using these drugs for the first time in the year prior to the survey. In 2004, 2.4 million people reported using prescription pain relievers without prescription; 1.2 million used tranquilizers; 793,000 used stimulants, and 240,000 used sedatives. The number of new non-medical users of Oxycontin was 615,000, with an average age at first use of 24.5 years.

3. Increasing Non-prescription Use of Addictive Pharmaceutical Drugs by Adolescents.

Non-prescription use of opioids, sedatives and tranquilizers by adolescents is increasing. Of particular concern is the rapid rate of initiation of Oxycontin and Vicodin use among adolescents (Johnston et al 2005). Physicians generally prescribe these opiates to relieve severe pain, but they now are becoming widely used for non-medical purposes by young people. The 2005 *MTF* survey reported that 5.5 percent of 12th graders, 3.2 percent of 10th graders, and 1.8 percent of 8th graders said they used Oxycontin at least once in the past year—a 29 percent increase since 2002. It is important to note that questions regarding Oxycontin and Vicodin use were not added to *MTF* until 2002 so that earlier information on the prevalence of adolescent non-medical use of these drugs is not available. Even higher rates of annual use were reported in 2005 for Vicodin: 9.5 percent of 12th graders, 5.9 percent of 10th graders, and 2.6 percent of 8th graders said they used Vicodin without prescription in the previous year. (In 2005, 68.6 percent of 12th graders reported alcohol use and 33.6 percent reported marijuana use.) Vicodin is now the third most widely reported drug used by 12th graders. Heroin, on the other hand, has an annual prevalence rate of less than 1 percent among 12th, 10th, and 8th graders (Johnston et al 2005).

The *NSDUH* reported that in 2004, 14 percent of youths ages 12-17 said they had tried psychotherapeutics for non-medical use at least once in their lifetime, including 1.2 percent using Oxycontin, 3.2 percent using tranquilizers, 6.9 percent using Vicodin, Lortab or Lorcet, 2.5 percent using hydrocodone, and 2.8 percent using codeine (SAMHSA 2005). According to *MTF*, students also reported significant rates of non-prescription use of sedatives and tranquilizers. The annual *MTF* survey asks only 12th graders about barbiturate use: in 2005, 7.2% of 12th graders reported using non-prescribed barbiturates in the previous year, more than double the rate reported in 1992 (2.8 percent). Similar increases in non-prescribed use of tranquilizers were reported by 12th graders (6.8 percent in 2005 vs 2.8 percent in 1992) (Johnston et al 2005).

Nearly one in five teens (19 percent) report non-medical use of prescription medications, according to a recent survey by the Partnership for a Drug-Free America (PDFA 2006). As for prescription painkillers, around 18 percent of teenagers reported using Vicodin, and one in ten reported using Oxycontin. More than one third of teenagers (37 percent) said they have close friends who have used prescription painkillers such as Vicodin, Oxycontin and Tylox, without prescription. One in 10 teenagers, or 2.3 million young people, have tried prescription stimulants, such as Ritalin or Adderall without a prescription (PDFA 2006).

A 2003 study conducted via a web-based survey examined non-medical use of prescription drugs in a sample of 1,017 public school students ages 10-18 in the Detroit metropolitan area (Boyd et al 2006). The study found that 22 percent of girls and 10 percent of boys reported non-medical use of a pain medication at least once in their lifetime, while 15 percent of girls and 7 percent of boys reported such use within the year prior to the survey. The students reported that the single largest source for drugs was family members, followed by friends and dealers. The study did not include any youths who had obtained prescription drugs on the Internet. Furthermore, a 2006 study investigating non-medical use of prescription medications among undergraduate students found that college men are more likely than women to obtain prescription opioid medications for non-medical use from peer sources, while women are more likely to get them from family members (McCabe, Teter and Boyd 2006).

The *NSDUH* is the most recent source of information on the demographic characteristics of adolescents in drug treatment nationwide. The survey reports that in 2004, 276,000 youth ages 12-17 received treatment for non-medical use of an illicit drug during the previous year (SAMHSA 2005). Non-medical use of prescription drugs is the reason why many youth are in treatment: 15% of youths who received treatment reported use of pain relievers, 7% reported use of tranquilizers, and 3% reported use of sedatives.

4. Perceptions of Non-Medical Prescription Drug Use among Adolescents.

According to a 2005 survey by the Partnership for a Drug Free America, two in five teens, or around 9.4 million, said they believe that getting high from prescription medications is "much safer" than street drugs (PDFA 2005). Thirty one percent of adolescents, or 7.3 million, believe there's "nothing wrong" with using prescription drugs without a prescription "once in a while". Nearly three out of 10, or 6.8 million, believe that prescription painkillers, even if taken without a prescription, are not addictive. The majority of teens (13.4 million) agreed that prescription drugs are easier to get than illegal street drugs, and that prescription painkillers are "available everywhere".

5. Ease of Finding Internet Drug Pharmacies.

With more than 200 million Internet users in the United States, the web is a vital medium for communication, entertainment, and commerce (Clickz Network Statistics 2006). The Pew Internet &

American Life Project reported that 87% of 12-17 year olds, and 82 percent of 18-24 year old go online at least monthly. Similarly, 43 percent of teens and two-thirds of adult internet users go online to make purchases, and a large number of adults (79 percent) use the internet to look for health and medical information (Fox and Madden 2005, Lenart 2004). The digital divide between African-Americans, Hispanics and whites appears to be closing. A 2006 Pew national survey reports that 74 percent of whites, 61 percent of African-Americans and 80 percent of English-speaking Hispanic-Americans go on-line (Marriott 2006). In 1998, a Pew survey found that 42 percent of whites and 23 percent of African-Americans used the Internet.

About half of all adult Americans take a prescription medication regularly, and one in four have used the Internet to learn about prescription medications. The majority of Americans have greater confidence in their local pharmacy than Internet-based pharmacies, and only about 4 percent report having purchased medications online (Fox 2004). A wide range of controlled substances is offered for sale online including stimulants, steroids, sedatives, hallucinogens and marijuana (SAMHSA 2003). In addition to the many legitimate online pharmacies that operate in accordance with state and federal laws, hundreds of websites have appeared offering to sell controlled substances such as Vicodin and Oxycontin without prescription. No prescription websites (NPWs) are online pharmacies that supply consumers with controlled substances without a valid prescription. There are two general categories of NPWs: *Retail* NPWs directly offer to sell opioid medications without prescription while *Portal* NPWs provide multiple links to Retail NPWs. The majority of the NPWs identified in monitoring studies conducted since 2003 were classified as Portals (Gordon et al 2006).

While legitimate online pharmacies require a valid prescription from the consumer's physician, there are hundreds of NPWs that sell prescription medications based solely on an online questionnaire, a telephone interview, or a simple online order without any interaction with a physician or other licensed healthcare professional. To assess the relative availability of NPWs versus websites that offered addiction health information (e.g. WebMD), during the first two weeks of August 2004, Gordon et al (2006) conducted 27 Google searches using a wide variety of opioid search terms. Two search terms - *no prescription Vicodin*, and *no prescription hydrocodone* –yielded 80-90 percent NPWs and no links to addiction health information websites. On the other hand, searches for several opioid medications, including Fentanyl, Duragesic, buprenorphine, and Subutex – with and without the no prescription prefix – yielded a majority of addiction health information websites and few or no NPWs.

Beyond qualitative examinations of typical NPWs, there has been no systematic study of the content of current Retail NPWs. Forman and Block (Manuscript) looked at fifty NPWs by examining links within the top three portal NPWs identified during a search in June 2005. During the coding process, any website found to be a legitimate retailer that only sold medications to customers with a doctor's prescription was eliminated from consideration and replaced by the next linked website until a total of fifty NPWs was reached. Nearly all (92 percent) of the NPWs contained an implied legitimacy or credibility claim of some kind. Over 80 percent of NPWs contained a medical legitimacy claim. Fewer NPWs displayed a retailer legitimacy claim (24 percent). 88 percent of NPWs accept payment via one of the major credit cards and over half (52 percent) mention delivery through a reputable carrier like FedEx or DHL. These findings suggest that working with credit card and shipping companies may be a viable mechanism for identifying ownership of NPWs and potentially suspending their credit card contracts. Approximately half (52 percent) of NPWs require some kind of online questionnaire to be filled out by the patient; a much smaller percentage offer a telephone consultation, either for free (8percent) or a fee (20 percent).

Research conducted since 2002 by Dr. Robert Forman and his colleagues at the Treatment Research Institute (TRI) (Forman, 2003; Forman et al in press) has identified more than 300 unique websites offering to sell non-prescription opioid drugs. In over 50 Internet monitoring replications in which search terms such as *codeine*, or *Vicodin* were used, more than 50 percent of the links returned for these terms led to websites offering to sell opioid medications without a prescription (Forman et al in press). When the search prefix *"no prescription"* was added to the drug term (e.g. *no prescription Vicodin*), the proportion of NPWs obtained increased to 60-80 percent. During a one week investigation, the National Center on Addiction and Substance Abuse (CASA 2004) identified 495 web sites that offered to sell drugs listed on Schedules II-IV of the Controlled Substances Act requiring a prescription and found that only 10 percent of those websites required prescription verification.

6. Difficulty in Shutting Down These Websites.

Legitimate online pharmacies (e.g., www.drugstore.com, www.caremark.com) provide convenience and efficiency to consumers while complying with state and federal regulations that require a valid prescription from the consumer's physician. The American Medical Association (AMA) and the National Association of Boards of Pharmacy (NABP) have issued policy statements that support the Internet as a medium for processing legitimate prescriptions. However, hundreds of websites now sell prescription medications based solely on an online questionnaire, a telephone interview, or a simple online order without any interaction with a licensed healthcare professional (See Forman et al in press). This has been recognized as a threat to public health (American Medical Association Policy H-120.956 – 3, American Medical Association Policy H-120.949, National Association Boards of Pharmacy 2003).

The benefits of the Internet are available to everyone, including individuals who commit unlawful acts such as software piracy, virus releases, identity theft, espionage, the sale of child pornography, illegal weapons, and controlled substances (White House Executive Order). Online stores can be hosted and registered anywhere in the world, advertising, selling, and delivering products internationally with relative anonymity and convenience – and with little regard for the laws of other countries. The United States Controlled Substances Act (CSA 2006) prohibits the sale of Schedule I drugs such as marijuana, heroin, crack cocaine, and ecstasy and regulates access to Schedule II-V drugs, including opioid analgesics, sedatives, tranquilizers, stimulants and steroids by requiring a valid prescription from an appropriately licensed healthcare professional (U.S. Department of Justice 1970). However, many countries have drug policies that differ from those of the United States, or have similar laws but less enforcement.

The fluidity and virtual reality of cyberspace are ideally suited to illicit drug transactions, creating a complex challenge for law enforcement, policy makers and the general public (White House Executive Order 1999, U.S. General Accounting Office 2004). Businesses wishing to circumvent the U.S. Controlled Substances Act may do so by establishing multiple websites, in multiple countries, under multiple online identities (Forman and Block Manuscript). Many of the websites selling drugs are hosted outside the United States, and drug suppliers guarantee to (and actually do) replace any drugs intercepted by U.S. Customs or other law enforcement agencies. Recent studies indicate that Russia, Ukraine, and the South Asian countries are emerging as key locations for drug sales websites. For example, a "no prescription website" can be physically located on a computer in Uzbekistan; registered to a business address in Mexico; ship its drugs from Pakistan; deposit payments to a Cayman Island bank - while the owner resides in Miami. Importantly, all links in this online enterprise can be quickly dismantled and resurrected under a new set of virtual identities. The effect of this was seen following the April 2005 report of the DEA's Operation "CyberChase" which resulted in the arrest of 20 individuals in eight U.S. cities and four foreign countries, operating over 100 websites (U.S. Department of Justice 2005a, 2005b). However, this widely publicized DEA operation did not have any measurable impact on the availability of non-prescription controlled substances over the Internet (Forman et al. personal communication based on May through October 2005 searches of NPW sites).

7. Intercepting NPW Deliveries.

Since it is illegal to purchase prescription opioids and other controlled substances without prescription, there are limited data on the actual delivery rate of NPWs. It is easy to think that, like so many other Internet "scams," there is no reality to the offers of sale from these websites. However, the U.S. General Accounting Office (GAO) recently conducted an investigation in which they attempted 11 purchases of opioids without prescription (including hydrocodone and oxycodone). Of those 11 attempted purchases, 10 were delivered. The GAO also found that many Internet suppliers promise to replace any drugs intercepted by U.S. law enforcement agencies and they actually do so. (GAO 2004). In June 2005, the Miami DEA announced the arrest of eight operators of illegal drug sales websites. Seized

- 8 -

records showed these websites delivered over 28,000 orders for controlled substances without prescription <u>per week</u>, particularly hydrocodone (Vicodin).

On July 30, 1999, U.S. Deputy Attorney General Ivan Fong testified before the Subcommittee on Oversight and Investigations, Commerce Committee, United States House of Representatives, that "...online pharmacies allow consumers to purchase prescription drugs without any pretense of a prescription" and that these websites introduce "potential risks to public health and safety" (Fong 1999). A week later the White House issued Executive Order 13133 creating the "Working Group on Unlawful Conduct on the Internet" leading to the publication of "*The Electronic Frontier*" (Attorney General's Office 2000). The Drug Enforcement Administration (DEA) subsequently published guidance (Department of Justice 2001) which specified <u>four</u> conditions under which legal prescriptions can be issued over the Internet: a) a patient presents a medical complaint; b) a medical history is obtained; c) a physical examination is performed; and d) some logical connection exists between the medical complaint, the medical history, the physical examination, and the drug prescribed. Prescriptions based on telephone interviews or online questionnaires are not considered valid. In support of these guidelines, the American Medical Association subsequently issued guidance for physicians on Internet prescribing that largely parallels the DEA's position (American Medical Association Policy (Policy H-120.949).

8. Enforcement.

Since 2001, the sale of controlled substances over the Internet has been cited in U.S. Justice Department reports (National Drug Intelligence Center 2001, 2002; DEA 2002) and has led to criminal investigations for Internet sales of non-prescription drugs such as ecstasy, gamma hydroxyl butyrate (GHB) and methamphetamines, (Drug Enforcement Administration News Release 2002, 2003; National Drug Intelligence Center 2003) and the illicit sale of prescription drugs online (NDAS 2001, National Drug Intelligence Center 2003, U.S. Department of Justice 2002, Hutchinson 2002). Similarly, the U.S. Food and Drug Administration (FDA) has provided testimony (Hubbard 2002), and reports (Henney 2000, FDA 2003, Center for Drug Evaluation and Research 2003) on the risks of online prescription practices. In conjunction with U.S. Customs, the FDA participated in an investigation of illicit prescription drug sales originating overseas (FDA 2003). On March 1, 2004, the White House Office of National Drug Control Policy (ONDCP issued the 2004 National Drug Control Strategy Update (White House 2004) which for the first time described plans to monitor illicit Internet drug offers (p. 28). Concurrent with the issuance of this strategy update, ONDCP issued a press release (ONDCP 2004) entitled "*U.S. Drug Prevention, Treatment, Enforcement Agencies Take on 'Doctor Shoppers,' 'Pill Mills'*" and a fact sheet entitled "*Reducing Prescription Drug Abuse*" (ONDCP 2004) which announce initiatives to stop illicit online prescription drug sales. There are four potential "choke points" for NPW enforcement efforts: a) search engines that list NPWs when searches are conducted; b) credit card companies with which NPWs and their customers have accounts; c) package delivery companies; and d) Iinternet service providers (ISPs) where NPWs files are hosted (Forman and Block Manuscript).

The existing regulation of Internet prescription drug sales is very clear on paper, but quite murky in practice. At its most basic, the purchase of any prescription drug must be done through a properly accredited Internet site, which requires a valid prescription. To oversee this regime, the National Association of Boards of Pharmacy (NABP) has established a certification program to enable the approved sales of prescription medications over the Internet. The program, known as Verified Internet Pharmacy Practice Sites (VIPPS) certification, allows merchants in the United States to sell prescription medications over the Internet. To achieve VIPPS accreditation, a pharmacy site must comply with the licensing and inspection requirements of the state in which it does business, and must demonstrate to the NABP compliance with certain specified criteria, including patient rights to privacy, authentication and security of prescription orders, maintenance of quality assurance and improvement program, and provision of meaningful consultation between patients and pharmacists.

Even with certification, there are limits on what a pharmacy can sell based on Federal regulation. These rules apply equally to physical and virtual pharmacies. Physicians can prescribe and pharmacies can dispense drugs listed in the Controlled Substances Act Schedules II through V, which are defined as drugs with a legitimate medical purpose, but dangerous if not properly controlled. Drugs listed in Schedule I are considered to have no legitimate medical purpose and are illegal to sell under any circumstance, such as heroin. The powerful drugs currently most prone to abuse are Oxycontin (Schedule II) and Vicodin (Schedule III). Schedule II drugs cannot be provided legally over the Internet, while Schedule III drugs can prescribed through a VIPPS Internet pharmacy.

Despite this regulatory regime and the fact that purchasing controlled substances overseas is illegal, traditional enforcement efforts towards illicit purchases have generally been lax. This is because of the overwhelming volume of pharmaceuticals entering the United States and the political controversy around individuals attempting to purchase cheaper prescription drugs for legitimate medical problems overseas. As a result, despite a clear regulatory regime, the actual flow of prescription drugs (legal and illegal) into the United States continues to accelerate.

9. Increasing Awareness of Drug Availability Online.

Beginning in the fall of 2003, the popular press began reporting on the availability of prescription opioids over the Internet without prescription (Forman et al in press). The earliest newspaper report on NPWs was published on October 18, 2003, in the *New York Times* (Harris 2003) in an article describing a joint DEA/FDA taskforce targeting "rogue online pharmacies" that sold prescription drugs without a prescription. Two days later the *Washington Post* released a five-part series detailing the results of a one-year investigation into the availability of prescription drugs without a prescription (Gaul and Flaherty 2003a, b, c, d, e, f). A month after the *Washington Post* series, *USA Today* (Rubin 2003) reported on the "uncontrolled sale of controlled substances" over the Internet and then, in December 2003, news coverage about NPWs became widespread with the *Los Angeles Times, Philadelphia Daily News, Boston Herald, Miami Herald, Denver Post, San Jose Mercury News*, and the *Chicago Tribune* publishing stories about the online availability of controlled substances without a prescription (Anderson 2003, Caywood 2003, DeWolf 2003, Frates 2003, Gaul 2003, Healy 2003, Higgins 2003). Since then, press and broadcast coverage of this phenomenon has accelerated. A recent example is the front-page story in *USA TODAY* on June 13, 2006, "Prescription Drugs Find Place in Teen Culture." The press reports that the term "pharm party" where youth swallow fistfuls of prescription drugs is now widespread.

Next Steps in Developing Comprehensive Strategy

I. More Research Needed Specifically on:

A. Accurate Information on Extent of Controlled Substances Availability without Prescription over the Internet.

In contrast with the many reports in the law enforcement literature and popular press, there are few publications in the public health or medical literature concerning the availability of prescription opioids without prescription over the Internet. In a recent Medline search using combinations of terms including "online," "opioids," "Internet," and "narcotics" only one publication addressing the availability of prescription opioids over the Internet was found: the principal investigator's preliminary research report (Forman 2003). This, and other searches conducted using Medline and PsychINFO, identified general articles about topics such as online pharmacy prescribing practices, the Internet as a source of drug information, and the online sale of sexual performance enhancement drugs, but no articles were found about websites selling prescription opioids without a prescription.

The European Union has funded the Psychonaut 2002 Project, which is searching the Internet for drug-related websites using a controlled search methodology (www.psychonaut2002.org). Its primary aim is to collect and analyze the information available on these websites, and to develop an Early Warning System for professionals providing information and suggestions concerning emerging drug markets, new drugs and new trends in drug use. This is a multi-site research project involving 15 centers from nine European countries and to date has analyzed more than 4,000 sites in 8 languages. Investigators in this project have published articles about the availability of controlled substances on the Internet (Schifano et al 2003).

114

B. Data on Internet Role in Supplying Prescription Drug Abusers.

There is an overall lack of information about who is using the Internet to obtain psychoactive prescription drugs without a prescription. The original impetus for TRI's research on NPW websites came from reports in AA meetings and to clinicians that advertisements for drugs on the Internet were becoming an important cause of relapse. To explore this carefully, a study was undertaken in 2004 in a collaborating private adult residential treatment program outside Philadelphia (Gordon, Forman and Siatkowski 2006). One hundred consecutive adult patients were interviewed concerning how they had obtained the drugs they had used 30 days prior to entering treatment. Nine percent reported having purchased their drugs online and an additional 2 percent stated they had found their dealer online. In addition, 29 percent indicated that they knew they could purchase drugs over the Internet without prescription and 11percent reported they had used the Internet either to buy drugs or locate a drug dealer. Among the respondents who knew the Internet was a drug source, reasons given for not using it were: it was too expensive; the desired drug could not be obtained (e.g. cocaine); and fear of being identified by authorities or other family members using the same computer. The results of this preliminary study suggest that the Iinternet has become a source of controlled substances for some addicted individuals (Gordon et al 2006).

Although we have anecdotal evidence of the Internet's role in distributing drugs, we still do not have solid information about the amounts of controlled substances that are being purchased without a prescription over the Internet, both by adults and adolescents. There has not yet been research based on actual interviews with non-medical users of controlled substances. Neither of the two annual drug use surveys, *MTF* and *NSDUH*, contain questions asking non-prescription drug users where they obtain their drugs (e.g., friends, internet, doctors, dealers, family medicine cabinets), although they could do so in the future.

Relatively little is known about how demographic and socioeconomic factors as well as race, gender and ethnicity relate to adolescent non-medical prescription drug use. Some research indicates that female adolescents have significantly greater severity of substance use (Stevens et al 2003, Warner and Leukefeld 2001), in particular non-medical use of prescription drugs. (SAMHSA 2005). In terms of location, it has been observed that drug use patterns among adolescents from rural areas may be different from those of non-rural youth (Gordon and Caltabiano 1996, Warner and Leukefeld 2001, Ruiz et al 2005). However, some publications show rural youth exceed urban youth in their drug use and some find the contrary (Ruiz et al 2005). The role of the Internet as a source of drugs for these groups has not been explored. For example, could the Internet be a more important source for rural youth than for urban youth who have more immediate access to dealers? Or, would female adolescents (who already show greater non-medical use of prescription drugs) be more likely than males to use the internet to purchase

- 12 -

these drugs, since the Internet does not involve direct contact with dealers and purchases can be made in privacy rather than on the street?

C. New Treatment and Prevention Strategies.

Most adults do not realize that many adolescents and even younger children may find it easier to buy drugs online than on street corners. Even at very young ages, they can navigate easily among websites, which offer information, entertainment, consumer goods and now drugs. Websites aggressively advertise controlled substances, so that a seventh-grader researching a paper for health class might enter the term "Vicodin" in any major search engine and see sites that sell these narcotics, without a prescription, on a majority of the listings provided. Even websites that claim they require prescriptions often allow users to generate a "prescription" by simply checking off a series of quick questions; no direct interaction with a physician is required.

Although media coverage of the misuse of pharmaceutical drugs by adolescents is increasing, many parents and youth do not believe that these drugs are a threat. A recent national survey by the Partnership for a Drug Free America (2005) reported that almost half of teens said they believe that prescription drugs, even if not prescribed by a doctor, are much safer than street drugs and almost a third said that prescription pain killers, even if not prescribed, are not addictive. The survey also reported that adults and youth do not view controlled substances such as Vicodin as equally "dangerous" as narcotics that can be bought from street dealers or classmates, especially since these drugs are widely prescribed by doctors for legitimate medical purposes. The ease with which these drugs are obtained over the Internet, their packaging, and their appearance of legitimacy can contribute to the belief that such drugs are relatively safe when in fact these drugs can be lethal when taken in high doses or in combination with alcohol. The risk for overdose and dependence derives from the dosage, potency of the drug and the vulnerability of the person using it – not the source of the drug or its brand name.

There are some indications from treatment centers that Internet drug availability may play a role both in developing drug dependence and in relapse. For both adolescents and adults who purchase drugs over the Internet, the computer seemingly can become a relapse trigger, which may need to be avoided until a stable recovery has been secured. More research is needed regarding the effect that Internet access and the ubiquity of computers have on relapse, both in terms of the client being confronted with unsolicited offers for prescription drugs via email, and the role of NPW's in facilitating access that can lead to relapse.

The powerful addictive properties of some of these drugs further complicate treatment and prevention. Given the rapid path to addiction and the fact that many adolescents are using opioids such as Vicodin and Oxycontin as their first or second drug of abuse, there is less time for intervention. Given the ubiquity of computers with Internet access, treatment for adolescents purchasing drugs over the internet may require more comprehensive and long-term intervention than treatment for traditional gateway drugs. Even more pressing is the substantial risk for overdose and death resulting from the use of prescription opioids and sedatives obtained over the Internet.

Treatment, intervention and prevention efforts face new challenges related to the emergence of the Internet as a drug source. Current drug education and prevention programs, designed largely for classroom use, may have little impact on the emerging phenomenon of Internet drug sales to youth, since parents, teachers, and the students themselves do not view drugs obtained over the Internet as equally "dangerous" as those bought from street pushers or even classmates. The skills taught in most school drug education curricula may not prove relevant in the very new technological context of the isolated world of the Internet, where children can buy drugs without physical contact with sellers or peers. A 14-year old can now access over the Internet a tremendous amount of information about dangerous drugs, including how to purchase them without a prescription. New prevention strategies will be required to deal with this new reality, including ways to use Internet technology to teach prevention.

D. Public and Private Enforcement Strategies.

As is the case with any drug epidemic, if we wait too long, the problem will become far more difficult to control. Based on our extensive research, particularly our contacts with treatment professionals in the field, we are convinced that now is the time to develop a comprehensive approach to combating the illicit sale and shipment of these drugs to youth. We do not believe this is solely a Government responsibility. The private sector has a powerful role to play and our early experience in our public private partnership confirms that the private sector will play an important role.

We believe that all parties involved in Internet commerce, from advertising, to ISPs, to the financial institutions that make electronic payments possible, to the common carriers that ship merchandise, need to embrace the problem of internet sales of controlled substances without prescription as a top priority. Each sector has a different interaction with the eco-system that drives this commerce. Each sector will have different strategies to employ.

We look forward to providing Congress with an update on our progress toward concrete solutions toward the end of this year. Below is a brief list of the efforts now underway. These go far beyond theoretical approaches. Each of these areas incorporates the research we have to develop actionable strategies to keep our children safer in the global community and in their global neighborhoods, which the Internet has become.

II. Future Policy Initiatives Currently Under Consideration by the "Keep Internet Neighborhoods Safe" Collaboration.

117

A. Prohibit websites from offering to sell controlled substances without legitimate prescriptions from wherever in the world they originate and develop real-time information about violators.

B. Empower Families to Limit Home Access To Websites Illegally Selling Controlled Substances.

C. Prevent Misuse of Financial Institutions.

D. Strengthen Law Enforcement and International Cooperation.

E. Enhance Border Interdiction.

F. Launch nationwide education and prevention campaigns.

This project was made possible by support from the Miriam and Peter Haas Fund, the Bonderman Family Foundation, the Center for International Criminal Justice at Harvard Law School and the Brody Family Foundation. The background research was supported by the National Institute on Drug Abuse.

"Keep Internet Neighborhoods Safe" is a collaborative effort of Drug Strategies, the Center for International Criminal Justice and the Berkman Center for Internet and Society at Harvard Law School, Weill Medical Center of Cornell University and the Treatment Research Institute at the University of Pennsylvania. For additional information, please contact Mathea Falco, President, Drug Strategies at 202-289-9070 or dspolicy@aol.com.

118

Bibliography

American Medical Association Policy (Policy H-120.956 - 3).

American Medical Association Policy (Policy H-120.949).

Anderson, Curt. (2003). "Web Sites Charged In Internet Drug Case: Feds Say Diet Pill, Viagra Sales Illegal," *San Jose Mercury*, December 4: 2C.

Attorney General's Office, U.S. Justice Department, The Electronic Frontier: The Challenge Of Unlawful Conduct Involving The Use Of The Internet A Report Of The President's Working Group On Unlawful Conduct On The Internet, Mar 2000.

Boyd, Carol J., McCabe, Sean E., and Christian J. Teter. (2006). "Medical and nonmedical use of prescription pain medication by youth in a Detroit-area public school district." *Drug and Alcohol Dependence* 81: 37-45.

Caywood, Thomas. (2003). "Online Drug Buying Can Turn Into Nasty Habit: Deals Are Illegal, Dangerous." *Boston Herald*, December 14: 4.

Center for Drug Evaluation and Research, Cyber Letters 2003: Contact Us by Email if You Suspect Illegal Online Drug Sales, February 2, 2000.

Clickz Network Statistics. http://www.clickz.com/stats/web_worldwide/ Accessed January 26, 2006.

DeWolf, Rose. (2003). "Conn. A.G.'s OxyContin Hunt Leads To Us." *Philadelphia Daily News* December 4: 15.

Domestic Strategic Intelligence Unit (NDAS) of the Office of Domestic Intelligence. *Drug Trafficking in the United States*, Drug Enforcement Administration, 2001.

Drug Enforcement Administration, State Factsheets 2002, U.S. Department of Justice.

Drug Enforcement Administration News Release, Operation Webslinger, September 19, 2002.

Drug Enforcement Administration News Release, DEA suspends online drug activity, December 20, 2002.

Drug Enforcement Administration News Release, DEA Brings 'Operation X-OUT' to Ohio, May 1, 2003.

Fong, Ivan. *Statement Of Ivan Fong, Deputy Associate Attorney General Department Of Justice, Before The Subcommittee On Oversight And Investigations, Committee On Commerce, United States House Of Representatives Concerning Sale Of Prescription Drugs Over The Internet.* July 30, 1999.

Forman, Robert F. (2003). "Availability of Opioids on the Internet." *Journal of the American Medical Association* 290: 889.

Forman, Robert F. (In Press). "Narcotics on the Net: The Availability of Websites Selling Controlled Substances." *Psychiatric Services.*

Forman, R.F. and L.G. Block. "The marketing of opioid medications without prescription over the internet." (*manuscript*)

Forman, Robert F., Woody, George E., McLellan, Thomas A., and Kevin Lynch. (In Press). "Availability Of Websites Offering To Sell Opioid-Containing Medications Without A Prescription." *American Journal of Psychiatry.*

Fox, Susannah, (2004), "Prescription Drugs Online," Pew Internet & American Life Project, October 10, 2004. [available at www.pewinternet.org].

Fox, Susannah and Mary Madden. (2005). "Generations Online." Pew Internet and American Life Project, December. http://www.pewinternet.org/pdfs/PIP_Generations_Memo.pdf.

Frates, Chris (2003). "AG Targets Importing Of Drugs Through Unlicensed Pharmacies." *The Denver Post*, August 25: B-04.

Gaul, Gilbert M. (2003). "Net Doctor Racks Up Business." *The Miami Herald*, December 28: 9A.

Gaul, Gilbert M. and Mary Pat Flaherty (2003a). "Internet Trafficking in Narcotics Has Surged." *Washington Post*, October 20: A1.

Gaul, Gilbert M. and Mary Pat Flaherty (2003b). " Web Physician Says He Did No Harm; Thousands of Patients Received Painkillers Without Being Examined." *Washington Post*, October 21: A14.

Gaul, Gilbert M. and Mary Pat Flaherty (2003c). "Lax System Allows Criminals to Invade the Supply Chain." *Washington Post*, October 22: A1.

Gaul, Gilbert M. and Mary Pat Flaherty (2003d). "Canada is a Discount Pharmacy for Americans; FDA Doing Little to Stop Cross-Border Trade in Drugs." *Washington Post*, October 23: A17.

Gaul, Gilbert M. and Mary Pat Flaherty (2003e). "Warnings Target Rogue Drug Sites; Drugstore.com Campaign Aimed at Illegal Pharmacies." *Washington Post*, October 24: A7.

Gaul, Gilbert M. and Mary Pat Flaherty (2003f). "Google To Limit Some Drug Ads: Giants Asked To Help Discourage Illicit Online Pharmacies." *Washington Post*, December 1: A1.

Gordon, Susan M., Forman, Robert F. and Siatkowski, Candis. (2006). "Knowledge and Use of the Internet as a Source of Controlled Substances." *Journal of Substance Abuse Treatment* 30(3): 271-4.

Harris, Gardiner (2003). "Two Agencies to Fight Online Narcotics Sales," *New York Times*, October 18.

Healy, Mary (2003). "A Web of Drugs; Online 'Rogue Pharmacies' Offer Quick Access to Prescription Drugs, Many of Them Addictive and Dangerous." *Los Angeles Times*, December 1: F1.

Jane E. Henney, E-Regulation and Public Health, 2000 Leonard Davis Institute of Health Economics, University of Pennsylvania Health Policy Seminar Series, Philadelphia, PA, September 29, 2000.

Higgins, Michael (2003). "Lawmakers Target Rogue e-pharmacies." *Chicago Tribune*, December 6: 1.

Hubbard, William K. Statement of William K. Hubbard Associate Commissioner For Policy, Planning, And Legislation Before The Committee On Government Reform. U.S. House Of Representatives, March 27, 2003 Hutchinson, A. DEA Congressional Testimony before the House Judiciary Subcommittee on Crime, Terrorism, and Homeland Security, October 10, 2002.

Johnston, L. D., O'Malley, P. M., Bachman, J. G., and J.E. Schulenberg. (2005). Monitoring the Future: national results on adolescent drug use: Overview of key findings, 2005. Bethesda, MD: National Institute on Drug Abuse.

Kissinger, Meg. (2004). "Internet becoming lax pharmacist: Addicts easily obtain drugs without prescriptions." *Milwaukee Journal Sentinel Online Edition*, May 3, 2004.

Lenhart, A. (2004). "Teens, Students, Parents and Internet Technology: The Findings of the Pew Internet & American Life Project." Presented at the Lawlor Group Summer Seminar, June 18, 2004 Minneapolis, MN.

Littlejohn, C., Baldacchino, A., Schifano, F., & Deluca, P. (2004). Internet pharmacies and online prescription drug sales: A cross-sectional study. Paper submitted for publication.

Marriott, Michael. (2006). "Digital Divide Closing as Blacks Turn to Internet." *New York Times*, March 31, 2006.

McCabe SE, Teter CJ and C.J. Boyd. (2006). "Medical use, illicit use, and diversion of abusable prescription drugs." *Journal of American College Health* 54(5): 269- 278.

National Association Board Pharmacy. Accessed June 23, 2003, [available at http://www.nabp.net/vipps/intro.asp].

National Center on Addiction and Substance Abuse at Columbia University (CASA). (2004). *"You've got drugs!" Prescription drug pushers on the internet: A CASA white paper.* New York, NY: Author. [On-line]. [available at www.casacolumbia.org/pdshopprov/shop/item.asp?item=61].

National Drug Intelligence Center. *National Threat Assessment 2002.* U.S. Department of Justice, 2001.

121

National Drug Intelligence Center. *Information Bulletin: Drugs, Youth and the Internet.* U.S. Department of Justice, 2002.

National Drug Intelligence Center, Hyphophorous acid in methamphetamine production, reprinted in Drug Enforcement Administration Microgram, VOL. XXXVI, NO. 9, September 2003.

National Drug Intelligence Center. *National Threat Assessment 2003.* U.S. Department of Justice, 2003.

Office of National Drug Control Policy (2004), "Reducing Prescription Drug Abuse," (accessed on March 4, 2004) [available at http://www.whitehousedrugpolicy.gov/news/press04/030104.html].

Office of National Drug Control Policy, U.S. Drug Prevention, Treatment, Enforcement Agencies Take on "Doctor Shoppers," "Pill Mills." Press release March 1, 2004 [accessed on March 4, 2004: http://www.whitehousedrugpolicy.gov/news/press04/030104.html].

Partnership for a Drug-Free America. (2005). "Generation Rx: National Study Reveals New Category of Substance Abuse Emerging." April 21, 2005.

Salman, R. & Schifano, F. (2000). The Internet, children, young people and substance misuse: Co-ordinated approaches are needed to minimise the use of E-commerce to obtain drugs and prevent substance misuse. Public Health Medicine, 2 (3), 96.

Schifano, F., Leoni, M., Martinotti, G., Rawaf, S., and Rovetto, F. (2003). Importance of Cyberspace for the Assessment of the Drug Abuse Market: Preliminary Results from the Psychonaut 2002 Project. CyberPsychology, 6 (4), 405-410.

Schifano, F., Leoni, M., Deluca, P., & Rovetto, F. (2003). Surfing the net whilst wandering around for drugs: The Psychonaut 2002 preliminary results. Paper presented at the European Association for Behaviour Analysis Conference, July 23rd-25th 2003, Parma - Italy.

Schifano, F., P. Deluca, L. Agosti, G. Martinotti and the Psychonaut 2002 research group (2004). Hallucinogenic phenethylamines on the web; the case of 2C-T-7 ("Blue Mystic") Submitted to Journal of CyberPsychology.

Schifano, F., & Deluca, P. (2003). The quest for drugs: New tools, old habit. Paper presented at the 2nd PrevNet Conference of Telematics in Addiction Prevention, October 23rd-25th 2003, Dublin - Ireland.

Schifano, F., Deluca, P., & Baldacchino, A. (2004). Online prescription drugs' availability; the case of dextropropoxyphene. Paper submitted for publication.

Substance Abuse and Mental Health Services Administration. (2005). Results from the 2004 National Survey on Drug Use and Health: National Findings (Office of Applied Studies, NSDUH Series H-28, DHHS Publication No. SMA 05-4062). Rockville, MD.

Substance Abuse and Mental Health Services Administration, Office of Applied Studies (2003), The *DAWN Report: Trends in Drug Related Emergency Visits, 1994-2002.*

U.S. Department of Justice, Drug Enforcement Administration. (1970). Controlled Substances Act.

U.S. Department of Justice, Drug Enforcement Administration, Dispensing and Purchasing Controlled Substances over the Internet, *Federal Register,* April 27, 2001, Volume 66, Number 82. Notices, p. 21181-21184.

U.S. Department of Justice, Press Release: Defendants Sentenced for Selling Prescription Drugs on Norfolk Men's Clinic Web Site, June 18, 2002.

U.S. Department of Justice, Press Release: Internet Doctor Sentenced to Over 4 Years in Prison, May 29, 2002.

U.S. Food and Drug Administration, Buying Medicines and Medical Products Online, [accessed August 4, 2003 at http://www.fda.gov/oc/buyonline/default.htm].

U.S. Food and Drug Administration, Press Release: FDA/U.S. Customs Import Blitz Exams Reveal Hundreds of Potentially Dangerous Imported Drug Shipments, September 29, 2003.

U.S. General Accounting Office. (2004). "Internet Pharmacies: Hydrocodone, An Addictive Narcotic Pain Medication Is Available Without A Prescription Through The Internet," testimony before the Permanent Subcommittee on Investigations, Committee on Governmental Affairs, U.S. Senate, June 17.

Volkow, Nora. (2004). Keynote address to the College on Problems in Drug Dependence Annual Conference, June 12, San Juan, Puerto Rico.

The White House. Executive Order 13133 Working Group on Unlawful Conduct on the Internet, Aug 5, 1999.

The White House, National Drug Control Strategy Update, March 2004.

Zickler, Patrick. (2004). "Early Nicotine Initiation Increases Severity of Addiction, Vulnerability to Some Effects of Cocaine." *NIDA Notes* 19(2), July.

PARTICIPANTS
"KEEP INTERNET NEIGHBORHOODS SAFE" CONFERENCE
HARVARD LAW SCHOOL
JULY 6-7, 2006

David Aufhauser
Managing Director
UBS

Elizabeth Banker
Associate General Counsel
Yahoo! Inc.

Scott Bradner
Technology Security Officer
Harvard University

Brian Burke
Northeast Regional Government Affairs Director
Microsoft

Sean Clarkin
Executive Vice President
Director of Strategy and Program Management
Partnership for a Drug-Free America

Thomas M. Dailey
General Counsel
Verizon Online

Sarah Deutsch
Vice President and Associate General Counsel
Verizon Communications

James Dirksen
Technology Strategy and Customer Relationships
RuleSpace

Rob Dorfman
Director, Strategic Initiatives
Earthlink

Mathea Falco
President
Drug Strategies

Jodi Golinsky
Vice President and U.S. Regulatory Counsel
MasterCard Worldwide

124

Michelle Gress
Counsel
U.S. House of Representatives Subcommittee on Criminal Justice, Drug Policy and Human Resources

Lydia Kay Griggsby
Counsel
Senator Patrick Leahy on the U.S. Senate Judiciary Committee

Julian A. (Tony) Haywood
Counsel
U.S. House of Representatives Reform Committee

Philip Heymann
James Barr Ames Professor of Law
Harvard Law School

Stephen Heymann
Chief of the Computer Crime Unit
U.S. Attorney's Office
Boston, Massachusetts

Ramsey Homsany
Senior Corporate Counsel
Google, Inc.

William Langford
Senior Vice President and Director of Global Anti-Money Laundering
J.P. Morgan Chase & Co.

Mark MacCarthy
Senior Vice President for Public Policy
Visa U.S.A.

John J. Manning
Assistant U.S. Attorney
U.S. Department of Justice

Douglas B. Marlowe
Director of the Division on Law & Ethics Research
Treatment Research Institute
Adjunct Associate Professor of Psychiatry
University of Pennsylvania

Christy McCampbell
Deputy Assistant Secretary for International Narcotics and Law Enforcement Affairs
U.S. Department of State

Michael McEneney
Partner
Sidley Austin

125

A. Thomas McLellan
Executive Director
Treatment Research Institute
Professor of Psychiatry
University of Pennsylvania

Robert Millman, MD
Director
Treatment and Research Service at the New York Presbyterian Hospital
Saul Steinberg Distinguished Professor of Psychiatry and Public Health
Weill Medical Center, Cornell University

John Muller
Vice President and General Counsel
PayPal

Kevin Omiliak
General Manager
G2 Web Services

Morris Panner
CEO
OpenAir, Inc.

Stacey Parker
Senior Director of Regulatory Affairs (Northern Division)
Comcast

Jules Polonetsky
Vice President, Integrity Assurance
America Online

Joseph Rannazzisi
Deputy Chief of Enforcement Operations
U.S. Drug Enforcement Administration

Steve Schorr
Chief, Cargo Control Branch
U.S. Customs and Border Patrol

Alexander Slater
Student Research Assistant
Harvard Law School

Michael Standard
Senior Counsel
AT&T Internet Services

Jack Stein
Deputy Director, Division of Epidemiology, Services and Prevention Research
National Institute on Drug Abuse

Marcia Lee Taylor
Vice President for Government Affairs
Partnership for a Drug-Free America

J. Marc Wheat
Staff Director and Chief Counsel
Subcommittee on Criminal Justice, Drug Policy & Human Resources

Jonathan Zittrain
Professor of Internet Governance and Regulation
Oxford University

Mr. SOUDER. Next, Mr. Stephen Johnson.

STATEMENT OF STEPHEN E. JOHNSON

Mr. JOHNSON. Chairman Souder, Ranking Member Cummings, and members of the committee, I'm Steve Johnson, executive director of commercial planning at Pain Therapeutics, Inc.

Pain Therapeutics is a biopharmaceutical company specializing in the research and development of safer drugs for use in pain management. We commend the subcommittee for holding this hearing, and I'm grateful for this opportunity to discuss what is becoming an enormous health problem.

As the subcommittee knows all too well, prescription drug abuse continues to have a widespread and devastating effect on American families, businesses, and our society as a whole. For abusers, the appeal of a prescription drug typically depends on its dose strength and the ease with which it can be abused. Illustrative is OxyContin, a strong oral opioid drug, typically prescribed to treat moderate to severe pain. That is also reported to be one of the most commonly abused prescription products.

Drug abusers, however, can quickly and simply disable OxyContin's controlled release mechanism, usually by crushing, breaking or chewing a tablet. The extracted active ingredient, oxycodone, is then ingested, snorted or injected, immediately releasing into the body a dose that was intended to be delivered over a 12-hour period.

Despite the tireless efforts of thousands of Federal, State and local officials, the incidents of prescription drug abuse has continued to rise even as the rate at which other categories of illicit drug use have decreased or remained stable.

The criminal and civil liability and theft associated with products such as OxyContin are discouraging some doctors from prescribing the pain treatments their patients need and dissuading some pharmacists from stopping them. This is a tragedy, for pain is already too often undertreated. Clearly, additional methods of combating prescription drug abuse are necessary.

At Pain Therapeutics, we believe pharmaceutical technology is a potential critical tool in the battle against prescription drug abuse. For example, our investigational drug product, Remoxy, is a novel form of oxydodone contained in a highly viscous fluid formulated to resist tampering or accidental misuse. While Remoxy is not intended to be abuse-proof, it is formulated to resist breaking, chewing or crushing. We believe this investigational drug will also reduce the potential for accidental overdose among patients who may innocently crush or chew a tablet.

Moreover, we expect Remoxy's advanced technology to be useful in reformulating other commonly abused opioid drugs, as well as other drugs, rendering them similarly abuse-resistant.

We are taking a very different approach to reducing prescription drug abuse in developing Oxytrex, an investigational drug product that combines oxycodone, an opioid agonist, with an ultra-low dose of opioid antagonist. Research has shown that the addition of an ultra-low dose opioid antagonist blocks activation of the body's excited opioid receptors, while allowing the agonist to block the transmission of pain signals. We are working to demonstrate that

Oxytrex can significantly inhibit pain while simultaneously reducing the risk of physical dependence.

In addition to potential law enforcement benefits, the development of such products represents a new and efficient means of addressing current concerns regarding prescription drug safety without further restricting or discouraging access for patients who need such care.

Pain Therapeutics is not alone in recognizing the potential benefits of formulating prescription drugs to reduce abuse. In recent years, Congress and various governmental entities and private organizations have recognized the need to develop abuse-resistant prescription drugs. Most recently, the Office of National Drug Control Policy recommended continuing to support the efforts of firms that manufacture frequently diverted prescription drugs to reformulate their products so as to reduce diversion and abuse.

Additionally, NIDA Director Dr. Nora Volkow recently co-authored a paper on opioid analgesic abuse, calling for development of less abusable but still potent forms of opioid agents, as well as combinations of medications that can be given to treat pain, but to minimize the chances of addiction.

In 2005, the comprehensive report by the National Center on Addiction and Substance Abuse at Columbia University went even further, asserting the FDA should require pharmaceutical companies manufacturing controlled drugs to formulate or reformulate the drugs where possible to minimize the risk of abuse. "pharmaceutical companies should be required to demonstrate in their application materials for FDA approval of new drugs that they have made every effort to formulate the drug in such a way that avoids or least minimizes the drug's potential for abuse."

Now we must turn these statements into real public health and law enforcement achievements. Currently, there are no Schedule II prescription drugs on the market specifically formulated to resist or reduce abuse. Moreover, no statute, regulation or guidance specifically addresses issues that are critical to determining whether it will continue to be worthwhile to invest in the research and development to bring such products to market.

This subcommittee can play a unique role in ensuring that agencies across the government coordinate their efforts to maximize the benefits of pharmaceutical technology and addressing drug abuse and misuse.

To conclude, we have four recommendations:

No. 1, applications to market prescription drugs that are especially formulated to deter abuse or misuse should be eligible for priority review.

No. 2, FDA should permit labeling that accurately conveys the specific means of abuse or misuse to which a product has been shown to be resistant; and the agency should not require companies to demonstrate resistance to all potential methods of abuse and misuse such as those that are relatively uncommon.

We welcome FDA's recent announcement that it intends to develop this year guidance for industry in this area. We are hopeful that prompt issuance of these documents will eliminate some of the current ambiguity by framing reasonable standards for approval and accurate labeling that clearly differentiates products incorporating such technologies for products providing no abuse.

No. 3, risk management plans for potentially abusable drug products should take into account these innovative safeguards and encourage physicians to prescribe those products that deter abuse and misuse, while also discouraging use of prescription drugs known to be readily abusable.

And No. 4, given the cost to our health care system, we must ensure that both private and governmental payers and Medicare and Medicaid recognize the benefits of these products and favor their use and formularies.

Mr. Chairman, we are especially grateful to you and the other members of the subcommittee for calling attention to this issue today. We look forward to working with Congress and other governmental agencies to continue to develop the innovative approaches to more effectively approach the epidemic of prescription drug abuse. Thank you.

Mr. SOUDER. It would be nice if they took a normal definition of prompt.

[The prepared statement of Mr. Johnson follows:]

Pain Therapeutics, Inc.

STATEMENT OF STEPHEN E. JOHNSON
EXECUTIVE DIRECTOR, COMMERCIAL PLANNING
PAIN THERAPEUTICS, INC.

BEFORE THE SUBCOMMITTEE ON
CRIMINAL JUSTICE, DRUG POLICY AND HUMAN RESOURCES
COMMITTEE ON GOVERNMENT REFORM
UNITED STATES HOUSE OF REPRESENTATIVES

PRESCRIPTION DRUG ABUSE:
WHAT IS BEING DONE TO ADDRESS THIS NEW DRUG EPIDEMIC?

JULY 26, 2006

Mr. Chairman and Members of the Subcommittee, I am Stephen Johnson, Executive Director of Commercial Planning at Pain Therapeutics, Inc. Pain Therapeutics is one of a handful of biopharmaceutical companies in the United States specializing in the research and development of safer drugs for use in pain management, particularly opioid analgesics specially formulated to reduce prescription drug abuse and misuse. We commend the Subcommittee for holding this hearing, and I am grateful for this opportunity to discuss what has become an enormous public health problem. I would like to begin by reviewing the problem of prescription drug abuse, then turn to a brief and non-technical discussion of how novel pharmaceutical technology might address this new drug epidemic. I will then close with four recommendations for your review and consideration.

As this Subcommittee knows all too well, prescription drug abuse continues to have a widespread and devastating effect on American families, businesses, and our society as a whole.

416 Browning Way, South San Francisco, CA 94080
Phone: 650-624-8200 Fax: 650-624-8222

Non-medical use of prescription drugs is the second-most prevalent category of drug abuse, after marijuana.[1] In fact, 56 percent more Americans abuse prescription drugs than abuse cocaine, heroin, hallucinogens, and inhalants – combined.[2] Among teenagers, the problem of prescription drug abuse is even more worrisome. According to recent data published by the Partnership for a Drug-Free America, 19 percent of children ages 12 to 17 report having abused prescription drugs, of which the largest category is pain relievers.[3]

Prescription drug abuse inflicts enormous costs on our society. In 2002 alone, abuse of prescription drugs cost Americans nearly $181 billion.[4] Direct costs related to non-medical use of prescription drugs are considerable – for example, 25 percent of visits to hospital emergency departments are associated with abuse of prescription drugs.[5] Indirect costs result from drug theft, the commission of crimes to support addiction, "doctor shopping," lost productivity and wages, and the administration of law enforcement.

The largest group of prescription drug abusers is comprised of individuals who abuse opioids,[6] a class of drugs widely prescribed to treat pain. Examples of prescription opioid drugs include oxycodone, hydrocodone, morphine, and fentanyl. When both appropriately prescribed by a physician and used properly by a patient, opioid drugs can manage pain, especially severe chronic pain due to cancer, failed back syndrome, or advanced forms of arthritis. When abused, however, opioid drugs can also induce some sort of extreme euphoria. Chronic drug abusers will repeatedly pursue the experience of such euphoria without regard for their well-being or the welfare of others. Interestingly, there currently is no way to predict which patients will end up abusing opioid drugs. Moreover, just this week, researchers at the Centers for Disease Control and Prevention published a study revealing that opioids account for more overdose deaths in the United States than either heroin or cocaine.[7] For these reasons, and many others, I believe the pharmaceutical industry must have a leadership role in preventing the abuse and misuse of opioid drugs.

For abusers, the appeal of a prescription drug typically depends on its dose strength and the ease with which it can be abused. Illustrative is OxyContin®, a strong, oral opioid drug typically prescribed to treat moderate to severe pain. Unfortunately, it is also reported to be one of the most commonly abused, branded, prescription controlled substances in the United States. The active ingredient in OxyContin® is oxycodone, a potent opioid which is a Schedule II controlled substance because it has an abuse liability similar to morphine. OxyContin® contains a very high dose of oxycodone that, when used properly, is intended to be slowly released over 12 hours. Drug abusers, however, can quickly and simply disable OxyContin's® controlled release mechanism – usually by crushing, breaking, or chewing a tablet, or by stirring it in high-proof alcohol for a few minutes. The extracted oxycodone is then ingested, snorted, or injected, immediately releasing into the body a dose of drug that was intended to be slowly delivered over a 12-hour period. The ease of abuse, combined with the potency of the active drug ingredient, allows drug abusers to experience a very powerful and immediate high

According to the Drug Enforcement Administration (DEA), criminal activity related to OxyContin® abuse and diversion is rapidly depleting the resources of law enforcement.[8] In fact, DEA reports record the theft of 1,369,667 dosage units of OxyContin® between January 2000 and June 2003.[9] Moreover, fully 25 percent of the Schedule II investigations conducted by DEA between Fiscal Year (FY) 2001 and FY 2003 involved OxyContin®.[10]

While urgent action is needed to more adequately address this epidemic, it is also critically important that any efforts to prevent prescription drug abuse not unduly restrict appropriate access to effective pain therapies for the patients who need them. In fact, pain already is too often undertreated.[11] Unfortunately, criminal and civil liability and theft associated with OxyContin® are discouraging some doctors from prescribing the pain treatments their patients need, and dissuading some pharmacists from stocking them.

3

133

Under the Controlled Substances Act (CSA), DEA is responsible for maintaining a closed system of distribution for controlled substances by administering stringent requirements applicable to manufacturers, distributors, physicians, and pharmacists.[12]   Such requirements include registration, recordkeeping, reporting, security, scheduling, production quotas, and import/export authorization.   Over the years, these controls have been particularly effective in dramatically reducing diversion at the manufacturer and distributor level, a significant source of diversion when the CSA was passed.   However, traffickers and abusers currently divert Schedule II opiates from the retail level (physicians and pharmacists), where the federal government has less control.   Currently, Federal efforts to address prescription drug abuse principally rely on costly and sustained risk management approaches, including: physician and patient education, surveillance of the distribution and dispensing of controlled substances, marketing restrictions, warning labels, and law enforcement.

Unfortunately, despite the tireless efforts of thousands of Federal, State, and local officials working to implement these practices, as well as the enormous financial resources appropriated to support them, the incidence of prescription drug abuse has continued to rise -- even as the rate at which other categories of illicit drug use have decreased or remained stable.[13]   In fact, the number of Americans abusing prescription drugs rose 94 percent between 1992 and 2003, a period during which the U.S. population increased only 14 percent.[14]   Moreover, during the same period, there was a 212 percent increase in the number of children ages 12 to 17 abusing prescription drugs, and, remarkably, a 542 percent increase in teens initiating abuse of prescription opioids.[15]   Notably, approximately 600,000 Americans became new abusers of OxyContin® in 2004 alone.[16]   Clearly, additional methods of combating prescription drug abuse are necessary.

At Pain Therapeutics, we believe that the battle against prescription drug abuse is a shared responsibility among government, the healthcare community, and the pharmaceutical industry.   The

4

use of novel pharmaceutical technology can help combat the problem of prescription drug abuse. In fact, our scientists are using innovative chemical advances to develop a tamper-resistant capsule that provides long-acting, effective pain relief when used properly, while also resisting degradation under conditions of abuse.

For example, our investigational drug product Remoxy™ is a novel form of long-acting oxycodone. The capsule, which contains oxycodone in a highly viscous fluid, is formulated to be resistant to tampering or accidental misuse. While Remoxy™ is not intended to be abuse-proof – a sophisticated chemical laboratory might still manage to extract its active ingredient – it cannot be readily broken, chewed, or crushed, which are the principal means by which abusers disable the extended release mechanism of OxyContin® and other sustained release opioid drug products. Importantly, although the labeling for Remoxy™ will ultimately be determined in the course of Food and Drug Administration (FDA) review, we believe this investigational drug will also reduce the potential for accidental overdose, which too often occurs when elderly patients and others who find an OxyContin® tablet difficult to swallow ingest its contents after crushing, breaking, or chewing it. Moreover, we expect Remoxy's™ advanced technology to be useful in reformulating other commonly abused opioid drug products to similarly render them abuse-resistant. Remoxy™ is currently in late-stage testing in nearly 40 clinical sites across the United States. We hope to be able to file for approval to market this novel formulation in late-2007.

We are taking a very different approach to reducing prescription drug abuse in developing Oxytrex™, an investigational drug product that combines oxycodone, an opioid agonist, with an ultra-low-dose of an opioid antagonist. Research has shown that the addition of an ultra-low-dose opioid antagonist blocks activation of the body's excitatory opioid receptors, while allowing the agonist to block the transmission of pain signals.[17] We are working to demonstrate that Oxytrex™ can significantly inhibit pain while simultaneously reducing the risk of physical dependence, which is a physiological adaptation to the continued use of a drug that can often lead to both a diminished physiological sensitivity to the drug's effects (tolerance) and adverse physical symptoms upon withdrawal of the drug's use.

We believe that prescription drugs that are specially formulated to reduce the risk of abuse can significantly contribute to current efforts to address the nation's prescription drug abuse epidemic. Importantly, abuse resistant prescription drugs could also diminish the burden on law enforcement. Additionally, the development of such products represents a new and efficient means of addressing Congress' increasing concern regarding prescription drug safety, and could do so without further restricting or discouraging access for patients who need such care. In fact, the availability of such products could enhance appropriate prescribing of opioid drugs by diminishing the stigma associated with commonly abused drugs and reducing the threat of civil and criminal liability that can discourage physicians from prescribing more readily abused prescription controlled drugs.

Pain Therapeutics is not alone in recognizing the potential benefits of formulating prescription drugs to reduce abuse. In fact, several governmental entities and organizations have been urging the development of abuse-resistant prescription drugs. For example, over the past several years, DEA has repeatedly indicated that it is working closely with the FDA "to strongly urge the rapid reformulation of OxyContin by Purdue Pharma, to the extent that is technically possible, in order to reduce the abuse of the product, particularly by injection."[18] Additionally, the FY 2006 House Appropriations Committee report notes that "[p]roviders and patients alike will benefit from the expedited review of safer drugs, as well as the provision of information that accurately differentiates abuse-resistant formulations."[19] Meanwhile, the corresponding House-Senate Conference report advises that "new drug applications and supplements seeking approval for replacement or alternative abuse-resistant formulations of currently available drug products that include an active ingredient that is a listed chemical under the Controlled Substances Act . . . may be considered under the expedited, priority review process at FDA."[20]

.

Further, the 2006 "Synthetic Drug Control Strategy" issued by the Office of National Drug Control Policy lists as its third of 46 recommendations: "Continue to support the efforts of firms that manufacture frequently diverted pharmaceutical products to reformulate their products so as to reduce diversion and abuse."[21] A comprehensive report issued in 2005 by the National Center on Addiction and Substance Abuse at Columbia University goes even further, urging:

> The FDA should require pharmaceutical companies manufacturing controlled drugs to formulate or reformulate the drugs where possible to minimize the risk of abuse. Pharmaceutical companies should be required to demonstrate in their application materials for FDA approval of new drugs that they have made every effort to formulate the drug in such a way that avoids or at least minimizes the drug's potential for abuse.[22]

Earlier this year, National Institute on Drug Abuse Director Dr. Nora Volkow coauthored a paper on opioid analgesic abuse calling for development of "less abusable, but still potent, forms of opioid agents," as well as "combinations of medications that can be given to treat pain but to minimize the chances of addiction."[23]

Now we must turn these statements into real public health and law enforcement achievements. Currently, there are no Schedule II prescription controlled drugs on the market specifically formulated to resist or reduce abuse. No trailblazer exists to guide industry in determining whether and how to pursue development of such products. Moreover no statute, regulation, or administrative guidance specifically addresses issues that are critical to determining whether it will continue to be worthwhile to invest in the research and development to bring such products to market. This Subcommittee can play a unique role in ensuring that agencies across the government coordinate their efforts to maximize the benefits of pharmaceutical technology in addressing drug abuse and misuse.

We recommend the following:

1. Applications to market prescription drugs that are specially formulated to deter abuse or misuse should be eligible for priority review.

2. FDA should permit labeling that accurately conveys the specific means of abuse or misuse to which a product has been shown to be resistant; and the agency should not require companies to demonstrate resistance to all potential methods of abuse and misuse, such as those that are relatively uncommon.

3. Risk management plans for abuse-resistant products should reflect their inherent safeguards. Appropriate risk management plans could encourage physicians to prescribe those products that deter abuse and misuse, while also discouraging use of prescription drugs known to be readily abusable.

4. We must recognize that achieving approval and meaningful labeling for these products will be a pyrrhic victory if patients are not given access to products incorporating abuse- and misuse-resistant technologies. Given the cost of prescription drug abuse and misuse to our healthcare system, we must ensure that both private and governmental payors, such as Medicare Part D plans and the Medicaid program, recognize the benefits of these products, and favor their use in their formularies.

As a first step, we welcome FDA's recent announcement that it intends to develop this year guidance for industry on both "Assessment of Abuse Potential of Drugs"[24] and "Developing Analgesic Products for the Treatment of Pain,"[25] and we are hopeful that the prompt issuance of these documents will eliminate some of the current ambiguity that may be discouraging development of prescription drugs formulated for reduced abuse potential. We hope such guidance will seek to encourage the development of abuse-resistant prescription drugs by instituting

138

reasonable standards for accurate labeling that clearly differentiates products incorporating such technologies from products providing no abuse- or misuse-deterrent benefit.

Mr. Chairman, we are especially grateful to you and the other Members of the Subcommittee for calling attention to this issue today. Pain Therapeutics looks forward to working with Congress, FDA, DEA, and other government agencies to continue to promote the development of innovative approaches to more effectively address the epidemic of prescription drug abuse.

Thank you. I would be pleased to answer any questions.

[1] Substance Abuse and Mental Health Services Administration, Office of Applied Studies, *Results from the 2005 National Survey on Drug Use and Health: National Findings*, DHHS Pub. No. SMA 05-4062, at 232 (Sept. 8, 2005).
[2] *Id.*
[3] The Partnership for a Drug-Free America, *The Partnership Attitude Tracking Study (PATS): Teens in Grades 7 through 12*, at 21 (May 2006).
[4] Office of National Drug Control Policy, *The Economic Costs of Drug Abuse in the United States, 1992-2002*, Pub. No. 207303, at vi (Dec. 2004).
[5] Substance Abuse and Mental Health Services Administration, Office of Applied Studies, Drug Abuse *Warning Network, 2004: National Estimates of Drug-Related Emergency Department Visits*, DHHS Pub. No. (SMA) 06-4143, at 21 (Apr. 2006).
[6] The National Center on Addiction and Substance Abuse, *Under the Counter: The Diversion and Abuse of Controlled Prescription Drugs in the U.S.* 32 (July 2005) *available at* http://www.casacolumbia.org/absolutenm/articlefiles/380-under_the_counter_-_diversion.pdf (last viewed July 23, 2006).
[7] Opiate Painkiller ODS Now Top Those for Cocaine, Heroin, Forbes On-Line (July 24, 2006) *available at* http://www.forbes.com/forbeslife/health/feeds/hscout/2006/07/24/hscout533964.html (last viewed July 24, 2006).
[8] Drug Enforcement Administration, Office of Diversion Control, *Action Plan to Prevent the Diversion and Abuse of OxyContin®*, *available at* http://www.deadiversion.usdoj.gov/drugs_concern/oxycodone/abuse_oxy.htm (last viewed July 23, 2006).
[9] Office of National Drug Control Policy, *Drug Fact Sheet: OxyContin* (last updated June 16, 2006) *available at* http://www.deadiversion.usdoj.gov/drugs_concern/oxycodone/abuse_oxy.htm (last visited July 23, 2006).
[10] *Overview of the President's Fiscal Year 2007 Request for the Dep't of Justice: Hearing Before the Subcomm. on Commerce, Justice and Science of the Senate Comm. On Appropriations*, 109th Cong. (Apr. 5, 2006) (attachment accompanying statement of Karen P. Tandy, Administrator, Drug Enforcement Admin.) *available at* http://www.usdoj.gov/dea/pubs/cngrtest/ct040506_attachp.html (last viewed July 23, 2006).
[11] *See, e.g., OxyContin and Beyond: Examining the Role of FDA and DEA in Regulating Prescription Painkillers: Hearing Before the Subcomm. on Regulatory Affairs of the House Comm. On Government Reform*, 109th Cong. 26-27 (2005) (statement of Robert J. Meyer, Director, Off. of Drug Evaluation II, Center for Drug Evaluation & Research, Food & Drug Admin.).
[12] 21 U.S.C. § 802 (2001).
[13] *See, e.g., OxyContin and Beyond: Examining the Role of FDA and DEA in Regulating Prescription Painkillers: Hearing Before the Subcomm. on Regulatory Affairs of the House Comm. On Government Reform*, 109th Cong. 27 (2005) (statement of Robert J. Meyer, Director, Off. of Drug Evaluation II, Center for Drug Evaluation & Research, Food & Drug Admin.)

[14] The National Center on Addiction and Substance Abuse, *Under the Counter: The Diversion and Abuse of Controlled Prescription Drugs in the U.S.*, at i (July 2005) *available at* http://www.casacolumbia.org/absolutenm/articlefiles/380-under_the_counter_-_diversion.pdf (last viewed July 23, 2006).

[15] *Id.*

[16] Substance Abuse and Mental Health Services Administration, Office of Applied Studies, *Results from the 2005 National Survey on Drug Use and Health: National Findings*, DHHS Pub. No. SMA 05-4062, at 50 (Sept. 8, 2005).

[17] Lynn R. Webster et al., *Oxytrex Minimizes Physical Dependence While Providing Effective Analgesia: A Randomized Controlled Trial in Low Back Pain*, J. Pain (forthcoming 2006); Walter Ling et al., *Abuse of Prescription Opioids, in* Principles of Addiction Medicine (Allan W. Graham et al. eds., 2003).

[18] *See, e.g.*, Drug Enforcement Administration, Office of Diversion Control, *Action Plan to Prevent the Diversion and Abuse of OxyContin®*, *available at* http://www.deadiversion.usdoj.gov/drugs_concern/oxycodone/abuse_oxy.htm (last viewed July 23, 2006); Drug Enforcement Admin., Office of Diversion Control, OxyContin®: Diversion & Abuse, at 9 (Oct. 2003) *available at* http://www.deadiversion.usdoj.gov/drugs_concern/oxycodone/oxy_oct2003.pdf (last viewed July 23, 2006).

[19] H.R. Rep. No. 109-102, at 81 (2005).

[20] H.R. Rep. No. 109-255, at 102 (2005).

[21] Office of National Drug Control Policy, *Synthetic Drug Control Strategy: A Focus on Methamphetamine and Prescription Drug Abuse* 44 (2006) *available at*
http://www.whitehousedrugpolicy.gov/publications/synthetic_drg_control_strat/synth_strat.pdf.

[22] The National Center on Addiction and Substance Abuse, *Under the Counter: The Diversion and Abuse of Controlled Prescription Drugs in the U.S.*, at 101-102 (July 2005) *available at* http://www.casacolumbia.org/absolutenm/articlefiles/380-under_the_counter_-_diversion.pdf (last viewed July 23, 2006).

[23] Wilson M. Compton and Nora D. Volkow, *Major Increases in Opioid Analgesic Abuse in the United States: Concerns and Strategies*, 81 Drug & Alcohol Dependence 103, 106 (2006).

[24] Center for Drug Evaluation & Research, Food & Drug Admin., *Guidance Agenda: Guidances CDER Is Planning to Develop During Calendar Year 2006* (2006) *available at* http://www.fda.gov/cder/guidance/CY06.pdf (last viewed July 23, 2006).

[25] *Id.*

Mr. SOUDER. Dr. Manchikanti.

STATEMENT OF LAXMAIAH MANCHIKANTI, M.D.

Dr. MANCHIKANTI. Mr. Chairman, I would like to thank you, the committee members, and staff for giving us this opportunity to speak.

My name is Laxmaiah Manchikanti. I am a practicing physician from Paducah, KY. I am also the president and CEO of the American Society of Interventional Pain Physicians. The issues are very close to me as a physician and as the CEO of a group representing approximately 3,700 members. I have published multiple articles on this subject as part of the education and certification programs and controlled substance management published guidelines that were instrumental in the design and passage of the National All Schedules Prescription and Electronic Reporting Act [NASPER].

Our members are involved in prescribing controlled substances. However, our primary modality of treatment is intervention techniques. I have provided the committee with information. During the next few minutes I would like to discuss specific issues related to chronic pain and prescription drugs.

Today, chronic pain is estimated in approximately 10 to 30 percent of the population in the United States. As we heard from the earlier witnesses, psychotherapeutic drugs, which include pain deliveries, tranquilizers, stimulants, and sedatives are the second leading category of illicit drug use. Between 1992 to—sorry—2003 the U.S. population increased 14 percent, but the number of people abusing prescription controlled substances increased 94 percent. Mr. Chairman, as you have stated in your opening statement, the increase of prescription controlled substances was double the increase of marijuana, five times that of cocaine and 60 times the increase of heroin.

In recent years there have been sharp increases in the therapeutic use of controlled substances coupled with misuse and abuse. Today, 90 percent of the patients presenting in pain management centers are on opioids; opioid prescriptions sales are increasing rapidly.

Drug abuse in chronic pain management is common. Today, with all the available tools, with prescription monitoring programs, random drug testing and vehicle license, it has been reported that 9 to 20 percent of the patients still abuse their drugs. In addition, illicit drug use is common in as many as 32 percent of the patients.

Drug diversion is an epidemic in the United States. The majority of physicians perceive doctor shopping as the major mechanism of diversion. Patients and physicians alike are facing a multitude of problems. Physicians feel that patients deceive and manipulate the doctors and authorities around their tale. We have patients that feel undertreated for their pain and it is their fundamental right to be pain free by whatever means.

Many programs are in place to deal with this. The Drug Enforcement Agency is in the forefront of it. NASPER was signed in to law on August 11, 2005, but it is moving extremely slow with no funding coming yet.

At the present time, there are approximately 32 or 33 State programs under DEA that had programs. Many of these programs are reactive rather than proactive, and they are limited to a single State. With this—to combat this epidemic and improve patient care, we must include mandated care and continuing education care for physicians, pharmacists and the public.

The public must be educated on non-opioid techniques of pain management and the effects of opioid treatments. In addition, the program is ideal and necessary. Enactment of NASPER in all States is the major solution for the existing problems. This will benefit physicians, patients and the DEA with honest patients receiving a proper treatment and physicians providing proper treatment without hassles.

Other strategies may include increased strategy of methadone treatment, increased eligibility of outpatient detoxification and rehabilitation—improvement of rehabilitation, and finally, elimination of Internet pharmacies.

Thank you.

Mr. SOUDER. Thank you.

[The prepared statement of Dr. Manchikanti follows:]

PRESCRIPTION DRUG ABUSE:
WHAT IS BEING DONE TO ADDRESS
THIS DRUG EPIDEMIC?

STATEMENT OF:
LAXMAIAH MANCHIKANTI, MD

CHIEF EXECUTIVE OFFICER
AMERICAN SOCIETY OF INTERVENTIONAL PAIN PHYSICIANS

2831 LONE OAK ROAD • PADUCAH, KY 42003
PHONE: 270-554-8373 EXT. 107 • FAX: 270-554-8987 • E-MAIL: DRM@APEX.NET

BEFORE:
SUBCOMMITTEE ON CRIMINAL JUSTICE,
DRUG POLICY, AND HUMAN RESOURCES

JULY 26, 2006

143

The American Society of Interventional Pain Physicians is an organization representing interventional pain physicians and other health care professionals involved in interventional pain management. Our membership is 3,700 at the present time. It is estimated that there are 6,500 interventional pain physicians across the country practicing interventional pain management. Interventional pain management, as per NUCC, is defined as – "the discipline of medicine devoted to the diagnosis and treatment of pain related disorders principally with the application of interventional techniques in managing subacute, chronic, persistent, and intractable pain, independently or in conjunction with other modalities of treatment." As interventional pain physicians, our members are involved extensively in prescribing controlled substances, even though not to the same extent as non-interventional pain physicians whose mainstay of treatment of chronic pain is controlled substances.

The misuse and abuse of controlled substances, especially those containing opiates, among the general public and in patients suffering with chronic pain is a problem attracting nationwide attention. This fact is reinforced by multiple committees with jurisdiction over the epidemic, numerous hearings conducted by various committees, and the focus of numerous agencies. As an interventional pain physician, I am always humbled to note the course of two pioneers with diametrically opposing views that conveyed the same message: "We physicians know little and sometimes can do less."

> Voltaire said,
> "Doctors are men who give drugs of which they know little, into bodies of which they know less, for diseases of which they know nothing at all."
>
> Albert Schweitzer said,
> "Pain is a more terrible lord of mankind, than even death itself"

Both views remain true even today, despite numerous scientific advances in medicine. America and the world have entered into an era where we have to look at a different problem – prescription drug abuse, the byproduct of compassion coupled with a lack of understanding of the complex puzzle of pain and its management. Our nation is facing an epidemic of prescription drug abuse and addiction. Abuse of prescription drugs has been steadily, but sharply, rising.

1. Chronic pain is an epidemic in the United States

- Chronic pain is pain that persists beyond the usual course of an acute disease or a reasonable time for an injury to heal that is associated with chronic pathological processes that cause continuous pain or pain at intervals for months or years (1, 2); or
  - Persistent pain that is not amenable to routine pain control methods; or
  - Pain where healing may never occur.
- The prevalence of chronic pain in the adult population ranges from 2% to 40%, with a median point prevalence of 15% (3-5).
  - Persistent pain was reported with an overall prevalence of 20% of primary care patients, with approximately 48% reporting back pain (6).
- Chronic pain spares no one. It involves children and elderly alike (1-12).
  - Even though, historically, back pain research has primarily focused on younger, working adults, there is evidence that back pain is one of the most frequent complaints in older persons (11-14), and is an independent correlate of functional limitations (15, 16), perceived difficulty in performing daily life activities (17), and a risk factor for future disability.

144

- Chronic pain with involvement of multiple regions is a common occurrence in over 60% of the patients (18).

♦ Duration of pain and its chronicity are topics of controversy, with conventional beliefs that most episodes of low back pain will be short-lived with 80% to 90% of attacks resolving in about 6 weeks irrespective of the administration or type of treatment, and with 5% to 10% of patients developing persistent back pain.

- This concept has been questioned as the condition tends to relapse and most patients will experience recurrent episodes.

- Modern evidence has shown that chronic persistent low back pain and neck pain, not only in adults but also in children, are seen in up to 60% of patients for 5 years or longer after the initial episode (3, 7).

♦ Chronic non-cancer pain is associated with significant economic, societal, and health impact (1, 2, 23-26).

- The cost of uncontrolled chronic pain is enormous both to individuals and society as it leads to a decline in quality of life and disability (1, 2).

- Estimated in patterns of direct healthcare expenditures among individuals with back pain in the United States reached $90.7 billion for the year 1998 (23).

- On average, individuals with back pain generate healthcare expenditures about 60% higher than individuals without back pain.

- The healthcare for patients with chronic pain might exceed the combined cost of treating patients with coronary artery disease, cancer, and AIDS (27).

♦ In the last several years, health policy-makers, health professionals, regulators and the public have become increasingly interested in better pain therapy provisions.

2. Prescription drug abuse for non-medical purposes is becoming an epidemic

♦ Non-medical uses of psychotherapeutics as described in multiple surveys include non-medical use of any prescription type of drugs (not including OTC):

- Pain relievers
- Tranquilizers
- Stimulants
- Sedatives

♦ The 2004 Survey on Drug Use and Health (NSDUH) (28) showed startling statistics.

- An estimated **19.1 million** Americans or 7.9 percent of the population aged 12 and older **used illicit drugs** in 2004.

2

- 2.4 million persons used pain relievers non-medically for the first time within the past 12 months.

- Almost **half of all Americans** have **tried an illicit drug** at least once in their lifetime.

- The rate of **illicit drug use** among **youth was 10.6 percent.**

- 2.1 million persons had used marijuana for the first time within the past 12 months.

- Approximately **one in six youths is approached** by someone selling drugs.

- While the true extent of prescription drug abuse and diversion is unknown, estimates from a national survey indicate that the principle drug of abuse for nearly 10% of U.S. patients in treatment is a prescription drug.

- The most commonly abused drugs include oxycodone (Percodan®, Percocet®, Roxicet®, Tylox®, OxyContin®), hydrocodone (Vicodin®, Vicoprofen®, Lorcet®, Lortab®), hydromorphone, morphine (Astramorph®, Duramorph®, MS Contin®, Roxanol®), codeine, clonazepam (Klonopin®), alprazolam (Xanax®), lorazepam (Ativan®), diazepam (Valium®) and carisoprodol (Soma®) (28-30).

- The survey of Diversion and Abuse of Controlled Prescription drugs in the United States by the Center on Addiction and Substance Abuse (CASA) (30) revealed startling statistics.

  - **Between 1992 and 2003:**

    - The U.S. population increased 14%
    - The number of people abusing prescription controlled substances increased by 94%
    - 200% ↑ of Marijuana use
    - 500% ↑ of Cocaine use
    - 6,000% ↑ of Heroin use

  - **212% ↑ in 12-17 years olds**

  - **542% ↑ new drug use among teens**

  - **Most people (75%) are polysubstance abusers**

- The 2004 NSDUH survey showed lifetime non-medical use of psychotherapeutics has increased to 20% of the population or 48 million adults in America.

		Current (millions)	Past Year (millions)	Lifetime (millions)
•	Pain relievers	4.4	11.3	31.8
•	OxyContin®	0.33	1.2	3.1
•	Tranquilizers	1.6	5.1	19.9
•	Stimulants	1.2	3.0	20.0
•	Methamphetamine	0.6	1.4	11.7
•	Sedatives	0.27	0.7	9.9
	Total	**6.0**	**14.6**	**48.0**
	Percentage	**(2.5%)**	**(6.1%)**	**(20%)**

- From 2003 to 2004, there were significant increases in lifetime prevalence use for specific pain relievers.

  - Hydrocodone products
    ↑ from 31.3% to 33.9%
  - Oxycodone products (OxyContin® not included)
    ↑ from 16.7% to 18.8%
  - OxyContin®
    ↑ from 3.6% to 4.3%

- The Drug Abuse Warning Network (DAWN) (31) examined the involvement of opiates and deaths related to drug misuse.

  - Nearly 1.3 million emergency department (ED) visits in 2004 were associated with drug misuse/abuse.
    - Nonmedical use of pharmaceuticals was involved in nearly a half million of these ED visits.
    - Opioids > 158,000
    - Benzodiazepines > 144,000

  - Opiates/opioid analgesics (pain killers) and benzodiazepines were each present in more than 100,000 ED visits in 2004.

  - Muscle relaxants, particularly carisoprodol and cyclobenzaprine, were involved in an estimated 28,000 ED visits.

  - Two-thirds or more of ED visits associated with opiates/opioids, benzodiazepines, and muscle relaxants involved multiple drugs, and alcohol was one of the other drugs in about a quarter of such visits.

- Characteristics of recent initiatives for non-medical use of pain relievers is as follows (28):

- In 2004, among persons aged 12 or older, 2.4 million initiated non-medical use of prescription pain relievers within the past year
- There were 615,000 new non-medical users of OxyContin® in 2004
- Three-fourths (73.8 percent) of past year initiates of non-medical pain reliever use had used another illicit drug prior to using pain relievers non-medically
- Nearly all (99.1 percent) past-year initiates of non-medical OxyContin® use had used another illicit drug prior to using OxyContin® non-medically

♦ Non-medical use of OxyContin® has been skyrocketing.

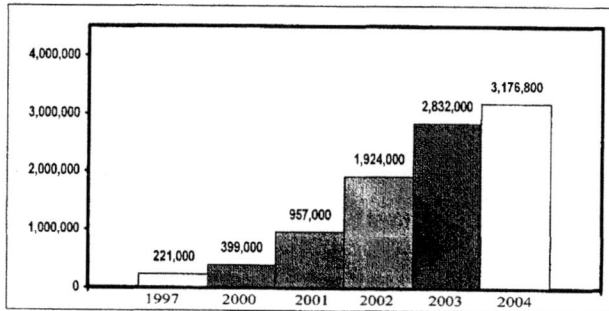

♦ A recent survey of *USA Today* published on July 20, 2006 stated that 1 in 5 adults have a close relative who is or was addicted to drugs or alcohol.

3. Sharp increases in therapeutic use of controlled substances and misuse or abuse of controlled substances

♦ Considerable controversy exists about the use of opioids for treatment of chronic pain of non-cancer origin.

- Inadequate treatment of pain has been attributed to a lack of knowledge about pain management options, inadequate understanding of addiction, or to fears of investigation or sanction by federal, state, and local regulatory agencies (2, 29).
- Many authors contend that drug therapy with opioid analgesics plays an important role in pain management and should be available when needed for all types of pain.
- The DEA also took the position that clinicians should be knowledgeable about using opioids to treat pain and should not hesitate to prescribe them when opioids are the best clinical choice of treatment.
- The alleged undertreatment of pain as a major health problem in the United States led to the development of initiatives to address the multiple alleged barriers responsible for the undertreatment of pain.
- Patient advocacy groups and professional organizations have been formed with a

148

focus on improving the management of pain.
- Numerous clinical guidelines also have been developed, even though none of them have been developed using evidence-based medicine.
- **Extensive systematic review of the literature (2) showed that long-term use of opioids has not been well studied. Among the studies presented, it has been shown that opioids generally provide approximately 40% relief in 40% of the patients.**

- Opioid use and subsequent use of other controlled substances for chronic pain has been increasing rapidly.

  - Over 90% of patients presenting to and in pain management centers are on opioids (32-35).

  - U.S. Office-based prescriptions have increased

    - **All opioids**
      - 8% in 1980
      - 16% in 2000
    - **Schedule II**
      - 2% in 1980
      - 9% in 2000

  - The increase in therapeutic opioid use in the U.S. from 1997 to 2002 has been substantial.

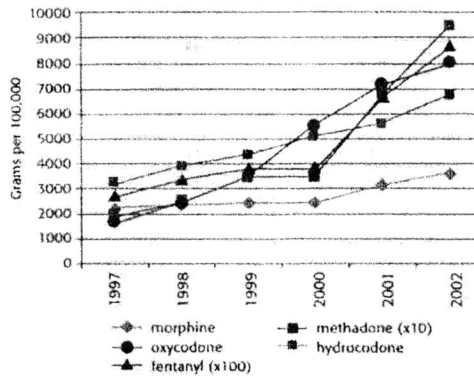

Data taken from: U.S. Drug Enforcement Administration. Automation of Reports and Consolidated Orders System (ARCOS); http://www.deadiversion.usdoj.gov/arcos/retail_drug_summary/index.html

149

- Another frequent form of obtaining opioids included "street purchase" by 26% of the patients.
- In Methadone maintenance treatment (56), 83% of patients at admission had been using prescription opioids with or without heroin.

♦ Between 1992 and 2002, while the population of the United States increased by 13% and the number of prescriptions written for non-controlled drugs increased by 57%, the number of prescriptions filled for controlled drugs increased by 154%.

- During this same period, there was a 90% increase (from 7.8 million to 14.8 million) in the number of people who admitted abusing controlled prescription drugs (30).

♦ Sales of opioids in grams increased significantly from 1997 to 2002 with an approximate 400% increase for oxycodone and methadone and over 110% increase for hydrocodone use. The following shows opioid sales in grams from 1997 to 2002.

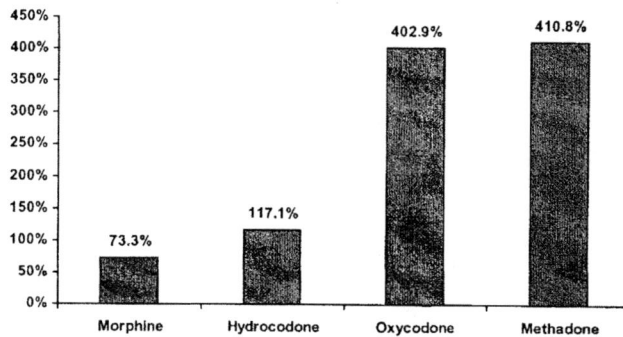

♦ *Drug abuse in chronic pain management is common.*
- Substance abuse in interventional pain management settings has been shown to be 9% to 24% (33, 34, 36-50).
- With prevalence of chronic pain ranging from 15% to 30% in the United States (25 to 45 million persons), the prescription drug abuse or misuse is seen in 9% to 24% (approximately 3 million to 9 million persons).
- *The illicit drug use among patients in chronic pain receiving controlled substances has been shown to be 14% to 32%.*

- Based on their type of insurance, the prevalence of illicit drug use among individuals with chronic pain was shown to be highest in patients on Medicaid (51).

♦ Prevalence of mental illness is almost double in patients with drug abuse (28).

♦ The interest in managing chronic pain has lead to increased prescription of controlled substances, fueled by:
  - Pharmaceutical companies providing marketing and gifts.
  - Numerous organizations providing guidelines and standards.
  - Patient advocacy groups demanding opioids for benign pain.
  - Enactment of the Patient's Bill of Rights in many states.
  - Unproven JCAHO regulations mandating monitoring and appropriate treatment of pain, which is misunderstood by the media and the public.
  - Patient's right to pain relief.
  - Easy availability on internet.
  - Unscrupulous providers.
  - Street value of prescription drugs.
  - Legitimacy provided by prescription drugs.
  - Safety and purity of prescription drugs.

4. Drug diversion is an epidemic in the United States

♦ Drugs can be diverted from their lawful purpose to illicit ease at any point in the pharmaceutical manufacturing and distribution process. The diversion of prescription drugs among adults is typically described to occur through one of the following:
  - Doctor shopping
  - Illegal internet pharmacies
  - Prescription forgery
  - Illicit prescriptions by physicians
  - Youths typically acquire drugs by stealing from their relatives or buying from classmates who sell their legitimate prescriptions.

♦ Doctor shopping is one of the most common methods of obtaining prescription drugs for legal and illegal use (2, 31-50).

  - The majority of physicians perceive doctor shopping as the major mechanism of diversion (30).
  - Doctor shopping typically involves an individual going to several different doctors complaining of a wide array of symptoms in order to get prescriptions. This type of diversion can also involve individuals who use people with legitimate medical needs, like cancer patients, to go to various physicians in several cities to get prescription medications.
  - Patients practicing doctor shopping may target physicians who readily dispense prescriptions without physical examination or screening.
  - Some patients with a legitimate medical condition may get prescriptions from multiple physicians in various states or in the same state (52). It has been reported that individuals may collect thousands of pills during a one-year period and sell them on the street.

- Recently, some elderly have been supplementing their Social Security checks by selling part of their prescriptions.

♦ One specific area in which diversion has increased dramatically is through the use of the internet.
  - CASA (30) has reported the number of internet pharmacies in operation at any one time has reached as high as 1,400.
  - In 2001, prescription drug abuse and misuse was estimated to impose approximately $100 billion annually in healthcare costs.
  - ComScore networks reported that 17.4 million people visited an online pharmacy in the fourth quarter of 2004, an increase of 14% from the previous quarter (54).
    - Sixty-three percent of these sites did not require a prescription to obtain controlled substances.

♦ Prescription forgery can occur at any point from manufacturer to the patient. Thefts are on the rise, largely due to drastic increases in prescription drug abuse and high street prices (52).

  - Prescription forgery is also fairly common either by altering the prescription or stealing blank prescription pads in order to write fake prescriptions or creating prescriptions by a computer program.
  - The vast majority of prescription forgery is from non-health care professionals.
  - Illicit prescriptions written by physicians, is rare, but a real phenomenon.
  - Headlines are made describing criminal cases involving physicians who become involved in diverting prescription drugs for huge profits.
    - However, malprescribing, either due to lack of knowledge or due to prescribing inappropriately through "pill mills" is more common. *Adverse actions taken by the DEA against physician prescribers has, in fact, decreased from 0.9% in 1999 to 0.05% in 2003, even though actions by medical licensure boards have been increasing slightly.*

♦ The diversion and abuse of prescription drugs are associated with incalculable costs to society in terms of addiction, overdose, death, and related criminal activities. The DEA has stated that the diversion and abuse of legitimately produced controlled pharmaceuticals constitute a multi-billion dollar illicit market nationwide (53). As of February 2002, OxyContin® has been involved in 464 deaths from prescription drug abuse, as reported by DEA on the basis of medical examiners autopsy findings for 2000 and 2001 from 32 states.

♦ A substantial amount of drug diversion or drug abuse may be coming from Methadone clinics.

  - Methadone clinics do not just treat heroin addiction.
  - Patients are in the clinic as long as they can afford to stay.
  - High doses of methadone are given, creating addiction.

♦ Patients may be receiving Schedule II, III, and IV prescriptions from multiple practitioners who are unaware of the potential for drug interactions or of the potential for abuse, and diversion of certain medications.

152

• Drug spending is skyrocketing. Significant amounts of Medicaid funds are spent on abused drugs. Drug spending in some states has increased by 65% in 2003.

• Source of payment for specialty treatment or drug abuse and addiction treatment is highest for federal funds:

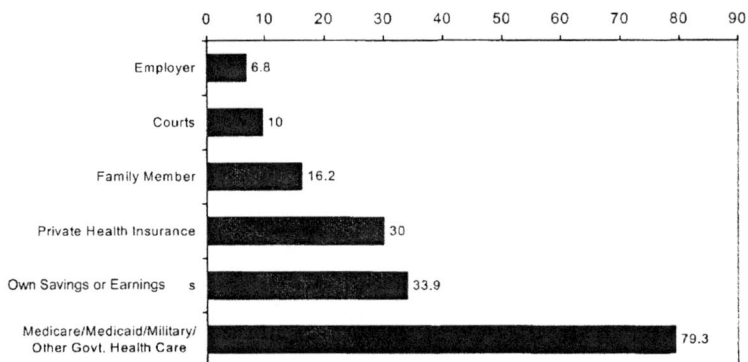

Percent Source of Payment for Treatment
(Note that the estimates of treatment by source of payment include persons reporting more than one source.)
Source: 2002 National Survey on Drug Use and Health (NSDUH). Results from the 2002 National Survey on Drug Use and Health: National Findings. Department of Health and Human Services

• Costs to society of drug abuse has been skyrocketing. The following shows costs from 1992 to 2000 in millions of dollars.

Year	Healthcare costs	Productivity losses	Other	Total
1992	10,820	69,421	21,912	102,153
1994	11,279	82,685	24,440	118,404
1996	11,428	92,423	27,444	131,295
1998	12,862	98,467	32,083	143,412
2000	14,899	110,491	35,274	160,664

◆ Federal drug control spending has been gradually increasing over the years.

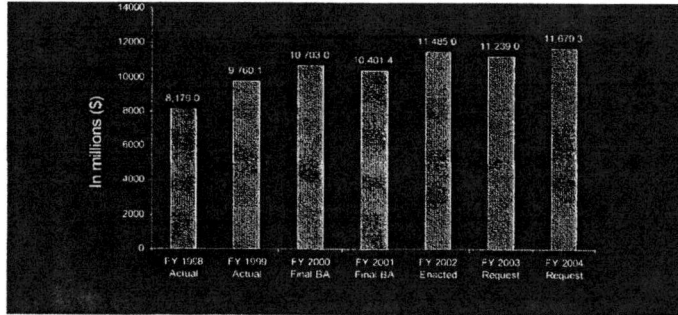

5. Problems facing physicians

♦ Role of physicians in controlling drug abuse.
A CASA survey (30) of 979 physicians regarding the diversion and abuse of controlled prescription drugs showed the following:

- Physicians perceive the three main mechanisms of diversion to be:
  - Doctor shopping (when patients obtain controlled drugs from multiple doctors) (96.4%)
  - Patient deception or manipulation of doctors (87.8%)
  - Forged or altered prescriptions (69.4%).
  - 59.1% believe that patients account for the bulk of the diversion problem.
  - 47.1% said that patients often try to pressure them into prescribing a controlled drug.
  - Only 19.1% of surveyed physicians received any medical school training in identifying prescription drug diversion.
  - Only 39.6% received any training in medical school in identifying prescription drug abuse and addiction.
  - 43.3% of physicians do not ask about prescription drug abuse when taking a patient's health history.
  - 33% do not regularly call or obtain records from the patient's previous (or other treating) physician before prescribing controlled drugs on a long-term basis. HIPPA regulations have made this step much more difficult.
  - 74.1% have refrained from prescribing controlled drugs during the past 12 months because of concern that a patient might become addicted to them.

♦ Every day physicians have to consider:

- Litigation for failure to treat pain
- Litigation for undertreatment
- Criminal charges for abuse, addiction, or death
- Numerous federal regulations
- State Board of Medical Examiners
- Drug Enforcement Agency
- State Bureau of Narcotics
- State Board of Pharmacy

♦ Options for Physicians

- Referral to Pain Medicine Clinics
  - Clinics with mainstay treatment of opioids
  - Very limited resource
  - Rare option for Interventional Pain Specialists

- Refuse to Prescribe Controlled Substances
  - Not an option for many practices
  - Inadequate treatment of pain lawsuits
  - Litigation for addiction
  - Criminal charges of murder

- Surrender Schedule II DEA License
  - Lose many patients
  - Lose hospital privileges
  - Lose all insurance patients
  - Not an option for interventionalists

6.   Problems facing pharmacists

♦ The role of pharmacists:
A CASA survey of 1,303 pharmacists regarding diversion and abuse of controlled prescription drugs showed the following:
- When a patient presents a prescription for a controlled drug:
- 78.4% of pharmacists become "somewhat or very" concerned about diversion or abuse when a patient asks for a controlled drug by its brand name;
- 26.5% "somewhat or very often" think it is for purposes of diversion or abuse.
  - 51.8% believe that patients account for the bulk of the diversion problem.
  - Only about half of the pharmacists surveyed received any training in identifying prescription drug diversion (48.1%) or abuse or addiction (49.6%) since pharmacy school.
  - 61% do not regularly ask if the patient is taking any other controlled drugs when dispensing a controlled medication; 25.8% rarely or never do so.
  - 28.9% have experienced a theft or robbery of controlled drugs at their pharmacy within the last five years; 20.9% do not stock certain controlled drugs in order to prevent diversion.

- 28.4% do not regularly validate the prescribing physician's DEA number when dispensing controlled drugs; one in 10 (10.5%) rarely or never do so.
- 83.1% have refused to dispense a controlled drug in the past year because of suspicions of diversion or abuse.

- Pharmacists may be involved in prescription drug diversion, first by selling the controlled substances and then, using their database of physicians and patients to write and forge prescriptions to cover their illegal sale.

7. Problems facing legitimate patients

- Problem list:

  - Undertreatment of pain.
  - All patients are under suspicion.
  - The interest in receiving opioids for chronic pain, fueled by advertising by pharmaceutical companies.
  - Unproven, misunderstood JCAHO regulations mandating monitoring and appropriate treatment of pain.
  - Media coverage of undertreatment of pain.
  - Numerous organizations providing advocacy guidelines and standards.
  - Patient advocacy groups advising them to demand more opioids.
  - Access to internet and daily bombardment of easy availability of drugs.
  - Patient beliefs that they have the right to total pain relief.

A study evaluating severe dependence on oral opioids illustrated that the majority of patients with severe dependence (39%) obtained opioids by going to different physicians (50).

8. What is being done to address prescription drug abuse epidemic?

Drug Enforcement Agency

- On October 27, 1970, Congress passed the Comprehensive Drug Abuse Prevention and Control Act. According to the DEA, Title 2 of this Act, The Controlled Substances Act, is a "consolidation of numerous laws regulating the manufacturing and distribution of narcotics, stimulants, depressants, hallucinogens, anabolic steroids and chemicals used in the illicit production of controlled substances" and is "the legal foundation of the governments fight against drugs and other substances" (57).

  - The Act also regulates all legal and illegal substances that are recognized as having potential for abuse or addiction (57).
  - The DEA's diversion control program oversees and regulates the legal manufacture and distribution of controlled pharmaceuticals (57).
  - DEA believes that controlled pharmaceuticals can be diverted intentionally or unintentionally by doctors, pharmacists, dentists, nurses, veterinarians, and individual users.
    - Diversion cases may involve physicians who sell prescriptions to drug dealers or abusers, pharmacists who falsify records to obtain and then

156

sell pharmaceuticals, employees who steal from physician or pharmacy inventories, individuals who forge prescriptions, individuals who commit armed robbery of pharmacies and drug distributors, "doctor shoppers" who routinely visit multiple doctors complaining of the same ailment to obtain multiple prescriptions for controlled substances, and individuals who establish internet pharmacies that sell controlled pharmaceuticals without requiring prescriptions.

- In 2005, Congress emphasized its concern regarding the diversion of controlled pharmaceuticals. The house report on the Justice Department's fiscal year (FY) 2005 appropriations stated, . . . "DEA has demonstrated a lack of effort to address this problem".
- The house report on the Justice Department's fiscal year 2006 appropriations repeated the concerns from the previous year. The final appropriation for FY 2006 included an additional $8.8 million and 41 positions for the DEA to improve intelligence support and $4.7 million and 23 positions for additional agents to assist diversion control.
- The DEA made diversion control one of its strategic goals.
- The DEA increased resources for diversion control. DEA added 75 diversion investigator positions in 2004, 75 positions in 2005 and 40 additional positions in 2006.
- The DEA undertook more criminal diversion investigations and established far more performance measures. The DEA's performance measures showed that from FY 2002 to FY 2005 the number of diversion drug organizations disrupted increased from 454 to 474 and the number of diversion drug organizations dismantled increased from 474 to 594. DEA developed then operational internet strategy.

Prescription controlled drug monitoring programs.
- The National All Schedules Prescription Electronic Reporting (NASPER) Act, which ASIPP initiated and worked through three sessions of Congress to pass, was signed into law on August 11, 2005.
  - It authorizes spending of $60 million from fiscal year 2006 to 2010 to create federal grants at the U.S. Department of Health and Human Services to help establish or improve state-run prescription drug monitoring programs.
  - NASPER is moving extremely slow with no funding committed yet.
- DEA/Harold Rogers and state monitoring programs. While state programs have been effective, the following deficiencies have been noted.

  - From 1940 to 1999, states have been able to establish only 15 functioning programs. The number of states with prescription drug monitoring programs has grown only slightly over the past decade, from 10 in 1992 to 15 in 2002.

  - It appears that now there are approximately 32 programs in the process.

  - The White House estimates an increase in drug monitoring programs within the next 10 years.

    - Even though the programs have a common goal of reducing prescription drug diversion and abuse, the programs vary in objectives, design, and operation.

14

- The major purpose of the state programs is to help law enforcement identify and prevent prescription drug diversion.

- Educational objectives to provide information to physicians, pharmacies, and the public is a secondary objective.

- Very few states are proactive to the extent that physicians can access the information to reduce or prevent abuse and diversion.

- Program design also varies across states in terms of which drugs are covered, how prescription information is collected, and which agency is given responsibility for the program.

- Methods for analyzing the data to detect potential diversion activity also differ among states.

- Only 4 of 15 states monitor Schedule IV drugs and only 5 of 15 monitor Schedule III drugs which are the subject of major controlled substance abuse.

- Challenges exist in establishing and expanding state programs, due to lack of awareness of the extent to which prescription drug abuse and diversion in a significant public health and law enforcement problem.

- Extent of diversion in abuse is not always recognized by the states.

- National efforts have focused only on providing guidance and technical assistance.

- **Incidents of drug diversion, however, are on the rise in neighboring states, indicating the problem is proliferating or shifting to states without monitoring programs.**

♦ **State Regulations**

- The state's regulation of practice of medicine and pharmacy and role in monitoring illegal use and diversion of prescription drugs. State laws govern the prescribing and dispensing of prescription drugs by licensed healthcare professionals.

- Multiple state agencies have responded to reports of drug abuse. However, complete information is not available from the directors of state Medicaid fraud control units in Kentucky, Maryland, Pennsylvania, Virginia, and West Virginia. They stated that drug abuse and diversion of OxyContin® is a problem in these states.

- State Medical Licensure Boards have also responded to complaints about physicians who were suspected of abuse and diversion of controlled substances, but like the Medicaid Fraud Control Units, the Boards generally do not maintain data on the number of investigations that were involved.

158

- Although Medical Boards may be tough, they can't always catch the bad apples
- The Board reacts to complaints and can't statutorily look for problems on its own

9. Strategies to combat the epidemic

- Education: Education is required at all levels including public, physicians and pharmacists.
  - Surveys have shown that less than 40% of physicians have received any training in medical school in identifying prescription drug abuse and addiction or identification of drug diversion. Similarly, only 50% of pharmacists received any training in identifying prescription drug diversion, abuse or addiction.
  - Controlled substance education must be mandated in medical schools, residency training programs, pharmacy schools, and supported by continuing education each year variable from 20 hours in the first year and 10 hours in subsequent years. The training must be accredited and approved and may be monitored mainly by DEA or State Board of Medical Licensures.
  - The public must be educated on nonopioid techniques of chronic pain management. In addition, public should be educated about overall ineffectiveness of opioid use, prevalence of misuse and adverse effects, even if used properly. The education should stress the disastrous consequences of misuse and abuse.
    - **A separate residency program is needed in interventional pain management.**

- Enactment of NASPER in all states:
  - NASPER is the best solution for a mounting problem in a proactive fashion.
  - NASPER is cost-effective and the information is shared by neighboring states. This will avoid all the disadvantages of people moving from one state to another.

    Table 1 shows the contiguous states for each of the 50 states.

  - NASPER is a physician friendly program, thus doctor shopping can be prevented rather than be dealt with by DEA with criminal charges.
  - DEA should work with provider community. At present, the relationship between DEA and provider community including pharmacists is at best lukewarm. This relationship has to be improved.
    - DEA should encourage NASPER program as it is a proactive, physician friendly, all schedules and shares information among the contiguous states.
    - Medicaid coverage for controlled substances should be looked at and regulated.
  - Benefits of NASPER are numerous as follows:

  - Benefits for Patients:
    - Improved access
    - Stable patient - physician relationship

Honest patients receive appropriate treatment

16

- Benefits for Physicians:
  - Decreased hassle factors
  - DEA, Medical Board, U.S. Attorneys, and Renegade Physicians

Proper treatment without hassles

- Benefits for Law Enforcement:
  - Improved identification
  - Rapid prosecution

♦ Improve relationships between DEA and providers

♦ Increased scrutiny of methadone clinics

♦ Increased comprehensive drug rehabilitation programs
  - Buprenorphine detoxification

♦ Elimination of internet pharmacies

Table 1. *Shows the contiguous states for each of the 50 states*

State	Surrounding States
Alabama	Florida, Georgia, Mississippi, Tennessee
Alaska	None
Arizona	California, Colorado, New Mexico, Nevada, Utah
Arkansas	Louisiana, Missouri, Mississippi, Oklahoma, Tennessee, Texas
California	Arizona, Nevada, Oregon
Colorado	Arizona, Kansas, Nebraska, New Mexico, Oklahoma, Utah, Wyoming
Connecticut	Massachusetts, New York, Rhode Island
Delaware	Maryland, New Jersey, Pennsylvania
Washington DC	Maryland, Virginia
Florida	Alabama, Georgia
Georgia	Alabama, Florida, North Carolina, South Carolina, Tennessee
Hawaii	None
Idaho	Montana, Nevada, Oregon, Utah, Washington, Wyoming
Illinois	Iowa, Indiana, Kentucky, Missouri, Wisconsin
Indiana	Illinois, Kentucky, Michigan, Ohio
Iowa	Illinois, Minnesota, Missouri, Nebraska, South Dakota, Wisconsin
Kansas	Colorado, Missouri, Nebraska, Oklahoma
Kentucky	Illinois, Indiana, Missouri, Ohio, Tennessee, Virginia, West Virginia
Louisiana	Arkansas, Mississippi, Texas
Maine	New Hampshire
Maryland	District Of Columbia, Delaware, Pennsylvania, Virginia, West Virginia
Massachusetts	Connecticut, New Hampshire, New York, Rhode Island, Vermont
Michigan	Indiana, Ohio, Wisconsin
Minnesota	Iowa, North Dakota, South Dakota, Wisconsin
Mississippi	Alabama, Arkansas, Louisiana, Tennessee
Missouri	Arkansas, Iowa, Illinois, Kansas, Kentucky, Nebraska, Oklahoma, Tennessee
Montana	Idaho, North Dakota, South Dakota, Wyoming
Nebraska	Colorado, Iowa, Kansas, Missouri, South Dakota, Wyoming
Nevada	Arizona, California, Idaho, Oregon, Utah
New Hampshire	Massachusetts, Maine, Vermont
New Jersey	Delaware, New York, Pennsylvania
New Mexico	Arizona, Colorado, Oklahoma, Texas, Utah
New York	Connecticut, Massachusetts, New Jersey, Pennsylvania, Vermont
North Carolina	Georgia, South Carolina, Tennessee, Virginia
North Dakota	Minnesota, Montana, South Dakota
Ohio	Indiana, Kentucky, Michigan, Pennsylvania, West Virginia
Oklahoma	Arkansas, Colorado, Kansas, Missouri, New Mexico, Texas

Oregon	California, Idaho, Nevada, Washington
Pennsylvania	Delaware, Maryland, New Jersey, New York, Ohio, West Virginia
Rhode Island	Connecticut, Massachusetts
South Carolina	Georgia, North Carolina
South Dakota	Iowa, Minnesota, Montana, North Dakota, Nebraska, Wyoming
Tennessee	Alabama, Arkansas, Georgia, Kentucky, Missouri, Mississippi, North Carolina, Virginia
Texas	Arkansas, Louisiana, New Mexico, Oklahoma
Utah	Arizona, Colorado, Idaho, New Mexico, Nevada, Wyoming
Vermont	Massachusetts, New Hampshire, New York
Virginia	District Of Columbia, Kentucky, Maryland, North Carolina, Tennessee, West Virginia
Washington	Idaho, Oregon
West Virginia	Kentucky, Maryland, Ohio, Pennsylvania, Virginia
Wisconsin	Iowa, Illinois, Michigan, Minnesota
Wyoming	Colorado, Idaho, Montana, Nebraska, South Dakota, Utah

REFERENCES

1. Boswell MV, Shah RV, Everett CR, Sehgal N, Mckenzie-Brown AM, Abdi S, Bowman RC, Deer TR, Datta S, Colson JD, Spillane WF, Smith HS, Lucas-Levin LF, Burton AW, Chopra P, Staats PS, Wasserman RA, Manchikanti L. Interventional techniques in the management of chronic spinal pain: Evidence-based practice guidelines. *Pain Physician* 2005; 8:1-47.

2. Trescot AM, Boswell MV, Atluri SL, Hansen HC, Deer TR, Abdi S, Jasper JF, Singh V, Jordan AE, Johnson BW, Cicala RS, Dunbar EE, Helm II S, Varley KG, Suchdev PK, Swicegood JR, Calodney AK, Ogoke BA, Minore WS, Manchikanti L. Opioid guidelines in the management of chronic non-cancer pain. *Pain Physician* 2006; 9:1-40.

3. Manchikanti L, Staats PS, Singh V, Schultz DM, Vilims BD, Jasper JF, Kloth DS, Trescot AM, Hansen HC, Falasca TD, Racz GB, Deer T, Burton AW, Helm S, Lou L, Bakhit CE, Dunbar EE, Atluri SL, Calodney AK, Hassenbusch S, Feler CA. Evidence-based practice guidelines for interventional techniques in the management of chronic spinal pain. *Pain Physician* 2003; 6:3-80.

4. Verhaak PF, Kerssens JJ, Dekker J, Sorbi MJ, Bensing JM. Prevalence of chronic benign pain disorder among adults: A review of the literature. *Pain* 1998; 77:231-239.

5. Blyth FM, March LM, Brnabic AJ, Jorm LR, Williamson M, Cousins MJ. Chronic pain in Australia: A prevalence study. *Pain* 2001; 89:127-134.

6. Gureje O, Von Korff M, Simon GE, Gater R. Persistent pain and well-being: A World Health Organization study in primary care. *JAMA* 1998; 280:147-151.

7. Elliott AM, Smith BH, Hannaford PC, Smith WC, Chambers WA. The course of chronic pain in the community: Results of a 4-year follow-up study. *Pain* 2002; 99:299-307.

8. Bressler HB, Keyes WJ, Rochon PA, Badley E. The prevalence of low back pain in the elderly. A systemic review of the literature. *Spine* 1999; 24:1813-1819.

9. Lawrence RC, Helmick CG, Arnett FC. Estimates of the prevalence of arthritis and selected musculoskeletal disorders in the United States. *Arthritis Rheum* 1998; 41:778-799.

10. Mallen C, Peat G, Thomas E, Croft P. Severely disabling chronic pain in young adults: prevalence from a population-based postal survey in North Staffordshire. *BMC Musculoskeletal Disords* 2005, 6:42.

11. Cecchi F, Debolini P, Lova RM, Macchi C, Bandinelli S, Bartali B, Lauretani F, Benvenuti E, Hicks G, Ferrucci L. Epidemiology of back pain in a representative cohort of Italian persons 65 years of age and older: the InCHIANTI study. *Spine* 2006; 31:1149-1155.

12. Lavsky-Shulhan M, Wallace RB, Kohout FJ, Lemke JH, Morris MC, Smith IM. Prevalence and functional correlates of low back pain in the elderly: the Iowa 65+ Rural Health Study. *J Am Geriatr Soc.*1985; 33:23-28.

13. Koch H, Smith MC. Office-based ambulatory care for patients 75 years old and over. National Ambulatory Medical Care Survey, 1980 and 1981. Advanced Data from Vital and Health Statistics (NCHS), No. 110 [DHHS Publication No, PHS 85-1250]. Hyattsville, MD: Public Health Service, 1985; 110:1-4.

14. Goel V, Iron k, Williams JL. Indicators of health determinants and health status. In: Goel V, Williams JI, Anderson GM, et al, eds. *Patterns of Health Care in Ontario: The ICES Pactice Atlas*, 2nd ed. Ottawa: Canadian Medical Association, 1996:5–26.

15. Hartley BB, Warren JK, Rachon PA, et al. The prevalence of low back pain in the elderly: a systematic review of the literature. *Spine* 1999;24:1813–9.

16. Edmond SL, Felson DT. Function and back symptoms in older adults. *J Am Geriatr Soc* 2003;51:1702–1709.

17. Leveille SG, Guralnik JM, Hochberg M, et al. Low back pain and disability in older women: independent association with difficulty but not inability to perform daily living activities. *J Gerontol* 1999; 54:M487–493.

18. Yeung SS, Genaidy A, Deddens J, Alhemood A, Leung PC. Prevalence of musculoskeletal symptoms in single and multiple body regions and effects of perceived risk of injury among manual handling workers. *Spine* 2002; 27:2166-2172.

164

19. Enthoven P, Skargren E, Oberg B. Clinical course in patients seeking primary care for back or neck pain: A prospective 5-year follow-up of outcome and health care consumption with subgroup analysis. *Spine* 2004; 29:2458-2465.

20. Hoving JL, de Vet HC, Twisk JW, Deville WL, van der Windt D, Koes BW, Bouter LM. Prognostic factors for neck pain in general practice. *Pain* 2004; 110:639-645.

21. Smith BH, Elliott AM, Hannaford PC, Chambers WA, Smith WC. Factors related to the onset and persistence of chronic back pain in the community: Results from a general population follow-up study. *Spine* 2004; 29:1032-1040.

22. Cote P, Cassidy JD, Carroll LJ, Kristman V. The annual incidence and course of neck pain in the general population: A population- based cohort study. *Pain* 2004; 112:267-273.

23. Luo X, Pietrobon R, Sun SX, Liu GG, Hey L. Estimates and patterns of direct health care expenditures among individuals with back pain in the United States. *Spine* 2004; 29:79-86.

24. Leigh JP, Markowitz SB, Fahs M, Shin C, Landrigan PJ. Occupational injury and illness in the United States. Estimates of costs, morbidity, and mortality. *Arch Intern Med* 1997; 157:1557-1568.

25. Freedman VA, Martin LG, Schoeni RF. Recent trends in disability and functioning among older adults in the United States. *JAMA* 2002; 288:3137-3146.

26. Turner JA, Franklin G, Heagerty PJ, Wu R, Egan K, Fulton-Kehoe D, Gluck JV, Wickizer TM. The association between pain and disability. *Pain* 2004; 112:307-314.

27. Hough J. Estimating the health care utilization costs associated with people with disabilities: Data from the 1996 Medical Expenditure Panel Survey (MEPS). *Annual meeting of the Association for Health Services Research*, Los Angeles, California, 2000.

28. Substance Abuse and Mental Health Services Administration (2004). Overview of Findings from the 2003 National Survey on Drug Use and Health (Office of Applied Studies, NSDUH Series H-24, DHHS Publication No. SMA 04-3963). Rockville MD.

29. Manchikanti L, Whitfield E, Pallone F. Evolution of the National All Schedules Prescription

Electronic Reporting Act (NASPER): A public law for balancing treatment of pain and drug abuse and diversion. *Pain Physician* 2005; 8:335-347.

30. Bollinger LC, Bush C, Califano JA, Chenault KI, Curtis JL, Dimon J, Dolan PR, Ganzi VF, Fisher M, Kelmenson LA, Keough DR, Kessler DA, Malloy EA, Pacheco MT, Plumeri II JJ, Redstone SE, Rosenwald Jr EJ, Schulhof MP, Sullivan LW, Sweeney JJ, Wiener MA. Under the counter. The diversion and abuse of controlled prescription drugs in the U.S. The National Center on Addition and Substance Abuse at Columbia University (CASA), July 2005.

31. US Department of Health and Human Services. Office of Applied Studies, Substance Abuse and Mental Health Services Administration (SAMHSA). Drug Abuse Warning Network. The DAWN Report. Opiate-related drug misuse deaths in six states: 2003. Issue 19, 2006.

32. Manchikanti L, Damron KS, McManus CD, Barnhill RC. Patterns of illicit drug use and opioid abuse in patients with chronic pain at initial evaluation: A prospective, observational study. *Pain Physician* 2004; 7: 431-437.

33. Chabal C, Erjavec MK, Jacobson L, Mariano A, Chaney E. Prescription opiate abuse in chronic pain patients: Clinical criteria, incidence, and predictors. *Clin J Pain* 1997; 13: 150-155.

34. Katz NP, Sherburne S, Beach M, Rose RJ, Vielguth J, Bradley J, Fanciullo GJ. Behavioral monitoring and urine toxicology testing in patients receiving long-term opioid therapy. *Anesth Analg* 2003; 97:1097-1102.

35. Gajraj N, Hervias-Sanz M. Opiate abuse or undertreatment? *Clin J Pain* 1998; 14:90-91.

36. Manchikanti L, Pampati V, Damron K, Fellows B, Barnhill RC, Beyer CD. Prevalence of opioid abuse in interventional pain medicine practice settings: A randomized clinical evaluation. *Pain Physician* 2001; 4: 358-365.

37. Manchikanti L, Pampati V, Damron K. Prevalence of prescription drug abuse and dependency in patients with chronic pain in western Kentucky. *J KY Med Assoc* 2003; 101:511-517.

38. Kell M. Monitoring compliance with Oxy-Contin prescriptions in 14,712 patients treated in 127 outpatient pain centers. *Pain Med* 2005; 6:186-187.

166

39. Vaglienti RM, Huber SJ, Noel KR, Johnstone RE. Misuse of prescribed controlled substances defined by urinalysis. *W V Med J* 2003; 99:67-70.

40. Passik SD, Kirsh KL, McDonald MV, Ahn S, Russak SM, Martin L, Rosenfeld B, Breitbart WS, Portenoy RK. A pilot survey of aberrant drug-taking attitudes and behaviors in samples of cancer and AIDS patients. *J Pain Symptom Manage* 2000; 19:274-286.

41. Atluri S, Sudarshan G. A screening tool to determine the risk of prescription opioid abuse among patients with chronic nonmalignant pain. *Pain Physician* 2002; 5: 447-448.

42. Lentner S. *Drug abuse.* Winer Zeitschrift fur Suchforschung 1991; 14:65-68.

43. Hurwitz W. The challenge of prescription drug misuse: A review and commentary. *Pain Med* 2005; 6:152-161.

44. Manchikanti L, Manchukonda R, Damron KS, Brandon D, McManus CD, Cash KA. Does adherence monitoring reduce controlled substance abuse in chronic pain patients? *Pain Physician* 2006; 9:57-60.

45. Manchikanti L, Cash KA, Damron KS, Manchukonda R, Pampati V, McManus CD. Controlled substance abuse and illicit drug use in chronic pain patients: An evaluation of multiple variables. *Pain Physician* 2006; 9:215-226.

46. Ives TJ, Chelminski PR, Hammett-Stabler CA, Malong RM, Perhac JS, Potisek NM, Shilliday BB, DeWalt DA, Pignone MP. Predictors of opioid misuse in patients with chronic pain: A prospective cohort study. *BMC Health Serv Res* 2006; 6:46.

47. Manchikanti L, Pampati V, Damron K, Beyer CD, Barnhill RC. Prevalence of illicit drug use in patients without controlled substance abuse in interventional pain management. *Pain Physician* 2003; 6:173-178.

48. Manchikanti L, Beyer C, Damron K, Pampati V. A comparative evaluation of illicit drug use in patients with or without controlled substance abuse in interventional pain management. *Pain Physician* 2003; 6:281-285.

49. Manchikanti L, Damron KS, Pampati V, McManus CD. Prevalence of illicit drug use among

individuals with chronic pain in the commonwealth of Kentucky: An evaluation of patterns and trends. *J KY Med Assoc* 2005; 103:55-62.

50. Manchikanti L, Manchukonda R, Pampati V, Damron KS, Brandon DE, Cash KA, McManus CD. Does random urine drug testing reduce illicit drug use in chronic pain patients receiving opioids? *Pain Physician* 2006; 9:123-129.

51. Manchikanti L, Manchukonda R, Pampati V, Damron KS. Evaluation of abuse of prescription and illicit drugs in chronic pain patients receiving short-acting (hydrocodone) or long-acting (methadone) opioids. *Pain Physician* 2005; 8:257-261.

52. Kraman P. Drug abuse in America – prescription drug diversion. The Council of State Governments. April 2004. www.csg.org

53. Drug Enforcement Administration and the National Alliance for Model State Drug Laws, *A closer Look at State Prescription Monitoring Programs* (http://www.deadiversion.usdoj.gov/pubs/program/prescription-monitor/summary.htm

54. ComScore is a global market research provider and consultant for Internet Usage, audience measurement, and e-commerce tracking data. The study is at www.comscore.com/press/release.asp?press=571.

55. Busto UE, Sproule BA, Knight K, Romach MK, Sellers EM. Severe dependence on oral opioids. *Can J Clin Pharmacol* 1998; 5: 23-28.

56. Brands B, Blake J, Sproule BA, Gourlay D, Busto UE. Prescription opioid abuse in patients presenting for methadone maintenance treatment. *Drug Alcohol Depend* 2004; 73:199-207.

57. US Department of Justice Office of the Inspector General Evaluation and Inspections Division. Follow Up Review of the Drug Enforcement Administration's Efforts to Control the Diversion of Controlled Pharmaceuticals. July 2006.

Mr. SOUDER. Mr. Pasierb.

STATEMENT OF STEPHEN J. PASIERB

Mr. PANSIERB. Thank you. Thanks to Ranking Member Cummings for inviting the Partnership here to testify today. I have also got to take the opportunity to thank the subcommittee for using its leadership in your steadfast dedication over the last 2 years in the drug issue, helping the American family navigate through the issues that we have been faced with. So, on behalf of all of us, I did want to get that one bit of thanks out before I got into my testimony.

We are encouraged, as you have heard in the testimony today, that drug use among teens has decreased 19 percent since 2001. However, when you examine individual drugs of abuse, there are very troubling trends, including the abuse of methamphetamine regionally, resurgence in inhalants and in prescription and over-the-counter medications.

The Partnership is particularly concerned about this new tier of teen abuse, that we have dubbed Generation Rx, which is really a cohort of young people for whom "pharming" with a "ph" or the behavior of partying or abusing a host of medicines to get high has become normative. This is not an issue of individual products, as we have heard, but rather it is a broad and negative behavior that has become far too common and acceptable in today's teen culture. These are medications that when used as directed improve health and even save lives. But there is a world of difference between good medicine and bad behavior.

The Partnership and our partners have been focused on this, doing research over the last year and a half. We're targeting this behavior now, and our dedication is to change this dangerous conduct.

Our 18th annual Partnership Attitude Tracking Study examines both teen drug use and attitudes, and that study confirmed alarming number of today's teenagers more likely to have abused medicines than a variety of illegal drugs like Ecstasy, cocaine, crack and methamphetamine. Nearly 1 in 5, or 4.5 million, teens has tried a prescription medication to get high, and 1 in 10, or 2.4 million, teens report abusing cough medicine to get high.

There is also a false sense of security about abusing medications because they are FDA-approved, legitimate and otherwise beneficial products in the medicine cabinet. The study shows that there is much work to be done to educate teens about the dangers of intentional abuse.

Two of five teens, or 9.4 million, mistakenly agree that prescription medicines even when not prescribed by a doctor are much safer to use than illicit drugs. Nearly one-third of teens, or 7.3 million, believe that there is nothing wrong with using prescription drugs once in a while without a prescription. More than half of teens, 13 million, don't strongly agree that using cough medicines to get high is risky.

Teens are also telling us in our studies that it's very easy for them to gain access to these medicines. Many teens say that they are easily available in the medicine cabinet at home or at a friend's house. They are easy to get through other people's prescriptions;

and teens say these medications are available everywhere, including the Internet.

Easy access combined with very little understanding of the consequences can be a lethal combination and has all of us quite concerned. What is more, today's parents are the most drug experienced in history, but they do not understand this new form of abuse among teenagers. As a result, they think that if they have talked about street drugs, they have done their job.

Parents need to be aware of the drugs teens abuse today, including medicines, are not the same drugs as in decades past. Only through education and parental involvement can we be successful. Once parents are educated about the intentional abuse of these products, then they can get through to kids about the dangers. We know kids who learn a lot about drug use at home are up to half as likely to use. But while 9 out of 10 parents say they've talked about the dangers, fewer than one-third of teens say they learn a lot at home about the risks of drugs.

And we know from the additional studies, only one-third of parents say they've talked to their kids specifically about the risks of abusing medicines to get high.

Focus groups show parents generally don't think their teens could be vulnerable to over-the-counter drug abuse. They don't understand the idea of this behavior. And like too many teens, they somehow think that abusing medicines is somehow safer than illicit street drugs and that has to change. That is why The Partnership and our partners, including the Consumer Health Care Product Association and its members, launched a new education campaign on May 1st that I can sum up in 3 words: educate, communicate and safeguard.

As a parent, educate yourself about the medicines kids are abusing; second, communicate with your kids on this subject and dispel the notion for yourself and your kids that these medicines can be safely abused; and finally, safeguard your medications, limiting access to them and keeping track of the quantities you have in your home and making sure your family and friends do the same. Parents are going to see that message on television, in newspapers, in magazine ads and on the radio.

The Internet also plays a role with resources for parents at Drugfree.org and specifically for teenagers who visit dxmstories.com. We would like to show examples of the campaign.

[Video presentation.]

[NOTE.—The DVD is on file with the subcommittee.]

Mr. PASIERB. So our bottom line is, we are going to be evaluating this effort over the next 3 to 5 years, and we know, through the research that has already been done, that received communications can change behaviors. This is a public health problem and we, The Partnership, are convinced that if this issue gets the attention it needs and industry is motivated in joining us to find solutions, and when this campaign gets the visibility it needs, we are going to be successful in rooting out this behavior and changing attitudes, changing behaviors.

I want to thank the committee. And please know that our dedication is to working with you to find solutions on this problem. Thanks.

[The prepared statement of Mr. Pasierb follows:]

The Partnership
for a Drug-Free
America®

Testimony of Stephen J. Pasierb, President and CEO
The Partnership for a Drug-Free America®

"Prescription Drug Abuse:
What is Being Done to Address This New Drug Epidemic?"
House Subcommittee on Criminal Justice, Drug Policy & Human Resources

The Honorable Mark E. Souder, Chairman
The Honorable Elijah Cummings, Ranking Member

United States House of Representatives, July 26, 2006

Mr. Chairman, Ranking Member Cummings, members of the subcommittee, thank you for inviting me to testify today about the problem of prescription drug abuse. I am Steve Pasierb, president and CEO of the Partnership for a Drug-Free America.®

Before I offer my testimony today, I want to take this opportunity to thank the subcommittee – and especially you, Mr. Chairman and you, Mr. Cummings – for your leadership on the drug issue. Year after year, you remain steadfast in your dedication to help the country contend with the issue of substance abuse. I have no doubt that your leadership and perseverance have contributed to the progress we have made in the last seven years in reducing the number of teenagers who use illicit drugs. All of us who work in prevention, law enforcement, and treatment are exceptionally grateful for the work of this subcommittee, and especially to both of you, for your unwavering commitment to this critical issue.

Overview

While overall substance abuse among teens has decreased 19 percent since 2001, when you examine individual drugs of abuse, there are some troubling trends, including the abuse of methamphetamine, inhalants, prescription drugs and over-the-counter drugs to get high. The Partnership is especially concerned about the advent of what we have dubbed "Generation Rx" – a cohort of young people for whom "pharming," or abusing a host of medicines and chemical products to get high has become normative.

The Partnership's 18th annual Partnership Attitude Tracking Study (PATS), which examines teen drug use and attitudes, showed that the intentional abuse of prescription and over-the-counter drugs to get high is now an entrenched behavior among teens.

Our study confirmed that an alarming number of today's teenagers are more likely to have abused prescription and over-the-counter drugs than a variety of illegal drugs like Ecstasy, cocaine, crack and methamphetamine. According to PATS:

- Nearly one in five (19 percent or 4.5 million) teens has tried a prescription medication to get high;

- One in 10 (10 percent or 2.4 million) teens report abusing cough medicine to get high; and

- Abuse of prescription and over-the-counter medications is on par with or higher than the abuse of illegal drugs such as Ecstasy (8 percent), powder/crack cocaine (10 percent), methamphetamine (8 percent) and heroin (5 percent).

The abuse of prescription medications has become "normalized" in teen culture. Two out of five teens report having a close friend who abuses prescription pain relievers to get high and nearly three out of 10 report having a close friend who abuses cough medicine to get high. So, even if teens are not abusing these medications themselves, one of their close friends may be. With this perception that "everyone is doing it" there is great risk that the "pharming" phenomenon will only grow larger.

The fact that prescription drugs are now the second most popular illegal drugs among teens, falling just behind marijuana, is certainly alarming. Equally disturbing is the number of people of all ages initiating use of this class of drugs. According to the National Survey on Drug Use & Health, in 2004 more people were initiating use of prescription pain relievers (2.4 million) than marijuana (2.1 million). Non-medical use of tranquilizers ranked third among initiates (1.2 million).

From talking to consumers, we know that this problem is not even on parents' radar screen. The Partnership has recently launched a nationwide media campaign to increase awareness and spur a dialogue about "pharming" between parents and teens. More information on this campaign follows.

Access and Perception of Risk

The Partnership's study found that two key factors are driving the "pharming" phenomenon: many teens have a misperception that intentionally abusing prescription and over-the-counter medicines is not harmful, and teens say there is easy access to these drugs through a medicine cabinet at home or at a friend's house or via the Internet.

When asked why they thought prescription drug abuse was becoming more of a problem among their peers, the most common response was the ease of access. In fact, 72 percent of teens say that it is easy to get these medications from their parents' medicine cabinets; 65 percent say that it is easy to get these medications using other people's prescriptions; 55 percent say that these drugs are available everywhere, and 36 percent say that it is easy to buy the drugs over the internet.

In addition to the ease with which these substances can be acquired, there is also a false sense of security about them because they are FDA-approved, legitimate medications from the medicine cabinet rather than street drugs imported into the United States and possibly cut with an unknown, dangerous substance. Because we know that the riskier a teen believes a drug is, the less likely they are to use it, The PATS study's findings on perception of risk is especially troubling:

- Two in five teens (40 percent or 9.4 million) agree that prescription medicines, even if they are not prescribed by a doctor are "much safer" to use than illegal drugs;

- Nearly one-third of teens (31 percent or 7.3 million) believe that there is "nothing wrong" with using prescription drugs without a prescription "once in a while;"

- Nearly three out of ten teens (29 percent or 6.8 million) believe prescription pain relievers, even if not prescribed by a doctor, are not addictive; and

- More than half of teens (55 percent or 13 million) don't strongly agree that using cough medicines to get high is risky.

The challenge is to get the message across to teens that there is a difference between good medicine and bad behavior. When these medications are abused, or used for anything other than their intended purpose under a doctor's supervision, they can be every bit as dangerous as illegal street drugs.

Motivation for Use

The Partnership's research shows that that teens see distinct benefits from different drugs and choose substances based on whether their motivation is simply to get high, to deal with problems such as stress or depression, to change their body or to help with school work.

Marijuana is the classic party drug; 81 percent of teens tell us that they use it to get high, and only 16 percent use it to deal with problems. Those numbers look quite different when you ask a teen about prescription drugs. A sizeable number of teens are self-medicating with these substances in order to get ahead in school or to deal with stress or depression. Forty three percent of teens report that they use prescription stimulants like Adderall or Ritalin without a doctor's prescription to help with school work, 31 percent say they use them to deal with problems, and 22 percent say they use them to get high. When it comes to prescription pain relievers, nearly half of kids say they use them to get high but 40 percent use them to help them to deal with a problem.

3

Parents Unaware of Teens' Intentional Misuse of Medications

Parents are crucial in helping prevent the abuse of prescription and over-the-counter medications but right now there is a huge disconnect between parents and teens about "pharming." Only one percent of parents say that it is "extremely or very likely" that their own teen has tried a prescription pain killer but 21 percent of teens admit to trying this type of drug to get high. The same holds true for prescription stimulants: two percent of parents say it is "extremely or very likely" that their own teen has used them to get high whereas 10 percent of teens actually have.

Today's cohort of parents is the most drug-experienced in history, but they do not understand this new drug abuse behavior among teens. As a result, they are looking for the classic signs of illegal drug use and are missing this trend. Parents need to be aware that the drugs their teens abuse today, including medicines, are not the drugs from decades past. Only through education and parental involvement can we reverse this trend. Once parents are educated about this problem, they can get through to their kids about the dangers of these substances.

We know that kids who learn a lot about the risk of drugs from their parents are up to 50% less likely to use drugs than teens who don't learn from their parents. Most parents say that they have talked to their kids about the dangers of drugs but our research shows that the message may not be getting through. Nine out of ten parents of teens say they have talked to their child about the dangers of drugs, yet fewer than one-third of teens (31 percent or 7.4 million) say they "learn a lot about the risks of drugs" from their parents.

Partnership research shows that parents are also the first place that teens turn for information about the risk of drugs. Fifty-six percent of teens report that they talk would turn to their mother and 45 percent would turn to their father when they have a question about drugs. Parents need to be educated so that they can seize that opportunity. The Partnership's efforts are helping parents understand the power that they have when it comes to their kids' decision about drugs and empower them to exercise it.

The Partnership is working to increase awareness about the dangers of "pharming" so that parents can talk to their kids about the dangers of abusing prescription and over-the-counter drugs. Our research shows that we need to target parents specifically on this issue: while three out of five parents report discussing drugs like marijuana "a lot" with their children, only a third of parents report discussing the risks of using prescription medicines or non-prescription cold or cough medicine to get high.

The Partnership's National Rx and OTC Medicine Abuse Campaign

The Partnership's annual tracking study – the largest, ongoing analysis of drug-related attitudes in the country – began measuring teen abuse of select medications in 2003. With three years of data in hand and last year's data heralding the emergence of this new category of substance abuse, the Partnership recognized this shift in teen drug abuse

175

behavior as one of the most significant in recent history and immediately began developing a necessary prevention and education campaign directed at parents.

In May, the Partnership launched a comprehensive, multi-year prevention communications effort targeting the abuse of prescription and over-the-counter medications. It is the first national campaign of its kind. The Partnership created this effort with support from the Consumer Healthcare Products Association and its member companies. The campaign speaks directly to parents by alerting them that their own homes are easily accessible sources for teens to obtain and abuse these medications. The campaign is comprised of hard-hitting television, newspaper, magazine and radio messages, a multifaceted interactive online component, and is supplemented by informational brochures to help parents get the conversation started with their teen. A multi-faceted public relations effort will provide media support for the campaign, in addition to the great coverage it has already received. When the Partnership released the research findings and launched the campaign in May, there was significant coverage around the country in the broadcast, print, and internet media, including on CNN, *CBS Evening News*, the Associated Press and the *Washington Post*.

The prescription and over-the-counter drug education effort is a priority campaign for the Partnership, which will work directly with national and local media to gain significant placements for the public service campaign messages. Television messages from the campaign will run nationally across all Comcast systems throughout the summer. Comcast will donate more than $2 million in advertising media exposure to support the campaign. In addition, Univision will also be lending extensive radio support to Spanish-language radio messages targeting the Hispanic community via Univision's national radio network. Univision will also be highlighting this issue in a special television program this Saturday, July 29.

The campaign also features an innovative online component consisting of unique and engaging Web sites focused on the dangers of abusing cough medicine/dextromethorphan (dextromethorphan, or DXM, is the active ingredient in cough medicine). And, in a first for the Partnership, we are driving visitors to the websites with a comprehensive search engine marketing campaign.

The Partnership's Web site www.drugfree.org features comprehensive online content on the abuse of prescription drugs. Original online content created specifically for parents and teens on the abuse of cough medicine can be found at:

- For parents - www.drugfree.org/Parent/

- For teens - www.dxmstories.com/

The message of this campaign can be summed up in three words: educate, communicate and safeguard. Educate yourself about the medications kids are abusing. Communicate with your kids and dispel the notion – for yourself as well as for your kids – that these medicines can be safely abused. And safeguard your medications by learning which ones

5

can be abused, limit access to them and keep track of the quantities you have in your home – and make sure your friends do the same.

As I mentioned, the Partnership has worked closely on this campaign with the Consumer Healthcare Products Association and its member companies, who are taking seriously the abuse of over-the-counter cough medications and helping find proactive solutions that reduce a negative behavior. They have been wonderful in this regard. We have seen similar positive actions by individual companies in the prescription drug industry. The prescription industry overall, however, thus far has focused its attention on the appropriate use of their products as well as on product safety and efficacy. This is an important step, but needs to be linked to complementary efforts to address the separate and very different consumer behavior of intentional abuse to get high. Again, this is an issue of good medicine meeting bad behavior, something both teens and parents do not fully understand. We are optimistic that the industry will do more to acknowledge the unfortunate fact that teens are abusing these products and take part in comprehensive, appropriate education and prevention efforts.

Effectiveness of Media Campaigns

The reason that the Partnership for Drug-Free America is focusing on a media campaign to educate parents about the problem of prescription and over-the-counter drug abuse is simple: anti-drug advertising works. This is documented in independent research, as well as in our own national tracking study, now in its 18th year.

A study published in the August 2002 *American Journal of Public Health* found anti-drug advertising is associated with a reduced probability of marijuana and cocaine/crack use among adolescents. A team including researchers from Yale University, New York University, the London Business School and Baruch College evaluated the effectiveness of drug-education messages from the Partnership for a Drug-Free America from 1987 through 1990. The researchers said that by 1990, "after three years of Partnership ads, approximately 9.25 percent fewer adolescents were using marijuana." The team also noted the decrease came at a time when anti-drug ads had increasing levels of media financial support - and thus were seen more often. "Given the results," the researchers said, "this increase appears to have been a worthwhile investment."

Previously, the February 2001 issue of the *American Journal of Public Health* reported television advertising contributed to a significant decline in marijuana use among teenagers. Research funded by the National Institute on Drug Abuse (NIDA) chronicled the impact of anti-drug TV ads on teens described as "sensation seekers" – adolescents attracted to risky activity and behavior. Conducted by Dr. Philip Palmgreen and a team of researchers at the University of Kentucky, the study tracked the impact of ad campaigns in select counties in Kentucky. The study showed a 26.7 decline in marijuana use among sensation-seeking teens exposed to anti-drug ads over a two-year period. Most ads used in the study were created by the Partnership for the Media Campaign.

National tracking data also support the effectiveness of anti-drug ads. Dr. Lloyd Johnston, lead researcher for the University of Michigan's Monitoring the Future study, said MTF research showed that:

> *"Over the past two years, there has been an increase in the proportion of students seeing marijuana use as dangerous; this change in beliefs may well explain some of the recent gradual decline in use. Quite possibly, the Media Campaign aimed at marijuana use, that has been undertaken by the White House Office of Drug Control Policy in collaboration with the Partnership for a Drug-Free America, has been having its intended effect. I am not aware of any other social influence process that could explain these changes in how young people view marijuana."*

Johnston also remarked of the Partnership's early efforts to combat inhalant abuse: "The use of inhalants began to turn downward in 1996, following the launching of an ad campaign by the Partnership for a Drug-Free America, and has been gradually and steadily declining since then."

Dr. Johnston has also said the survey consistently finds a very high degree of recalled exposure to Partnership ads, that the ads have high credibility with the audience and that they have high-judged impact on the behavior of that audience.

The effectiveness of anti-drug advertising is also underscored in findings from the Partnership Attitude Tracking Study: Year after year, tracking data show that teenagers who are exposed to anti-drug advertising frequently have stronger anti-drug attitudes and are considerably less likely to use drugs than teens who see and hear these messages infrequently.

There is also evidence of effectiveness from the National Youth Anti-Drug Media Campaign. The data cited below are drawn from the 2005 PATS Study. Last year, we sampled over 7,200 teenagers, in grades 7 through 12, across the country; we also over-sampled for African- and Hispanic-Americans to enable specific analysis of these two groups. Our findings in PATS track consistently with those of the Monitoring the Future study, conducted by the University of Michigan's Institute for Social Research under grants from the National Institute on Drug Abuse.

- Significantly fewer teenagers are using marijuana today when compared to 1998, the year the Media Campaign launched. Reductions are evident in all measured categories of prevalence – lifetime, past year and past month use. As you surely know, the Media Campaign focuses heavily on preventing adolescent use of marijuana – the most widely abused of all illicit substances.

- Marijuana-related attitudes among teenagers have improved significantly over the same time. In the past year, teen perception that marijuana use carries 'great risk' of getting in trouble with the law and dropping out of school increased significantly. Looking at risks by category, or type of risk, relational risks such as upsetting their parents, losing their friends or not being able to get a girlfriend or boyfriend are all significantly greater than in 1998.

- Teens are less likely to report that their close friends use marijuana. This is important because teens whose friends use drugs are more likely to use drugs themselves.

The Partnership for a Drug-Free America

The Partnership is a non-profit coalition of volunteers from the communications industry. Using a national drug-education advertising campaign and other forms of media communication, the Partnership exists to reduce illicit drug use in America.

The organization began in 1986 with seed money provided by the American Association of Advertising Agencies. The Partnership, which receives major funding from the Robert Wood Johnson Foundation and support from more than 200 corporations and companies, is strictly non-partisan and accepts no funding from manufacturers of alcohol and/or tobacco products. All actors in the Partnership's ads appear pro bono through the generosity of the Screen Actors Guild and the American Federation of Television and Radio Artists.

National research suggests that the Partnership's national advertising campaign – the largest public service campaign in the history of advertising – has played a contributing role in reducing overall drug use in America. Independent studies and expert interpretation of drug trends support its contributions. *The New York Times* has described the Partnership as "one of the most effective drug-education groups in the United States."

In addition to its work on the national level, the Partnership's State/City Alliance Program supports the organization's mission at the local level. Working with state and city governments and locally-based drug prevention organizations, the Partnership provides the guidance, on-site technical assistance and creative materials necessary to shape anti-substance abuse media campaigns tailored to the needs and activities of any given state or city.

The Partnership also participates in the National Youth Anti-Drug Media Campaign, coordinated by ONDCP. At the core of this multi-faceted initiative is a paid advertising program, featuring messages created by the Partnership.

Today, the Partnership is run by a professional staff of 50. Partnership campaigns have received every major award in the advertising and marketing industries for creative excellence and effectiveness, including the American Marketing Association's highest honor for marketing effectiveness.

Conclusion

The intentional abuse of medications among teens is a real issue threatening the health and well being of American families. We have a situation where a widespread and dangerous teen behavior has become normalized and has found our way into our homes. These findings should serve as a wake-up call to parents that their teens are facing a drug landscape that did not exist when they were teens. The abuse of prescription and over-the-counter drugs has taken root among America's teens and the behavior is not registering with parents. Unless we all take action, it is a problem that is only going to get worse.

Thank you for calling this important hearing today to shed light on this problem. The Partnership for Drug-Free America looks forward to working with this Committee and the Congress to educate the public about this problem and change teen attitudes and behavior regarding "pharming."

Mr. McHenry [presiding]. Thank you so much for your testimony and for showing the ads as well.

I have a few questions. Mr. Cummings, of course, will have, as I understand, a few questions as well.

But if we could start with Mr. Johnson. My understanding is, the makers of OxyContin said it would be more than a decade—it would take more than a decade to reformulate OxyContin to be abuse-resistant in that form. I am not asking you to divulge industry secrets or anything of that nature, but—you know, describing the specifics on how the product works, but there are some—what is the difference here?

It is a large company that produces OxyContin. What is the problem? Why—you know, why are they claiming this can't be done any time soon?

Mr. JOHNSON. I can't comment on or guess as to reasons why another company can't move forward in this area, but it's—our efforts are all about reformulating the drug to protect against the common methods of abuse which have been deliberated on the panel and by the DEA.

If you reformulate, using materials that are resistant or deterrent to abuse, then you essentially lock in drugs for patients who are trying to abuse or mechanically get drugs out of the system. If you take the drug as directed, then it delivers the dose to the patient over time.

Mr. McHenry. Can you describe how your product works differently?

Mr. JOHNSON. It is a gel-based delivery system. This is an example of the main ingredient. It's called sucrose acetate isobutyrate. I am not a scientist, but it is called SAIB. At any rate, it is a very viscous—it is called a creeping fluid. I turned it on its side about 15 minutes ago and it hasn't completely gone that way. That is the main ingredient.

Then we add another additional ingredient, I should say, to combat specific types of abuse.

So, again, if you take the drug as prescribed, it delivers the dose nicely over a 12-hour period and the patient gets pain relief. If, on the other hand, someone tries to abuse it, someone tries to crush it and snort it, you can't freeze it to a temperature that makes it brittle enough to actually defrag the delivery system and turn it into just a drug, as you can with some of the commonly available drugs. You can't.

We are doing studies to look at injecting the drug, and we have gotten down as far as an 18-gauge needle, which is very large, and even if you get the drug into a syringe, it still pops the needle off the end of the syringe.

When you challenge the drug with alcohol, which is a common method of abuse of some of the others, we have an excipient that locks in the drug. So some gets out, but a very small percentage; somewhere around 20 percent of the drug gets out. So if someone is playing with it, you know, hopefully they'll learn from a mistake and wake up the next morning.

Those are some of the differences.

Mr. McHenry. Do you think it is the absence of laws that are on the books about abuse-resistant prescription drugs that is contributing to very few of them being on the market?

Mr. Johnson. I think it creates a situation of ambivalence, or ambiguity rather; and this is where there is ambiguity, there is uncertainty.

From a business perspective, you don't want to invest your money in something that is highly risky unless you have money to throw away, which most companies don't, I think. You want to derisk it as much as possible.

There is no clinical path for approval of these drugs. There is no guide to tell industry what you need to do and what hurdles you need to cross to get these drugs approved, so I think the lack of guidance is a significant issue.

Mr. McHenry. Since this is sort of the general perception and understanding from industry, there is this perception that prescription drugs—as the ads outline, that they are somehow safe to abuse—as astronomically idiotic as that seems in this committee room, it is a reality outside, in America.

Do you think it is the idea that FDA approves drugs or that somehow they are safe, that they're approved, and this creates the perception among youth that it is OK?

I mean, if we could just have the whole panel to touch on that, give your comments on that.

Ms. Van Rooyan. In the hundreds and hundreds of college and high school students that I have spoken with over the past year, I would say unequivocally that is an issue. In addition to what I hear from young people is that they have grown up in a culture of taking some kind of medication for almost every ache and pain that comes along. And so, to them, you know, taking a prescription pill is almost in some instances like taking a vitamin or taking an aspirin if you have a headache; or gosh, if you have a stomachache, you know, take a little of this or take a little of that.

So many of the young people I speak to, taking a medication is nothing to them; they've grown up in that culture.

Mr. Pasierb. I think one of the things we saw was teens and parents shared the same view. I think parents were a little further beyond teens, thinking this was safer and there was less stigma attached to this. Many parents got that their own homes were a source of it, but they weren't doing anything to safeguard it, and I think it is the ubiquity of medicines in our lives. These are things that we all use to feel better and improve our lives, that safety veil which is so important, that is something in the American society that is now working against us in this case; and our kids are thinking this is a safer alternative.

And it is a tragically wrong conclusion, as you have heard this morning, from folks here.

Ms. Fetko. I just want to add, speaking with Carl's friends after he passed away, they just could not believe that something like this could have resulted from abusing these drugs. They were absolutely incredulous. They had no idea. And these were intelligent young men.

Ms. SURKS. I had the same experience. I spoke with a number of Jason's friends, and they just—they were amazed and shocked that this could have happened to him.

Ms. FALCO. I just wanted to add, the ready availability of these drugs beyond the family medicine cabinet. The Internet is going to emerge increasingly as the route for obtaining these drugs. Every kid in America is on line at least 3 or 4 hours a day. It is very easy to get these drugs without prescription, without the pretense of a prescription.

And as, in fact, we increase our ability to control the U.S. supplies and the U.S. requirements for prescriptions, this business will move offshore. It already has started to do so. And that will make control, at least from the supply end, even more difficult. That is why it is so important to engage the private sector players in this—the carriers who deliver the drugs, the credit card companies through which these drugs are purchased, the banks which approve the credit cards.

And, of course, there is this very important part of education, which by the way the search engines and the Internet service providers can also do through their huge networks and huge customer bases. That is what we are talking about right now coming back to you with recommendations along those lines.

Mr. MCHENRY. It is interesting you mention selling prescription drugs over the Internet. I had a pharmacy that was relieved of its license to issue drugs in the State of North Carolina because they were sending drugs across the country, which was strictly prohibited under North Carolina law. So it was interesting to see the pharmacy board in North Carolina really take on a challenge that may be largely, you know, a Midwest, a West Coast issue because this pharmacy was accepting orders for drugs across the country and how they were actually protecting people. So that is very helpful.

My time has expired, and we'll go to the ranking member, Mr. Cummings.

Mr. CUMMINGS. Thank you very much, Mr. Chairman. Let me just ask a few questions here.

Ms. Falco.

Ms. FALCO. Yes, sir.

Mr. CUMMINGS. How soon do you plan to come with those recommendations? And as I said a little bit earlier, this has been going on for a long time, and I am trying to figure out—I guess the older I get, the more I get frustrated. We study stuff and then we put it on a shelf, then we dust it off, warm it up, bring it back out; and a lot of times nothing happens.

And so and I am not—believe me, I am glad you are trying to do something. We are up here and we have just as much responsibility. But one of the things that I have concluded is that whenever something is driven by money and profit, it is hard. It is hard to stop it because basically it takes on a culture and a life of its own.

And so how soon do you think you'll see these recommendations, and what is the process of getting them to us?

Ms. FALCO. Fortunately, we have had the benefit of being able to work with committee staff. We are on a very fast track because we share your frustration. We hope that before the end of the year we will have developed very clear, specific recommendations that touch a wide range of private sector players in the Internet drug commerce, e-commerce. And I think that there will be some very— hopefully, some very specific recommendations that Congress might undertake.

I think the interest of this committee and your persistence in staying with this issue, in spite of the terrible frustration of studies that don't result in anything, have already begun to have an impact on the willingness of private companies to step up to the plate. They are not going to make—I am not speaking on behalf of any specific company, but let me just say that the credit card companies are not making most of their money off of this kind of commerce. They don't want to be associated with bringing these terrible drugs into the homes of our children.

I think there is a lot of common ground out there in the public sector and the private sector that we can really work on; and if we can continue to work with your staff, we will be back to you very soon.

Mr. CUMMINGS. Well, to Ms. Fetko, Ms. Surks and Ms. van Rooyan, I want to, first of all, express my sympathy to all of you. And I want to thank you for being a part of this and what you are doing.

I have often said that out of some of the most tragic things that happen can come some good things. Sadly, so often we have to suffer so that others might live and so that others might have a better life, and I thank you all for not taking your grief and going off into a corner, but coming out and saying, look, you know, I want to make sure that this doesn't happen to anyone else.

So I thank you not only on behalf of our committee, but on behalf of so many people that will be affected by what you do, that you will never meet and you will never know because they won't—and they may not know you. But because of what you do today, you may very well—I am sure you will save many, many people and save a lot of mothers from going through the pain that you have gone through.

Is there something that when you go back and you reflect on what you've seen and what you have experienced, is there anything, other than in the gist, that you would have loved to have seen government do?

Here we are in the business of trying to create laws, and one of the things that we did see is that when we took on the steroid issue, it was largely because of children. We were tired of seeing children emulating the great baseball, basketball, football players. And a lot of children did not understand that when they tried to emulate these big-time players, they could literally destroy their bodies.

And so we heard testimony from parents who came in here and said, We lost our son because he was trying to be like somebody he had seen on television. I'll never forget when we did that, when we held those hearings, a lot of people said, Oh, you are just grandstanding. You shouldn't be involved in this process; it is none of your business.

But I do believe that it has had a tremendous impact. And so what we are trying to figure out constantly is, what is it that we can do to try to—as legislators, try to help with the problem and understand with the steroid issue it wasn't just what we would do legislatively, but it would go back to what Ms. Falco is saying.

A lot of times when the voices come from the representatives of the people, industry and a whole lot of other folks begin to do things a little different than they would normally do them because they don't want laws to come down—you know, for us to create laws that affect them in a way that, you know, they may very well not feel comfortable with.

So are there any things that you can think of that you haven't already touched on that you would have loved to see the government do?

Ms. VAN ROOYAN. Yes. This is in my written testimony but not in my summation.

National prescription monitoring systems have to be in place, and there needs to be Federal appropriation of funds for that. Right now, in California, we most recently, as of January 2006, implemented and expanded a prescription drug monitoring program known as CURES. This is just the first leg of a monitoring system that, with the second leg, would involve having online access for all physicians and pharmacists to information on any patient's controlled substances.

The really unfortunate piece of this is that this expansion of the program in California only came about because Bob and Carmen Pack of Danville, California, lost their 7-year-old and 10-year-old children when a woman who was addicted to Vicodin and was under the influence of Vicodin ran into them with her car. And they found out during the trial that she had had six prior—prior to the crash, she had had six prior prescriptions filled from six different physicians all within the same HMO, none of whom corroborated any of the claims of injuries that she had.

So, obviously, our prescription monitoring system in our States are failing. And the Packs are at a point right now where this—there is only enough State funding for the first leg of it. They are looking to the pharmaceutical companies and the Federal Government for the funding in this prescription monitoring, CURES, in California.

So that is one way I see that the government can help.

Mr. CUMMINGS. Thank you.

Ms. Surks.

Ms. Fetko.

Ms. FETKO. A couple of things that, as I evaluated my experience: I wish that Carl was not able to walk into a pharmacy and purchase the cough syrups. Also, in regards to the Fentanyl, my suspicion is that it came from a home where a patient was being cared for at home. And finding ways to increase the accountability for the prescription drugs that are available to those patients in the home, as far as dispensing accountability for how many—how much drug is there and disposing of it after its use.

Mr. CUMMINGS. OK.

Ms. SURKS. It has already been mentioned. I think it is critical that we find a way to control the easy accessibility of these drugs over the Internet. The recommendations that the drug strategy is working sounds like it will approach that protection of our children.

I also think that education and prevention need to be supported. I know I work in prevention, and we do a lot to educate young people, parents; and that needs to be across the board, across the country. Everyone needs to have access to all of the information.

And so I think there needs to be support of the prevention efforts.

Mr. CUMMINGS. Are you—have you worked with these ladies, Ms. Falco?

Ms. FALCO. We are going to.

Mr. CUMMINGS. I was going to suggest that you do that.

Again, I want to thank all of you for your testimony. I don't know what is going to happen, but I can tell you that we are going to stick with the issue because it is so important. And thank all of you very much.

Mr. MCHENRY. We certainly appreciate your taking your time to come to Capitol Hill and tell your stories, and we certainly appreciate your input and guidance. For those that were not able to attend the committee hearing, they will read the testimony, as I did because of a prior engagement.

So thank you for your written testimony. Thank you for answering questions and thank you for your time. Thank you and have a wonderful afternoon.

This committee meeting is adjourned.

[Whereupon, at 1:10 p.m., the subcommittee was adjourned.]

[Additional information submitted for the hearing record follows:]

2004 Opiate Dependency Report
Part I: Waismann Institute Survey Reveals Over One-Third of Patients Battle OxyContin Dependency

According to The Waismann Institute's *2004 Opiate Dependency Report* , treatment for OxyContin dependency is catching up to that of the leading opiate, Vicodin, another powerful prescription painkiller. Based upon research conducted by the world-renowned opiate dependency center, 33 percent of patients were seeking treatment for a dependency to OxyContin, while a close 39 percent sought treatment for a Vicodin dependency. The findings are based on a survey conducted of patients receiving treatment for dependencies to various opiate-based drugs.

"A high percentage of the patients treated with the Waismann Method[sm] suffers from Vicodin dependencies; however, the number of patients that seek our help to battle an OxyContin dependency has steadily grown," said Clare W. Kavin, executive director of The Waismann Institute. "Although OxyContin is sometimes abused to achieve a high often compared to heroin, our survey revealed that 66 percent of respondents dependent on OxyContin indicated that their dependency stemmed from a desire to stop pain."

Of that 66 percent, 44 percent of respondents dependent on OxyContin said their dependency started after a doctor prescribed it as treatment, while 22 percent said they took OxyContin for pain, but obtained it from a friend or relative. Thirty-four percent of respondents indicated that they became dependent on the drug after taking it recreationally.

Additional findings include:

. Of those that were prescribed OxyContin by their doctors, 73 percent claimed the prescribing doctors gave directions for use that were clear, easy to understand and enforced
. Eleven percent indicated that they visited multiple doctors to acquire OxyContin prescriptions
. Seventy-two percent of those with OxyContin dependencies had not experienced dependency issues with any type of illegal drugs before seeking treatment for OxyContin use
. The age group with the most respondents to report a dependency to OxyContin was those between 46 and 56

"It is evident from the results of our *2004 Opiate Dependency Report* that both routine and recreational use of OxyContin can result in dependency," commented Waismann. "It is extremely important for those using the drug to understand the precautions and closely monitor intake, as dependency can occur in as little as two weeks."

For more information, please call (310) 205-0808 or (888) 987-HOPE or send us a confidential email.

The exclusive Waismann Method of Neuro-Regulation is administered by Drs. Clifford Bernstein and Michael Lowenstein to treat opiate dependency. Performed in a hospital intensive care unit, the Waismann Method involves cleansing the opiate receptors in the patient's brain of the narcotics while the patient is under anesthesia. During the procedure, the patient will experience no conscious withdrawal, and will be able to return home within days. Over 65 percent of patients treated with the Waismann Method remain drug free after one year.

2004 Opiate Dependency Report
Part II: Drug Dependencies Often Begin in the Doctor's Office

Waismann Institute's 2004 Opiate Dependency Report Reveals Challenges Faced by Pain Management Practitioners and Patients

The Waismann Institute released the findings of its *2004 Opiate Dependency Report*, which shows that 56 percent of patients' opiate dependencies began with medication prescribed by their doctors. (figure 1) The findings are based on a survey conducted of over 100 patients receiving treatment for dependency to opiates such as painkillers OxyContin, Vicodin and Lortab, and the illegal narcotic heroin.

"The results of our *2004 Opiate Dependency Report* indicate that there is a challenge faced by doctors treating patients in the evolving field of pain management," said Clare W. Kavin, executive director of The Waismann Institute. "The survey shows how painkiller dependencies often begin with a legal prescription to treat pain, and then the brain unsuspectingly develops a chemical reliance on the drug. These are not people who indulged in recreational drug use to achieve a high."

The Waismann Institute's *2004 Opiate Dependency Report* also reveals that 53 percent of patients who were dependent on a prescribed medication did not ask for assistance from the prescribing doctor to get off the drug after the dependency was realized. (figure 2)

"It is common to see patients who feel shame for their dependencies; therefore, they will not admit to their doctors that a problem has arisen," said Waismann. "They also harbor the fear that if they inform the doctor of the dependency, the doctor will immediately stop prescribing them the drug."

The study also found that 14 percent of patients visited multiple doctors to obtain their drugs. (figure 3) Additionally, for the majority of patients, the survey results indicated that dependency to prescription pain medication was their only experience with a drug dependency. Fifty-three percent of respondents reported they had never experienced dependency issues with any type of illegal drug. (figure 4)

For more information, please call (310) 205-0808 or (888) 987-HOPE or send us a confidential email.

For more information on the Waismann Institute, or to schedule an interview with Clare W. Kavin, contact Rachel Kay at 619-234-0345 or via email at kay@formulapr.com .

The exclusive Waismann Method of Neuro-Regulation is administered by Drs. Clifford Bernstein and Michael Lowenstein to treat opiate dependency. Performed in a hospital intensive care unit, the Waismann Method involves cleansing the opiate receptors in the patient's brain of the narcotics while the patient is under anesthesia. During the procedure, the patient will have no consciousness of withdrawal, and will be able to return home within a couple of days. Over 65 percent of patients treated with the Waismann Method remain drug free after one year.

Figure 1

How did your dependency begin?

Figure 2

Did you seek help in getting off the drug from the doctor that prescribed you the drug prior to the being treated with the Waismann Method?

Figure 3

What were your methods of obtaining the drug?

Figure 4

Have you experienced dependency issues with any type of illegal drug before seeking this help?

2004 Opiate Dependency Report
Part III: Majority of Female Patients with Opiate Dependencies are Reliant on Doctor-Prescribed Painkillers, According to Waismann Institute Survey

According to The Waismann Institute's *2004 Opiate Dependency Report* , 86 percent of female patients seeking treatment were battling a dependency to prescription painkillers. Based upon research conducted by the world-renowned opiate dependency treatment center, the drug most commonly found to be a problem for women was OxyContin at 21 percent, while 19 percent sought treatment for a Vicodin dependency. The findings are based on a survey conducted of patients receiving treatment for dependencies to various opiate-based drugs.

"As the results of our *2004 Opiate Dependency Report* show, dependency to prescription painkillers is a dangerous problem for women," said Clare W. Kavin, executive director of The Waismann Institute. "In addition to treatment for chronic pain from injury or disease, some women also seek doctor-prescribed relief from ailments like migraine headaches and menstrual cramps. They are commonly prescribed the same painkillers to treat these less serious ailments, but the risk of physical dependency is still there, and can pose a more destructive problem than the pain."

Of female respondents, 51 percent indicated that a doctor's prescription marked the beginning of the dependency, while another 18 percent said they were taking the drug to treat pain, but they obtained it through a friend or family member. Only ten percent reported taking it recreationally.

Additional findings include:

- Of female patients that were prescribed the medication by their doctors, 89 percent claimed the prescribing doctors gave directions for use that were clear, easy to understand and enforced
- Twenty percent of those dependent on prescription medication indicated that they visited multiple doctors to acquire prescriptions
- Sixty-three percent of women respondents with prescription drug dependencies did not seek help from the prescribing doctor after they realized they developed a physical dependency to the drug
- Of female survey respondents, 55 percent said they felt they had been dependent for over three years
- Fifty-five percent of women indicated that their family members noticed a dependency, while only 12 percent said their doctors were aware of one
- Many women reported health issues that they attributed to their opiate

dependencies, including memory loss (44 percent), decreases in mental health (26 percent) and extreme weight loss (12 percent).
. The age group with the most respondents to report a dependency to opiate-based drugs was between 33-45 (44 percent), while 40 percent were between 46-56 years of age

"It is evident from the results of our *2004 Opiate Dependency Report* that women using prescription medication must understand the precautions and monitor intake as they are at a high risk for dependency," explained Waismann. "Most women don't realize that simply taking an opiate-based painkiller for two weeks can be enough to create a physical dependency."

For more information, please call (310) 205-0808 or (888) 987-HOPE or send us a confidential email.

The exclusive Waismann Method of Neuro-Regulation is administered by Drs. Clifford Bernstein and Michael Lowenstein to treat opiate dependency. Performed in a hospital intensive care unit, the Waismann Method involves cleansing the opiate receptors in the patient's brain of the narcotics while the patient is under anesthesia. During the procedure, the patient will experience no conscious withdrawal, and will be able to return home within days. Over 65 percent of patients treated witht he Waismann Method remain drug free after one year.

SCIENCE

Drug Firms Trying to Make Painkillers Less Abusable

Efforts Include More Tamper-Proof Pills And Compounds That Suppress the 'High'

By Marc Kaufman
Washington Post Staff Writer

Millions of Americans suffer from intense but poorly treated pain that could be helped by today's broad array of morphine-based prescription painkillers. Millions of others abuse prescription narcotics, using them to get high rather than to ease pain, and many become addicted.

That dilemma—that rapid painkillers are both underused and abused—has become a pressing issue since the introduction in the mid-1990s of the extended-release opioid OxyContin. The drug has provided enormous relief to many pain sufferers and could help many more, but it has also become a drug of choice for many addicts, who promptly discovered how to disable the extended-release aspect of the drug to get high on the enhanced dose.

With the problem now clearly identified, dozens of researchers have embarked on a difficult and high-stakes race to find ways to keep the benefits of prescription painkillers available to pain sufferers while eliminating or reducing the possibility for abuse.

Officials at Purdue Pharma, the makers of OxyContin, say they and at least 10 other companies are actively working on ways to make nonaddictive or less addictive pain relievers. Some are working on compounds other than opioids, but most are trying to reformulate the large array of prescription narcotics already available.

Charles Grudzinskas, who has worked on these issues with industry and then the National Institute on Drug Abuse, said his recent search of patent applications found 250 issued since 1998 for ways to reduce the abuse potential of pain-killing drugs.

"Drug's a whole biology we're starting to pull apart," said Grudzinskas, who until recently chaired a session this week on the "Chemistry of Abuse: Opioid Analgesia" at the annual meeting in Puerto Rico of the College on Problems of Drug

Dependence, a group that has focused on addiction and pain relief since the 1950s. "We're making progress, but this is very hard—we're trying to thread a needle without any disaster can be met.

The reason is the unique set of demands placed on potential drug producers and existing pain-relieving painkiller. Drugs based on morphine, which is derived from the poppy plant, are the gold standard for relieving severe post-operative and chronic pain, and recent research has increasingly found that when used properly for pain sufferers, addiction is seldom a problem. Researchers and drug makers do not want to reduce the effectiveness of the drugs as they make them more abuse-resistant; in fact, they say, it would be unethical to do so.

Individuals respond quite differently to opioids, however, and with even greater variability to opioids that have been combined with another compound. As a result, some combination drugs that might reduce the abuse potential of painkillers are also likely to reduce their effectiveness.

And finally, any effort to make OxyContin or Lortab or other painkillers less prone to abuse has to make them unappealing to addicts while not causing them undue harm. It is a challenge unlike any other in drug formulation.

Nonetheless, industry, federal government and academic researchers are actively involved in the effort because the need—and potential profit—is so great. With doctors increasingly wary of prescribing painkillers to patients because of the possibility of abuse and the growing fear that the Drug Enforcement Administration will come after them if they prescribe the high dosages that some doctors now believe are appropriate—that issue is only expected to grow.

Purdue Pharma of Stamford, Conn., for instance, has concentrated on adding a compound that blocks the brain receptors that narcotics capture the opioids and relay their effects onward in the brain.

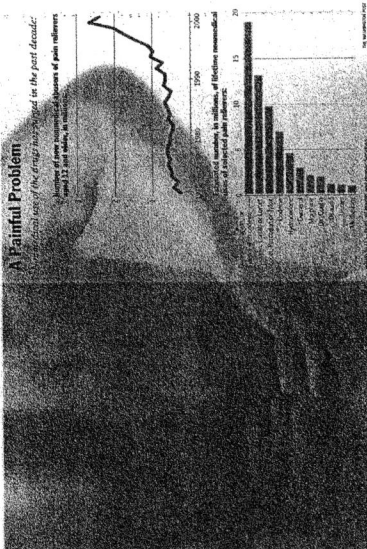

A Painful Problem

The compound would be added in contained, or "sequestered," form and would pass inertly through a patient taking the painkiller properly, but it would become an active antidote to the opioid if the pill were opened and crushed for a quick high. The added compound would, in effect, cause the abuser to go into withdrawal rather than feeling euphoric.

"We are very committed to making pain relief that can't be tampered with and abused," said David Haddox, Purdue Pharma's vice president for health policy. "It's our number one priority."

Harvard Medical School professor Clifford Woods has proposed adding capsaicin, the substance that makes chili peppers hot, to the painkiller in sequestered form. The drug would deliver the expected relief, but it would give an abuser snorting, chewing or injecting it a very unpleasant surprise.

Officials at Endo Pharmaceuticals of Chadds Ford, Pa, another major producer of painkillers, said they are experimenting with new ways to chemically encapsulate the opioids in their painkillers to make it far more difficult for abusers to extract the narcotic.

"We call it the Fort Knox approach," said Endo senior medical officer Bradley Galer. "We want to tweak the formulation, so if the abuser crushes a pill and takes some of the powder, the opioid would still be in extended release form and there would be no sudden burst of drug."

A variation on that idea, under development by a company that wants to remain anonymous, would reformulate painkillers into hard-to-open, gummy pills that opioid,

rather than split open, when hammered or cut. If perfected, they would deny abusers the narcotic they seek.

Frank Vocci of the National Institute on Drug Abuse said his agency is actively supporting further research into the basic science of how opioids work in the brain, and how they and other analgesics can be made less susceptible to abuse.

Another line of research supported by NIDA involves efforts to create a synthetic cannabinoid (the family that includes marijuana) that relieves pain but does not produce the buzz of the drug—and then explains Dr. Alexandros Makriyannis of the University of Connecticut, was reported last year in the Proceedings of the National Academy of Sciences. Other efforts are underway to develop nonaddictive, and po-

tentially very powerful, painkilling agents from spider, fish and sea snails and other shellfish.

Despite the money and effort going to this kind of research, experts doubt any breakthroughs are imminent. "To have a medication that's devoid of abuse potential and has good analgesic effect is highly desirable, but I know nothing at this point that would do it," said Vocci of NIDA. "We hope compounds will become available with reduced abuse liability, and that they will push the more abusable compounds out of the market. But this is such a complicated field that I see no magic, absolute solution or silver bullet."

"If this was easy to do," said Martin Adler, executive director of the College on Problems of Drug Dependence, "it would have been done long ago."

193

CHPA

<u>Subcommittee Hearing Statement</u>

Prescription Drug Abuse: What is Being Done to
Address this New Drug Epidemic?

**U.S. House of Representatives
Committee on Government Reform
Subcommittee on Criminal Justice, Drug Policy and Human Resources
2154 Rayburn House Office Building
Washington, DC
July 26, 2006**

The Consumer Healthcare Products Association (CHPA) appreciates the opportunity to submit this written statement to the Subcommittee on Criminal Justice, Drug Policy and Human Resources.

CHPA is the national trade association representing over 200 companies and organizations who are involved in the manufacturing, distribution, and promotion of nonprescription or over-the-counter (OTC) medicines. While several of our members also produce and distribute prescription medicines, this statement is submitted on behalf of the nonprescription side of the industry.

Dextromethorphan (DXM) is a safe and effective ingredient found in well over 100 over-the-counter cough and cold medicines. First approved by the U.S. Food and Drug Administration (FDA) in 1954, DXM is an effective, non-narcotic cough suppressant that works by raising the coughing threshold in the brain. It is the most widely used cough suppressant in the United States, has no pain relieving properties, and is not addictive. While dextromethorphan is used safely by millions of Americans each year to relieve coughs due to the common cold or flu, some teenagers and young adults are intentionally abusing large quantities of medicines containing dextromethorphan (up to 25 times the recommended dose) in an effort to get high.

The makers of nonprescription medicines take very seriously the intentional abuse of its products and sought out the experts at the Partnership for a Drug-Free America (the Partnership) for assistance in combating this problem. Together, CHPA and the Partnership began an ongoing initiative in 2003 to ensure that adults with influence and oversight of young people are

**Consumer Healthcare
Products Association**
900 19th Street, NW, Suite 700
Washington, DC 20006
T 202.429.9260 F 202.223.6835
www.chpa-info.org

aware that teens may be considering abusing medicines containing dextromethorphan. In addition to educating key audiences regarding the potential for abuse of OTC medicines containing dextromethorphan, CHPA, the Partnership, and the American Medical Association launched the Rx and OTC Medicine Abuse Education Campaign on May 16, 2006. This education campaign will be presented in greater detail at today's hearing by the Partnership's President and CEO Stephen J. Pasierb.

CHPA believes that there is also something that Congress can do prevent the abuse of dextromethorphan: **support HR 5280, the Dextromethorphan Distribution Act of 2006.** In addition to Rx and OTC medicine abuse, young people also have discovered that they can get the raw, unfinished, powdered form of dextromethorphan online. Teenagers and young adults are purchasing this bulk form of dextromethorphan on the Internet and ingesting it alone or with other drugs and alcohol. This type of abuse is particularly dangerous because it is the pure form of the drug. On May 20, 2005, FDA issued a talk paper warning against the sale of pure dextromethorphan in powdered form that is encapsulated by the "dealer" and offered for street use. The FDA paper acknowledged that dextromethorphan is generally recognized as safe and effective when ingested at recommended dosing levels.

Introduced on a bi-partisan basis by Congressman Fred Upton and Congressman Rick Larsen, H.R. 5280 would allow FDA to promulgate regulations on the sale of unfinished dextromethorphan and limit the distribution of the bulk ingredient to only those persons or entities which are registered with FDA. This important legislation would cut-off the supply of pure dextromethorphan to those who are using it to get high or who intend to sell it as a street drug. The bill now has 13 cosponsors and has been referred to the House Committee on Energy & Commerce. CHPA strongly commends Congressman Upton and Congressman Larsen for their leadership on this important issue.

The makers of OTC medicines are committed to stopping both of these types of abuse of dextromethorphan, and we appreciate the opportunity of sharing this information with the subcommittee.

195

July 31, 2001
Richard Sackler, M.D.
President
Purdue Pharma L. P.
One Stamford Forum
Stamford, CT 06901-3431

Dear Dr. Sackler:
I have been increasingly dismayed and alarmed about the problems and escalating abuse
of
OxyContin. As I have discussed with you and other Purdue officials, this extraordinarily
powerful medicine promises tremendous benefits to people who suffer from severe
chronic pain, but it also has led to widespread misuse, diversion, criminal wrongdoing,
and related problems. As you observed in your July 18 precautionary letter, OxyContin
is a synthetic narcotic "with an abuse liability similar to morphine." Addiction is a real,
present and growing danger. Once confined largely to a few eastern states and the
Appalachian region, such problems have now spread across the country. Once limited to
rural areas, abuse has migrated to the cities. It is the drug of choice for the middle class
and middle aged, along with teenagers and young adults. Nor are cancer patients now the
main recipients of such opioid painkillers. Of the six and one-half million OxyContin
prescriptions last year -- a staggering number -- oncologists accounted for only three
percent. As *The New YorkTimes* reported last Sunday, "The largest single group of
OxyContin prescribers is now family physicians who accounted for 21 percent of the
total." Physicians in that group tend to have little or no special training or skill-set in
prescribing such drugs. Connecticut, unfortunately, has not been spared problems relating
to improper use and criminal diversion of the prescription drug. As you are well aware,
at least one overdose death this month -- a teenager in Clinton -- has been linked to
OxyContin, and law enforcement is investigating
its role in other fatalities as part of the rave drug scene. (The state's Chief Medical
Examiner has reported increasing numbers of deaths in Connecticut related to
oxycodone: 16 reported in 1999, 26 in 2000, and an even higher number projected for
this year.) Recent events -- including the Bridgeport physician arrest -- highlight the
increased incidence of OxyContin-related criminal activity. The serious, almost epidemic
dimensions of these problems are reflected in: u☐Overdose deaths attributed, in whole
or in part, to OxyContin;
u☐Pharmacy robberies and other criminal wrongdoing related to the prescription drug;
and
u☐Growing addiction to OxyContin, whether acquired illegally or prescribed.
I have initiated an investigation of OxyContin abuse, involving cooperative and joint
action
with other state and federal law enforcement and regulatory authorities. One factor
prompting our heightened interest is the astonishing growth in state funding for
OxyContin prescriptions -- doubling this year, for example, to a projected $7.4 million
from $3.7 million last year, and far less the year before. I am advocating legislation to
establish a state electronic prescription monitoring program, and I have personally met
twice with representatives from Purdue Pharma so that I have now heard and read your

company's side of the story. While Purdue Pharma seems sincere in seeking to address the problems, no comprehensive effective solutions have yet been offered. A number of supposed anti abuse steps have been publicly touted in recent weeks -- tamperproof prescription pads, for example, or educational programs for children about general prescription drug dangers. These programs fail to address the fundamental and serious risks inherent in the drug itself, particularly its extraordinary potency and exploding availability. Each addresses only a small source of the abuse problem. The educational effort, for instance, deals generally with a broad array of prescription drugs, and only the very youngest age group, ignoring the steep pitfalls of addiction and misuse among adults. Similarly, I am encouraged and impressed by the strengthened warnings in labeling or letters to health care professionals -- recently required by the U.S. Food and Drug Administration (FDA). There is no assurance that such steps will stem (let alone stop) much of the illicit market or misuse. Very bluntly, initiatives must move beyond cosmetic and symbolic steps to deal directly with alarming andgrowing diversion, abuse, fraud, robbery, and other law breaking spawned by the present system of distribution. Purdue Pharma must overhaul and reform its marketing practices, eliminating the videos and other promotional materials aimed at persuading patients to pressure doctors into prescribing the prescription drug. Real reform will signal that the company is sincere, as it seems to be. OxyContin is not the only powerful prescription drug that may be abused, or pose other dangers. But OxyContin is different. It offers extraordinarily potent relief, but also raises special health care pitfalls and policy obligations. It is more powerful, more addictive, more widely sold, more illicitly available, and more publicized, than almost any other painkiller. These problems are different in magnitude and scope, if not in kind. Such problems provide an opportunity -- to create a
model for dealing effectively with similar dangers that inevitably accompany other powerful and useful pharmaceutical drugs. It is, indeed, an historic opportunity and a challenge. An important first step, which I commend, is indeed the announcement made in conjunction with the FDA to strengthen warnings on your labeling that improper use of OxyContin can lead toaddiction or death. Your vision and courage as a company could help lead the industry as well as save countless lives and social costs. Unfair as you may feel the public attention has been -- both to OxyContin and your company -- it may magnify all the more the impact of your actions. To that end I have some specific requests for immediate action which I feel will help address the problems while your company works to reformulate the drug, which may take three years to accomplish.

1. Centralized Pharmacies
Limiting availability of OxyContin to centralized pharmacies, initially suggested by the Drug Enforcement Administration, is a viable concept to stop the spread of armed robberies of drug stores. Reducing the number of pharmacies that carry OxyContin would facilitatepreventive patrols and help deter such robberies. Restricting the number of pharmacies would also help identify individuals who engage in "doctor shopping." It should not impede access for individuals who legitimately need it, so long as the dispensing pharmacies are wisely chosen. An alternative is that you work with your distributors and larger customers to reduce the of OxyContin available at each pharmacy and consolidate supplies at select locations within each state. Such an alternative, although not as effectiveas a centralized pharmacy, will still help to prevent robberies.

Independently, I plan to approach the large pharmaceutical chains in our state and make such a request.

2. Restricting Sales to Physicians with a Specialized Need and Expertise to Prescribe the Drug

According to your representatives, many medical schools fail to adequately teach their students about pain management. If so, the company should voluntarily limit the distribution of OxyContin only to physicians who have extensive experience or training in pain management, such as those physicians who regularly treat patients for chronic or severe pain.

3. Instituting a Physician Certification Program

A company sponsored training program to teach physicians about the proper use of OxyContin, including its attendant dangers and benefits, would help provide expertise. I am not advocating more seminars in Florida or Arizona to encourage more OxyContin prescriptions, but rather local workshops to train these physicians about the limited circumstances where such

prescriptions are appropriate. Following this training, the company could issue a certificate to the physician that attests to attendance at the training and acknowledgment of OxyContin's risks. Purdue Pharma could require such certification prior to selling the pharmaceutical to any physician.

4. The Use of Physician Risk Management Plans

Pain management experts advocate a multi-disciplinary approach to effectively treat pain. Schedule II opioids like OxyContin are a legitimate and necessary part of that approach, but the general consensus among experts is that these powerful drugs should be the treatment of last resort for chronic pain. As you well know, pain management is more than simply prescribing a pill. Purdue Pharma should adopt a plan that incorporates this approach to pain management and require a physician's acceptance of such a "contract."

5. Treatment and Rehabilitation Programs

Recognizing the powerful addiction dangers of OxyContin, the company must devote resources to treatment and rehabilitation programs, particularly among population groups most affected. The company has a responsibility, legal and moral, to individuals who are addicted, whether they acquired the drug legitimately or illicitly. Regardless of the source of the drug, they and their families must now cope with the addiction, and their communities must provide for their care. Addiction risks affect patients with legitimate prescriptions as well as illegal users. Eventually reformulation may reduce the risks, but the drug now does great harm as well as good. To diminish the damage, programs treating addiction are now essential. They also would serve to educate and emphasize to the general public that OxyContin's benefits may exact a great price. Such efforts would be more appropriate and effective than entrepreneurial or other general community programs currently sponsored by the company. I ask your company to devote a specific, set percentage of its OxyContin profits to fight addiction through such rehabilitation and treatment programs. The commitment could be implemented initially in areas hardest hit by addiction, but eventually in every state, since none has been completely spared such problems. While the details may depend on additional study and discussion, an immediate commitment will demonstrate your conviction and resolve to reach the right result and combat addiction.

Finally, three other points: First, I know that Purdue Pharma has offered to provide tamper

proof prescription pads to physicians. This step is welcome, but prescription forgeries are only a very small part of the overall problem. Second, while I must accept that your company does not market OxyContin directly to consumers, I take strong exception with the message conveyed in the "Patient Bill of Rights for Pain Management" on the Internet site "Partners Against Pain," which is financed by your company. Specifically, I am disturbed by the site's statement that addiction from prescribed opioids is "rare in patients without a history of drug/alcohol abuse" if prescribed under a physician's care. This statement is simply not true, and I have received letters and phone calls from patients attesting to the fact that they or family members became addicted to OxyContin after it was

prescribed by their physician. It must be changed. Third, as important as anything said so far, none of these proposed remedies is meant to minimize the state and federal governments' responsibility to enforce existing laws prohibiting illegal distribution or sale of controlled substance such as OxyContin, or seek stronger civil and criminal measures. We will continue to review current laws and advocate better ones.

I recognize that Purdue Pharma's adoption of one or more of these proposals will affect the

company's sales of OxyContin. I feel strongly that some decrease in sales of this very profitable prescription drug is a short term consequence Purdue Pharma must accept. OxyContin has been described as a great medical boon when prescribed responsibly for those who need it. Recognizing its perils as well as promise, Purdue Pharma has a moral, ethical and legal responsibility to take effective meaningful steps to rectify the problems. Whether or not the company should or could have readily foreseen how the time released formulation of OxyContin could be so easily compromised, the danger is now undeniable, and raises an unquestionable ethical and legal obligation. In short, it is time for Purdue Pharma to change it practices, not just its public relations strategy.

I would be open to further discussion on any of these strategies or on any other concrete proposals you may have to address the issues. If you disagree that they are viable short-term solutions, I would like to know why. My hope is that you will implement immediately a comprehensive affirmative and material plan of action to address these issues. While I cannot speak for all of the Attorneys General involved in our task force, I am confident that there would be a positive response to significant and effective measures dealing with distribution such as the ones I have suggested. In the meantime, this office will continue to identify and evaluate all of its options to remedy the problem.

Sincerely,
RICHARD BLUMENTHAL
RB:jb
c: Laura M. Nagel, Dep. Asst. Administrator Kim Herd, Coordinator
Office of Diversion Control Prescription Drug Abuse Task Force

199

Drug Enforcement Administration National Association of Attorneys General
2401 Jefferson Davis Highway 750 First Street, N.E. - Suite 1100
Alexandria, VA 22301 Washington, D.C. 20002 Richard Sackler, M.D.
August 07, 2001
Page 6

CPSIA information can be obtained at www.ICGtesting.com
Printed in the USA
238875LV00005B/23/P